# GLADIATORS
## AND CAESARS

THE POWER OF
SPECTACLE IN
ANCIENT ROME

# GLADIATORS
# AND CAESARS

EDITED BY

ECKART KÖHNE AND
CORNELIA EWIGLEBEN

ENGLISH VERSION EDITED BY

RALPH JACKSON

UNIVERSITY OF CALIFORNIA PRESS
Berkeley   Los Angeles

This book is published to accompany an exhibition held at the
British Museum from 21 October 2000 to 23 January 2001.
The exhibition is based on a concept designed by the Museum für Kunst
und Gewerbe, Hamburg, and shown at Hamburg from 11 February
to 18 June 2000 and at the Historisches Museum der Pfalz, Speyer,
from 9 July to 1 October 2000.

University of California Press
Berkeley and Los Angeles, California
Published by arrangement with
British Museum Press

First published 2000

Translated from the German by Anthea Bell
in association with First Edition Translations Ltd, Cambridge, UK

ISBN 0–520–22798–0

Printed in Spain

9 8 7 6 5 4 3 2 1 0

ENDPAPERS

**Graffiti showing fighting gladiators**
First century AD
Pompeii

On the left the novice *murmillo* Marcus Attilius has defeated
the *thraex* Lucius Raecius Felix, who kneels in submission

FRONTISPIECE

**Mosaic with gladiators: panel showing *equites***
First half of the third century AD
Römermuseum, Augst, 1961.13829

This floor mosaic panel decorated a rich Roman house in the town
of Augusta Raurica (Augst), Germany. The tunics show that the two
gladiators are *equites* (see pp. 47–9) who have dismounted from
their horses and are finishing their combat on foot. Mosaics with
gladiatorial scenes became part of the furnishings of private Roman
houses relatively late.

OPPOSITE

**Detail of a boxing glove from a statue of a victorious boxer**
Mid-first century BC
(See figs 87–8)

## Lenders to the British Museum Exhibition

Antikensammlung, Staatliche Museen zu Berlin

Ashmolean Museum, Oxford

British Museum, London: Departments of Greek and Roman Antiquities,
Prehistoric and Romano-British Antiquities, Coins and Medals, and Medieval
and Later Antiquities

Fitzwilliam Museum, Cambridge

Historisches Museum der Pfalz, Speyer

Kunsthistorisches Museum Wien, Antikensammlung

Landesmuseum Mainz

Monumenti Musei e Gallerie Pontificie, Città del Vaticano

Musée Archéologique, Vaison-La-Romaine

Musée de l'Arles Antique

Musée du Louvre, Paris

Musei Capitolini, Roma

Museo Archeologico di Verona

Museo Archeologico Nazionale di Napoli

Museo Nazionale Romano alla Terme di Diocleziano, Roma

Museum für Kunst und Gewerbe, Hamburg

Museum of London

Römerstadt Augusta Raurica, Römermuseum, Augst

Römisch-Germanisches Museum der Stadt Köln

Staatliche Kunstsammlungen Dresden, Skulpturensammlung

Württembergisches Landesmuseum Stuttgart, Antikensammlung

# Contents

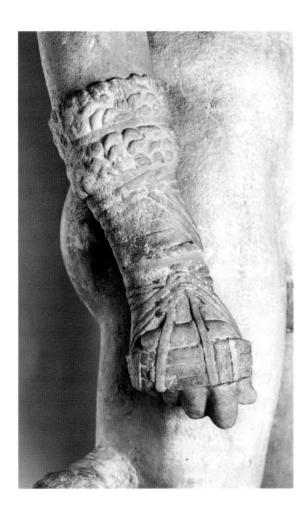

# Foreword

The exhibition *Gladiators and Caesars* displays the material remains of Roman mass entertainment, notably gladiatorial combat, chariot-racing and theatrical performance. Uniquely, exhibits from twenty museums throughout Europe have been brought together with the incomparable collections of the British Museum to give a vivid picture of the spectacle, danger, excitement, power and frequent brutality of games and shows in ancient Rome. It is an exhibition with wide and popular appeal, whether for its visual impact or its resonances with today's entertainment industry, but it is one that also raises deeper issues of state-sanctioned violence, political control and manipulation of the masses. Public interest in Roman sports, already whetted by the sensational film *Gladiator*, will be enriched by seeing real evidence.

The exhibition has had three venues: it was origi-nated in Hamburg, at the Museum für Kunst und Gewerbe, where it was conceived by Dr Eckart Köhne and Dr Cornelia Ewigleben, to both of whom we express our gratitude. It was then shown at the Historisches Museum der Pfalz in Speyer before transferring to the British Museum, where it has been consolidated by many additional exhibits.

The challenges and organisational complexities of such an exhibition are considerable and its success has been due to the vision, expertise, efforts and goodwill of many individuals and institutions. To all those and to the lenders listed above I extend my grateful thanks.

R.G.W. ANDERSON
*Director*
The British Museum

# Preface

Spectacular entertainment for the masses and the exercise of political power are the subjects of the exhibition *Gladiators and Caesars*. Bread and circuses – *panem et circenses* – were what the Roman people demanded of their emperor in a reciprocal relationship that generally suited both parties well. Giving to receive, euergetism, was a well-established practice of the power-brokers of the Roman world, and to receive the loyal support of their people Roman emperors gave spectacular games and entertainment from the first century BC to the end of the fourth century AD. The games, which originated in religious festivals, included chariot-racing, athletic events and theatre, and they grew in size, frequency and cost over the centuries. Gladiatorial combat had different origins, namely in the duels fought at the funerals of famous men, but they, too, grew into huge and spectacular events.

The famous actors of Rome were not so very different from those of today, and even the top charioteers in their fast and dangerous four-horse chariots equate quite well with our Formula One racing-car drivers, but Roman gladiators have no modern counterpart: fêted, loved and rewarded with huge sums of money, they differed from our top sports stars in one crucial respect – they fought, quite literally, for their life at every appearance. Some were professionals, some were slaves, many were captives or prisoners-of-war, but together in combat in the amphitheatre they were symbols of Rome's control over the ancient world. As Thracian was set against *murmillo*, and *secutor* against *retiarius*, in the contest of life and death, their fate was determined by a gesture of the emperor's hand, which might be influenced by the verdict of the crowd. The spectators expected and applauded a close-fought, exciting battle, which demonstrated warlike spirit and courage, for bravery was the foremost virtue of the Romans, who valued military service above the athletic achievements so beloved of the Greeks. Gladiatorial combat in the arena focused public attention on the ultimate expression of bravery.

But Roman society was complex, and so indeed were events in the arena, much more than people today tend to realize. The exhibition seeks to reveal the multi-faceted nature of these shows, from parades of exotic animals to animal hunts and from acrobats to gladiator pairs. Not to be confused with gladiatorial combat was the execution of criminals (*noxii*) and others charged with the most serious offences. Condemned to die as a lesson to others, they were brutally killed in the most public of spaces, the circus and amphitheatre. In front of tens of thousands of people they were burnt, crucified, put to the sword or exposed defenceless to wild animals. Some were Christians, who faced death for the treasonable offence of refusing to sacrifice to the emperor, thereby rejecting Roman state religion, and the wild animals sometimes included lions, but the reality was more complex and even more grotesque than 'Christians thrown to the lions'. Public executions and state-sanctioned violence are unpalatable today, but gladiatorial combat was evidently adapted to the conditions of the time. Until it was banned by the Christian emperors in the early fifth century AD there were few dissenting voices. In fact, theatre evoked sharper and more universal criticism for its stage nudity and erosion of public morality.

These spectacular shows were embedded in Roman society, and the imagery of the amphitheatre, circus and theatre permeated all classes, from top to bottom. For the first time a broad range of visual material has been brought together to illustrate the brilliance, danger, skills and brutality of those events and the political power that went with them. The exhibition was first conceived by Dr Eckart Köhne and Dr Cornelia Ewigleben, and it has been the greatest of pleasures to work with such friendly and generous-spirited colleagues on the staging of the London exhibition. I have also been fortunate to have had the assistance of many colleagues, both in my own department and throughout the British Museum. In particular, I have benefited from the constant support and advice of Dr Dyfri Williams, Keeper of the Department of Greek and Roman Antiquities, and especially Dr Paul Roberts, curator in that Department, while Teresa Francis of British Museum Press and Colin Grant have worked tirelessly to produce this fine English edition of the book.

RALPH JACKSON
*Curator*
Department of Prehistory
and Roman Britain, The British Museum

# Bread and Circuses:
# The Politics of Entertainment

The public has long since cast off its cares; the people that once bestowed commands, consulships, legions and all else, now meddles no more and longs eagerly for just two things: *panem et circenses* – bread and circuses.

The Roman poet Juvenal (*c.* AD 60–141) first made this famous statement in his Tenth Satire. Since then the quotation has been cited repeatedly as evidence of the decadence and irresponsibility of the population of Rome in the time of the Caesars. The author of the lines, however, was concerned less with fulminating against the games or the public distribution of grain than in condemning the Roman citizenry's lack of involvement in political life. The text describes the impotence of the people in the face of their autocratic sovereigns: the lethargy of those whom these sovereigns ruled and who, in Juvenal's opinion, had become mere non-political subjects.

The text does not, however, indicate that the inhabitants of Rome sat in the circus day in, day out, subsidized by the state and with no need to work for a living. Every recipient of *panis*, bread, was in fact allotted five *modii* (bushels) of grain a month, rather more than a single person needed. By way of comparison, the amount allotted for a legionary's consumption was four *modii* of grain a month. However, as only male Roman citizens resident in Rome had the right to receive this grain, families could certainly not live on state support alone. Additional grain had to be bought, not to mention other provisions, particularly oil. There were also the horrendous rents that had to be paid for accommodation in Rome. In view of the fact that the Roman community had no other regular welfare benefits in the modern sense, any idea that the state provided all-round care for its citizens is entirely erroneous. Naturally politicians and emperors made generous donations to the people on certain occasions – principally of money, but also of oil and other gifts in kind – but those occasions could not be predicted and were not regular enough to provide a living.

What about the second part of Juvenal's famous phrase, mentioning circuses? It is in fact confined to

1

**Circus Maximus, Rome**

Since the site of the Circus Maximus is not built over, the extent of the ancient layout can still be seen. This photograph was taken to the right of the *carceres* (starting boxes), looking down towards the *spina*, where a cypress marks the position of one of the turning posts. The ruins in the distance on the left are those of the imperial palaces on the Palatine hill.

*circenses*, games in the circus, not including theatrical performances or the contests of athletes and gladiators. The Circus Maximus could hold at least 150,000 people in the second century AD and, according to some sources, up to 250,000. If we agree with most scholars in assuming that Rome had about a million inhabitants at the time, then at least one-sixth or even a quarter of the population could have attended the races simultaneously. In terms of modern television, that would correspond to a staggering audience figure of 16 to 20 per cent, and the citizens of Rome were physically present, not just sitting in front of a screen at home. The circus offered a free mass spectacle to which everyone had access. The show was staged by the state itself, represented by the emperor or an official who made the arrangements for the games. Even in the heyday of racing in ancient Rome, however, there were not nearly enough races to constitute an uninterrupted programme. For the purposes of his satire Juvenal exaggerated the tendency he had observed for the citizens of Rome to seek an escape from reality. To this day, that image has determined the popularly held idea of the games of ancient Rome as a continual round of sporting events.

## THE OLDEST GAMES OF ROME – CHARIOT-RACING

According to legend, Rome owed the institution of 'games' to its mythical founder and first king, Romulus. These games were probably chariot-races and horseback races in honour of the god Consus, who was equated with Neptune, god of the sea and of horses. It was on the occasion of this festival, again according to legend, that the famous rape of the Sabine women took place. As well as the *consualia* (held on 21 August) there were other games with a long tradition behind them: the *equirria* (27 February and 14 March) and the feast of the *equus october* (15 October) in honour of Mars, as well as the *ludi taurii* (held every fifth year on 25 and 26 June). An important feature in the programmes of such games was the procession of those who were giving them and all participants (the *pompa*), together with sacrifices and other events. Athletic contests (running, wrestling and above all boxing) were probably a part of the games even at this early period.

Races on horseback subsequently took place rarely, and in later centuries must have seemed very old-fashioned. It is possible that a contest of this kind is shown on a marble vase found in the temple of Diana at Nemi, a small country town not far from Rome, and now in Copenhagen (fig. 2). The lap counter with eggs indicates that the scene is the Circus Maximus in Rome. In this form of the sport the jockeys (*desultores*) rode two horses each and had to change from one to the other at a full gallop several times during the race, a popular acrobatic variant on ordinary racing frequently described by classical writers. In this case the two *desultores* are not ordinary mortals: a small tail at

2

**Vase with horse-race**
Marble, first century BC
Ny Carlsberg Glyptotek, Copenhagen, 1518

The vase appears to show a horse-race, but the two jockeys (*desultores*) are not ordinary mortals. A small tail (not visible) on the rider in the picture shows that he is a satyr. He is in pursuit of a figure of Eros on the other side. The lap counter (left) indicates that the race is in its fifth lap. The shape of the marble vase resembles that of the Attic amphorae given as prizes. It was donated, with seven similar vessels, to the temple of Diana at Nemi, where it was found in 1895.

the rear of the rider shows that he is a satyr, a half-man, half-goat creature, who was among the retinue of the god of wine, Bacchus (Greek: Dionysos). His opponent may be the god of love, Amor (Greek: Eros).

The oldest games still regularly staged by the emperors

in later centuries were the *ludi romani*, held in honour of Jupiter. They are said to have been first given to celebrate the dedication of his great temple on the Capitol in Rome in 509 BC. At this period the city was still under the cultural and political influence of the Etruscans, who determined the organization and conduct of the games. There are few sources available for following centuries, so we do not know when the move towards holding certain festivals regularly every year was made. Again, the earliest indication of this change relates to the *ludi romani*, held annually after 366 BC at the latest.

Many events were traditionally held in the Circus Maximus, which occupied the natural hollow between the Palatine and Aventine hills. The shallow valley itself formed the racetrack, and the slopes of the two hills bordering it offered natural advantages as grandstands. It was not until Julius Caesar's time that permanent tiers of seating were built; previously spectators had to be satisfied with wooden benches for some, while most had to sit on the ground. Sometimes games were held on the Campus Martius (Field of Mars), a large and partly marshy area north of the city. Here, however, the only facilities were fenced-off racecourses, which at first had no buildings around them.

## THE GREEK THEATRE IN ROME

The year 364 BC was one of severe trial for Rome. An epidemic took its toll of many human lives, and in this desperate situation the Romans solemnly vowed to hold theatrical festivals in honour of the gods. They brought Etruscan actors to Rome to help them keep this vow – and a new branch of the entertainment industry was born. Its main inspiration came from the Greek cities of southern Italy with which the Romans came into increasingly close contact during the fourth century BC. Besides tragedy and comedy, burlesque folk plays were performed, and these were later to become the most popular pieces of all on the stages of Rome. However, it was over a hundred years before Greek tragedies and comedies were performed on stage in Latin; up to that point the Romans heard these plays in the original Greek.

There were still no stone theatres like those of Greece. Wooden buildings were constructed for theatrical festivals, and demolished again soon after the performances. The reason for this practice is to be sought in the dislike of the theatre felt by the influential conservatives of Rome. These critics regarded the content of the plays as being in stark opposition to the values usually connected with the city, and in view of the risqué verses and lewd subjects of many pieces, they did not intend to surrender the old Roman virtues without a struggle. This negative attitude to the theatre runs through the whole of ancient history, and was echoed by the moralizing Christian writers of the third and fourth centuries AD.

## THE GROWTH OF THE FESTIVAL CALENDAR

In the course of the third century BC there was an unprecedented expansion of the games and the Roman entertainment industry in general. The reasons for this cannot be clearly established. At this period Rome was becoming a major world power. It achieved domination of large parts of the Italian peninsula, and in two long wars, involving heavy losses, defeated Carthage, its one serious rival for supremacy in the western Mediterranean. Apart from the rich booty they won in these campaigns, the Romans now came into closer contact with other peoples, first the Greeks and the Campanian tribes of southern Italy, then the Hellenistic kingdoms to the east. In the difficult times of war a series of new games were pledged to the gods; these were organized annually and are thought to have been held until the end of the period of classical antiquity. In addition, the growing importance of Rome must certainly have been accompanied by a greater desire for display on the part of its citizens, and that desire found expression not only in the public buildings constructed by triumphant generals, funding them with their share of wartime booty, but also in the foundation of many new festivals.

These began with the *ludi plebeii* in honour of Jupiter, first held in 216 BC. They were given from 4 to 17 November, and chariot-racing, the most lavish of the spectacles involved, was staged on the last three days. A little later, in the year 208 BC, the *ludi apollinares* were dedicated to Apollo and ran from 6 to 13 July, with chariot-racing on two days. During the war with Hannibal the Romans had brought the sacred stone of Cybele, a goddess of Asia Minor, back to their city at the behest of an oracle. On this occasion games were promised to Cybele, too, and are known to have been held from 194 BC as the *ludi megalesia*, on 4 to 10 April, with one day of chariot-racing. They were closely followed, on 12 to 19 April, by the *ludi cereri* in honour of Ceres, goddess of fertility, and these games again included a day's chariot-racing. There is definite evidence of the existence of this festival from 202 BC, and it may go back further. April was an eventful month in general, since the *floralia* in honour of the goddess Flora were then held from 27 April to 3 May. At first these games were staged only sporadically, but in 173 BC they became a part of the regular festival calendar.

Another innovation in the festival programme consisted of the animal hunts and fights between animals (*venationes*). As early as the third century BC victorious generals riding in triumphal processions led with them exotic animals seized from their defeated enemies. The first animal fights were seen by the Romans in 186 BC at the celebrations held by Fulvius Nobilior on the occasion of his triumph over the Aetolians, a Greek people, when lions and panthers fought in the Circus Maximus. The conservative senators did not care for this novelty, and passed a senatorial decree prohibiting the import of wild animals from Africa, but the ban was lifted twenty years later, and imports of exotic animals for the games were permitted.

There was yet another innovation for the triumphal celebrations of Fulvius Nobilior: not only Greek actors but also Greek athletes appeared in Rome for the first time. Their performances do not seem to have been to the public taste – or at least, the sources show that the next athletic contest was not held in Rome until 80 BC. At that time the dictator Sulla recruited athletes from all over Greece, and as a result only a fraction of the events originally planned for the Olympic Games held in the same year could be staged, for lack of competitors. The 'Greek' competitive sports new to Rome were the long jump, javelin throwing and discus throwing; the Romans had already practised running, wrestling and boxing as sporting disciplines. However, social acceptance of Greek sport was slow in coming for one main reason: the athletes performed naked. Such nudity profoundly shocked the Roman sense of modesty, and many conservatives saw its adoption as a clear sign of the declining morals of Rome. Consequently, athletic competition was a matter of controversy for quite a long time. Not so with what today we would regard as a far more dubious form of entertainment: gladiatorial contests.

## A NEW SENSATION

The most successful innovation in the repertoire of Roman spectacular entertainment was undoubtedly the introduction of gladiatorial contests. A note by the historian Livy tells us the precise date of the first such contest, in 264 BC. At the magnificent funeral ceremonies of Decimus Junius Pero arranged by his two sons three pairs of gladiators appeared. The next reference is for the year 216 BC, when the three sons of Marcus Aemilius Lepidus organized fights between twenty-two pairs of gladiators. There are no written sources for the period between these two events, but we may suppose that gladiatorial contests were regularly staged as part of the funeral ceremonies for important citizens. In the following period the number of contestants appearing rose rapidly. The year 183 BC saw sixty pairs of gladiators fighting at the funeral of Publius Licinius. As a rule such performances took place in the Forum Romanum, since no permanent amphitheatre yet existed. Wooden seating was erected for the spectators.

While the public games (*ludi*) included theatrical performances and chariot-racing, gladiatorial contests of this kind were not part of them. They were generally held for the funerals of influential Romans, whose families took this opportunity to demonstrate their power and prosperity. Usually the dead man himself had left instructions for his funeral arrangements in his will. Fulfilling this part of his directions was an important

duty of his heirs, and was known as the *munus*. For this reason, the classical term for the gladiatorial contest was *munus* (plural: *munera*), in contrast to the games (*ludi*), which were dedicated to a deity and organized by representatives of the state.

## THE ORIGIN OF THE GLADIATORIAL GAMES

How did the gladiatorial contests of Rome come into being? The question was a subject of controversy among scholars for a long time, since it was not an issue that interested Roman authors. The sole mention in classical texts comes from the *Deipnosophistai* ('men learned in the arts of the banquet') by the Greek author Athenaeus, written in the first century AD. Athenaeus cites an older historian, Nikolaos of Damascus, as saying that the Romans adopted gladiatorial games from the Etruscans. This thesis was long regarded as valid, since Rome did follow the lead of the Etruscans in many other areas of life. However, those Etruscan monuments that are still extant contain no direct indication at all of the existence of gladiatorial contests, something that is all the more surprising in that the wall paintings found in the tombs of rich Etruscans show a wide variety of sporting contests, including horseback races and athletic competitions – but no gladiators. A famous painting in the so-called 'Tomb of the Augurs' in the city of Tarquinia could, however, be a reference; it shows a man with his head concealed by a hood, trying to defend himself with a club against a dog being set on him by a masked figure. The intention appears to be to kill a human being in the context of the games, but the scene does not, of course, show a fight between two men.

Not until lavish tomb paintings were found in southern Italy was it possible to answer the question of the origin of gladiatorial contests. These frescoes come chiefly from Paestum, a city in Campania, south of Naples. They were painted between 370 and 340 BC and depict various scenes at funeral games, generally including a chariot-race, fist fights, and a duel between two warriors armed with helmets, shields and spears. Since in some cases a referee is shown standing beside these pairs of men, they can only have been involved in contests in honour of the dead, a direct parallel to the later *munera* of Rome. It is doubtful whether the term 'gladiator' can be used at this early period, for nothing is known of the origin and position in life of any of the men depicted. None the less, there are other arguments in favour of identifying Campania as the area where gladiatorial fights originated: the first stone amphitheatres were built there, and it was the site of the most important gladiatorial schools.

The idea of shedding human blood beside a dead man's grave is very old, and occurs in most ancient Mediterranean cultures. The blood was supposed to reconcile the dead with the living. This is one possible explanation of the indication that the Romans took over gladiatorial contests from the Etruscans. The origin of the *munera* in religious worship was never forgotten in Rome, and the Christian author Tertullian, writing as late as AD 200, mentioned it in condemning the shameful nature of gladiatorial contests (*De spectaculis*, 12):

> For of old, in the belief that the souls of the dead are propitiated with human blood, they used at funerals to sacrifice captives or slaves of poor value whom they bought. Afterwards, it seemed good to obscure their impiety by making it a pleasure. So they found comfort for death in murder.

From a modern viewpoint it is difficult to understand the enthusiasm felt by the Romans for the bloody spectacle that will be described later in this book. However, we should not forget that our horror of watching the torture of human beings is an attitude that has arisen relatively late in the history of civilization, developing only slowly. Public torture and public executions were part of everyday life in many cultures, not least in Europe during the Middle Ages, and indeed, until quite recently, in the modern period. Both sacred and secular authorities were extensively involved, and no one saw these things as contradicting Christian ethics.

Even today, spectators relish pictures of catastrophes, or sports in which accidents or even the death of participants may be expected; they lend such spectacles a certain piquancy. Modern television transmissions of fatal crashes in motor racing spring to mind; the media bring them into our homes, and the danger to which the drivers in their powerful cars are exposed plays a considerable part in our enjoyment. It sets the final seal on the protagonists' victory. Other sports, such as Alpine skiing and three-day eventing, also benefit in the public mind from the similar risks they entail.

Naturally the gladiatorial contests of the ancient world are in no way comparable with the sports mentioned above. Those contests sanctioned mortal combat between one man and another, and made the death of the loser the general rule, displaying a total lack of the moral and ethical principles that are generally accepted in modern times. But the value system of Roman society differed fundamentally from our own in this point, and we cannot apply today's standards in making moral judgements. Roman civilization and culture is never so utterly remote from our understanding as in the matter of these life-and-death games.

## ROME IN THE FIRST AND SECOND CENTURIES BC

The Roman writer Livy (59 BC–AD 17) describes the origins of the Roman theatrical festivals in his history of the state, concluding with this summary: 'Amongst the humble origins of other institutions it has seemed worth while to set down the early history of the play, that it might be seen how sober were the beginnings of

**3**

**Forum Romanum, Rome**

This photograph was taken looking south-east from the Capitol. The foundations in the left foreground are those of the temple of Saturn, beyond which lies the paved area where gladiatorial contests were held until the early imperial period.

an art that has nowadays reached a point where opulent kingdoms could hardly support its mad extravagance' (*Ab urbe condita libri* 7, 2).

By the end of the Punic Wars against Carthage in 146 BC the Roman state had achieved the status of a world power. The western Mediterranean was entirely under its control, and it was about to confront the Graeco-Hellenistic kingdoms in the east. Little more than a century later the Romans were masters of the entire Mediterranean region, and finally, in 31 BC and

after the defeat of Cleopatra and Mark Antony, the future emperor Augustus incorporated Egypt, the last of the old kingdoms, into the Roman empire.

This period of expansion and the brilliant achievements of Roman foreign policy were accompanied by great difficulties at home. Power was in the hands of a few families whose members held all the major public offices. Rivalries were increasingly expressed in terms of open hostility. The conquered regions of the empire brought Rome first and foremost money, but also

luxury goods. The senate tried to control extravagance by constantly passing new laws. We are thus well informed about the extent of the changes; one example may suffice here. The *lex fannia* of 161 BC set the upper limit of expenditure on a banquet at 25 sestertii. In 81 BC the sum had risen to 300 sestertii for the same purpose, more than ten times as much. A generation later the army general Lucius Licinius Lucullus, who died in 57 BC, would spend up to 50,000 sestertii on a banquet – it is not surprising that his name has become

13

a byword for extravagance. At this time the annual pay of a legionary soldier was 480 sestertii.

The huge wealth of the upper classes of society was in contrast to the increasingly grave social and economic problems of the common people of Italy. The long wars required a great number of soldiers, who came from Rome and allied Italian cities. A soldier's regular period of service was twenty years. After that length of time, many veterans could not work in the fields to make a living, and did not want to. This constant drain on the male population meant that many farms had to be run entirely by slaves. The rich senators who possessed the requisite means to buy huge estates benefited, for many small farmers were forced to sell their unprofitable land and move to Rome. The discontented urban population, the *plebs urbana*, gradually developed into an important factor in the power struggle, and their rulers had to take account of them. From the late second century BC the *plebs* campaigned for cheap grain. They were supported by individual politicians from the families of the nobility, partly out of a desire to solve social problems, but also with an eye to their own careers, for they regarded their social commitment as an effective way of acquiring influence over potential voters and winning their support.

## THE ROMAN ARISTOCRACY AND THE GAMES

Today it would be unthinkable for prosperous citizens and the state to 'donate' extremely expensive entertainments to the rest of the population of a city on a regular basis, free and without any direct state commission. Translated into modern terms, it would be equivalent to the mayor and town council of a city making a large annual sum available from the civic budget for the upkeep of a football ground, the wages of the players and the manager – and free admission for the public. Such an expense would inevitably be too great a charge on the budget, and the civil servants would have to make up the deficit from their own pockets. Of course, it is absurd to transfer the ancient Roman situation to the present day in such terms, principally because our society is built on such different social and political foundations. To understand how publicly financed games came into being, a brief glance at the aristocratic families of ancient Rome will be helpful.

Roman society was divided into classes. The great mass of the people, free but without political influence (the *populus romanus*), were beneath the ranks of the knights (*ordo equester*) and senators (*ordo senatorius*). Property worth a minimum of 400,000 to 1,000,000 sestertii was a prerequisite for membership of the two last-named groups, and almost without exception the senators and their families provided candidates for political office. The senate had 300 members at first, later 600; under Caesar the number rose to 900. Formally speaking, the senate could take no decisions of its own, but it advised consuls and other officials, and in fact was the powerhouse of the Roman empire.

Candidates for high political office came from a small circle of about two dozen families of senatorial rank. Between 218 and 108 BC more than a third of the consuls, 83 out of 220, came from only eight families. The representatives of these rich and aristocratic families (*gens*, plural: *gentes*) were 'the state' – they ruled the Roman empire. In the protocol of ancient diplomacy they were on a par with the kings of the Hellenistic kingdoms in Greece, Egypt and Syria. Their influence (*auctoritas*) was expressed in terms of the offices they themselves and their ancestors had held in the state. Those offices gave access to military and political posts, which in their turn guaranteed income. The command of an army, or the governorship of one of the prosperous provinces, meant considerable prestige and large profits.

Roman magistrates held office for a year. Their posts were unpaid and honorary, so it would not be accurate to describe them as officials or civil servants in the modern sense. At the beginning of a man's career as an officer of the state – the *cursus honorum* – was the post of quaestor, for which a man must be at least thirty years old. One stage higher were the four aediles, who must be at least thirty-seven. Their chief concern was to look after the interests of the city of Rome, and they supervised the temples, markets, streets and squares, brothels, baths, and the water supply. They also organized the official games. The next step up the official ladder was the post of praetor. Praetors exercised functions of administration and jurisdiction, and after their period of office were usually appointed provincial administrators or given a military command. They too had to arrange some of the games after the first century BC. The lower age limit for a praetor was forty. At the head of the state were the two consuls, who were the highest magistrates, chiefly responsible for home policy, and must be at least forty-three.

Candidates for the above posts were elected, in a complicated system, by the people, who did not cast individual votes but voted according to electoral districts. However, the candidates can hardly be said to have represented any political programmes, since they all came from the same small upper class of society. There were no political parties in the modern sense. In the first century BC contenders for office differed chiefly in seeking to further their political aims either with the aid of the senate (the *optimates*) or through the support of the people and their tribunes (the *populares*). The sale of votes and electoral corruption were an established part of political life and provided many representatives of the people with a significant source of income.

Only the ambition of the aristocratic families and their image of themselves kept such a system of government going. The price this small circle had to pay for exclusive dominance was the making of donations to the people, who naturally wanted to profit by the extraordinary boom in the fortune of Rome them-selves. From a modern viewpoint the closest compari-son would be with the sheikhdoms of the Persian Gulf which have made billions from the exploitation of the oilfields. Political power and control of this source of wealth are in the hands of enormously rich families who, for their part, are morally and institutionally bound to provide their subjects with compensation in the form of social benefits, such as good medical care and other gifts. In ancient Rome the people also received such benefits – subsidies or bonuses, as they might be known today. They included first and fore-most cheap or free grain, banquets held regularly for the citizens, gifts in kind and money, and – last but not least – the staging of lavish games. The rich families used such subsidies to leave behind a record of their own power and political influence – influence that was displayed in the offices they held, and in having as great a number of supporters as possible.

## THE EXPENSES

The public games were organized by the aediles; later the praetors took over part of the task. The huge cost far exceeded the state funds made available for the purpose; two examples: the *ludi romani* (5 to 19 Sep-tember) received a contribution from the state of 760,000 sestertii, and the *ludi plebeii* (6 to 13 July) received 600,000 sestertii. These sums undoubtedly represented only a basic amount, and had to be sup-plemented by the holders of the games out of their own pockets. None the less, it was the accepted custom for a man to try outdoing his predecessors by coming up with increasingly unusual ideas for bigger and better games. Their usefulness to his career did not appear immediately obvious, since as a rule several years passed before a former aedile could stand for praetor, candidature for these offices being tied to a minimum age. But if he had succeeded in making a favourable impression with the memory of his own games, it usually furthered his chances of election. Other members of his family would also profit by his good reputation, for instance when political beginners from his own camp became candidates for a quaestor-ship. The people had their own ideas, and tried to choose candidates who might be expected to provide lavish spectacles, as the dictator Lucius Cornelius Sulla discovered at a later date. When he was quaestor he participated in the war against Jugurtha, king of Numidia, and he later applied for the rank of praetor without being an aedile first. The people felt cheated, since if Sulla had become an aedile in the usual way he would have had to hold games. They had hoped for exotic animals from Africa, which Sulla could easily have obtained through his connections on that conti-nent. His candidature failed, although he did become praetor a year later and he then thanked the people by providing African lions for the Circus Maximus.

In the endeavour to hold ever more magnificent and expensive games, the holders competed with one another in producing new ideas. First and foremost they had to engage the best actors and most famous charioteers – that is to say, it was incumbent on them to offer a really outstanding programme. However, there were other ways of making the expenditure rise steeply. As mentioned above, the public *ludi* were dedicated to individual deities and also comprised reli-gious ceremonies, particularly sacrifices. In the minds of the people of classical antiquity, a sacred act – and, legally speaking, the games were sacred acts – was not valid if it did not satisfy the ritual requirements in every respect. An unfavourable omen, the offering of sacri-fices in the wrong sequence or some mishap in the course of the ritual meant that it all had to start again from the beginning, for the gods demanded correct performance.

A famous episode from the year 211 BC clearly shows how important the smooth running of these events was. While the *ludi apollinares* were taking place in the theatre, a cry suddenly went up that the enemy was at the gates. The spectators in the theatre leaped to their feet and ran for their weapons. How-ever, it turned out to be a false alarm. When the citi-zens returned to the theatre they found that one of the actors had been dancing during their absence to the accompaniment of flute-playing. 'All is saved!' cried the crowd – for the correct conduct of the festival had been maintained by the brave singer's marathon per-formance. If it had been interrupted, the entire pro-gramme, lasting eight days, would have had to be repeated. The enemy who almost laid siege to Rome on this occasion was the Carthaginian general Hanni-bal, and the cry that struck alarm into the spectators became proverbial: '*Hannibal ante portas*'.

Very soon the holders of games hit upon the idea of deliberately devising reasons to repeat them, thus making them go on longer and appearing particularly generous. The historian Livy says that one year the magistrates held the *ludi romani* three times and the *ludi plebeii* five times because of infringements of reli-gious ritual. Finally a law had to be passed allowing only one repeat performance.

Another possible way for magistrates to endow their own games with particular brilliance was to build magnificent theatres. As mentioned above, the conser-vative senate would not at first tolerate any permanent stone-built theatre, for the senators were of the opinion that stage plays were a bad influence on the popula-tion of Rome. Consequently, the aediles had wooden constructions erected and demolished again after the festivities. The wooden theatre built in 58 BC by Marcus Aemilius Scaurus was particularly famous. The wall of the stage was adorned with pillars of African marble and with statues, and Scaurus used glass, gold, various kinds of marble and golden fabrics in the fur-nishings. In fact memorable games could considerably improve the prospects of a candidate for office. Scaurus profited from his lavish investment, since the people elected him praetor two years later, and he was still deriving benefit from it four years after the remarkable event, when he was a candidate for consul. In a letter of the year 54 BC the politician Cicero gave his views on this election:

> I have never seen candidates so evenly matched ...
> Scaurus has been prosecuted by Triarius. I may add that no very noticeable sympathy has been aroused on his behalf, but still his aedileship is not ungratefully remembered ...
> There remain the two plebeians, who are nicely balanced, Domitius having powerful friends and being helped by his show.

In fact Scaurus gained no further advantage from his magnificent theatre, since he was exiled for bribing electors, despite the brilliant advocacy of Cicero in his defence.

A curiosity was the double theatre financed by Gaius Scribonius Curio in 52/51 BC. Two movable theatres of traditional semi-circular construction, mounted on rollers, were pushed together to make a round amphitheatre. In this way plays could be performed in the morning and gladiatorial contests in the afternoon in the same building. The famous general Pompey had to resort to a trick to enable him to build the first stone theatre in Rome in 61–55 BC: he had a temple of Venus Victrix built above the semi-circular auditorium, and declared that the rows of seating in the theatre constituted the substructure and stairway of the temple itself.

Gladiatorial contests were held independently of state games. As described above, they formed an element in funeral ceremonies, and that remained the case almost without exception until the time of Caesar. Since the occasion for such a spectacle could not be planned in advance, certain adjustments were necessary if the *munera* were to be effectively staged as propaganda for the holder's own cause. The bereaved mourners would thus delay the games specified in the will until the best moment for them arrived. The fact that the dead might be kept waiting some time for their gladiatorial contests did not trouble the living much. Several times, a few politicians tried to pass laws putting an end to this abuse, but without success. After 63 BC a man was not allowed to stage *munera* for two years before becoming a candidate for any office, but the rules on exceptions were generously interpreted, making it possible to circumvent this ban without much difficulty.

## CAESAR

The career of Gaius Julius Caesar serves as the perfect example of the rise of a power-hungry politician in Rome in the middle of the first century BC. The future ruler of Rome, born in the year 100 BC, came from a very old but not prosperous family. He began his political career as a quaestor in 68 BC, and the people

elected him aedile in 65 BC. He impressed them with the buildings he constructed during his period of office, but above all with the games he arranged. Caesar knew how to create a great sensation by clever tactics and the investment of large sums of money. In particular, he succeeded in giving so many spectacles of his own that his colleague in office, the aedile Marcus Calpurnius Bibulus, was left lagging hopelessly

4
**Gaius Julius Caesar**
Lived 100–44 BC
Marble
Pisa, Campo Santo

This posthumous portrait was executed during the rule of Caesar's adopted son Augustus.

behind when it came to the organization of the public *ludi*. Apart from his political calculations, Caesar himself was an enthusiastic admirer of gladiatorial combats. Letters of Cicero show that he maintained a gladiatorial school of his own in Campania, the cradle of the gladiatorial system, and the fights he staged in honour of his father cast everything of the kind seen before into the shade. Caesar had delayed carrying out the stipulations in his father's will until his own period of office as aedile, which meant in this case that the dead man had to wait twenty years for his funeral celebrations. Even in advance, however, the occasion could be said to have hit the headlines, for it was known that the aedile planned to present more fighters than had ever been seen before. Caesar's political opponents succeeded in getting a law passed in the senate setting the highest number of pairs of gladiators that any one person might engage at 320. The measure was explained by fear of another gladiatorial revolt such as that led by Spartacus, which had held all Italy in suspense a few years before, in 73–71 BC. The real aim of this restriction, however, was to restrain the ambitious aedile, who in fact derived even more publicity from the action.

How did Caesar find the money for such ventures during his term of office? He ran up debts, like most of his colleagues in similar situations: the creditors speculated on their debtor obtaining money from profitable posts connected with his offices. First, however, Caesar had to invest yet again in his career. It will be useful to give a brief survey of this incident, since it sheds light on the situation in first-century Rome. To increase his reputation and influence, he stood in 63 BC for the office of chief pontiff or priest, the *pontifex maximus*, a post that was held for life. Suetonius, who wrote biographies of the first emperors of Rome in the second century AD, wrote (*Caesar* 13):

> He stood for the office of Chief Pontiff, and used the most flagrant bribery to secure it. The story goes that, reckoning up the enormous debts thus contracted, he told his mother, as she kissed him goodbye on the morning of the poll, that if he did not return to her as Chief Pontiff he would not return at all.

But the investment was worth it; Caesar won the election.

Next year he became praetor, and thus had the opportunity of being able to settle his debts, for after their year of office praetors took over the administration of a province, which they could then unscrupulously exploit to further their own interests. However, Caesar had almost overshot the mark, for his creditors did not want to see him leave for the province of Spain, which was allotted to him after his year as praetor. Only when the rich Marcus Licinius Crassus stood surety for him was he able to go. In less than two years Caesar had paid all his debts and become a rich man. It does not take much imagination to guess that the people of the provinces felt they had been sucked dry. In many cases their representatives in Rome brought legal charges, and such cases, in turn, could be won only by bribing the judges with large sums of money – money that usually came from the funds the defendant had already squeezed out of his province.

At this time the city of Rome was above all influenced by two politicians: Caesar and Pompey. Both were driven by such great personal ambition that a confrontation was unavoidable. The ensuing split ran right through the upper classes of Rome. In a long and bloody civil war Caesar finally succeeded in conquering his rival. He had himself proclaimed sole ruler (*dictator*) and from now on controlled the state. As head of state, Caesar now had much wider responsibilities to the people than ever before, and he met them by providing brilliant games and an abundance of other gifts. The four great victories he had won over his enemies were the occasion for games at his triumphs.

The festivities in the year 46 BC lasted for weeks, and

eclipsed anything that had ever been seen before. First the people were given presents: every citizen received ten bushels of grain (double the usual subsidized amount), ten pounds of oil and 400 sestertii. This bonus alone, at a rather low estimate of 150,000 recipients, would amount to a sum of 60 million sestertii. In addition, Caesar paid every citizen a year of rent up to the sum of 2,000 sestertii. There were allocations of free meat, and the *dictator* twice gave a breakfast for the whole people. Expenditure on the games in no way lagged behind the money spent on these gifts. First Caesar had new wooden seating erected in the Forum Romanum, and the fighting area was furnished with underground corridors and lifts to provide special effects for the entry of the performers. Besides the usual high spots on the programme, there were two battle scenes performed by hundreds of participants, one on land and one on water, the latter with ships on a specially dug artificial lake. There were some distinguished figures among the fighters, as Suetonius particularly notes. His account ends this section (Suetonius, *Caesar* 39):

> His public shows were of great variety. They included a gladiatorial contest, stage-plays for every quarter of Rome performed in several languages, chariot-races in the Circus, athletic competitions, and a mock naval battle. At the gladiatorial contest in the Forum, a man named Furius Leptinus, of patrician family, fought Quintus Calpenus, a barrister and former senator, to the death. The sons of petty kings from Asia and Bithynia danced the Pyrrhic sword dance … A broad ditch had been dug around the race-course, now extended at either end of the Circus, and the contestants were young noblemen who drove four-horse and two-horse chariots or rode pairs of horses, jumping from back to back. The so-called Troy Game, a sham fight … was performed by two troops of boys, one younger than the other. Wild-beast hunts took place five days running, and the entertainment ended with a battle between two armies, each consisting of 500 infantry, twenty elephants, and thirty cavalry. To let the camps be pitched facing each other, Caesar removed the central barrier of the Circus, around which the chariots ran. Athletic contests were held in a temporary stadium on the Campus Martius, and lasted for three days. The naval battle was fought on an artificial lake … between Tyrian and Egyptian ships, with two, three, or four banks of oars, and heavily manned. Such huge numbers of visitors flocked to these shows from all directions that many of them had to sleep in tents pitched along the streets or roads, or on roof tops; and often the pressure of the crowd crushed people to death. The victims included two senators.

## THE AGE OF AUGUSTUS

For all his skill as an army commander and in winning public favour, Caesar underestimated the resistance the conservative senators would put up to rule by one man. The forces of reaction saw only one way out of the concentration of all power in the person of the *dictator*, and that was the assassination of Caesar. Under the leadership of Brutus and Cassius a conspiracy formed. The actual murder of Caesar on the Ides of March (15 March) in 44 BC was the result of fears that he was about to declare himself king of Rome. Caesar was killed during a senate meeting in the *curia* of Pompey, part of the buildings belonging to the com-

5
**Cameo of Augustus**
Reigned 27 BC–AD 14
Agate
Römisch-Germanisches
Museum/Rheinisches
Bildarchiv der Stadt Köln, 70,3

This portrait of Augustus was probably executed during the century following his death in AD 14, although the setting dates to the sixteenth century. A cameo of this quality probably belonged to a member of an imperial or senatorial family.

plex of Pompey's theatre. The consequences of this deed were new and even bloodier civil wars. Caesar's adopted son Octavian (later to be the Emperor Augustus) and Mark Antony pursued and defeated the assassins, to clash with each other a little later for supremacy over the Roman empire. Antony was backed by the last Egyptian queen of the Greek Ptolemy family, Cleopatra. In 31 BC they were defeated in a sea battle off Actium in western Greece by Octavian's fleet, and committed suicide the following year when their situation had become hopeless. The victor thus became in effect sole ruler of the Roman empire, to which he could now add Egypt as an important province.

The new head of state had learned from the fate of his adoptive father. He avoided challenging the senate and making moves that would provoke its opposition. Only four years after the battle of Actium did he finally confirm his own position. Nominally, the senate and the two consuls continued to hold the highest authority in the state, but in fact Octavian reserved to himself the decisions on all important questions. He exercised this power by having major offices transferred to him for life. The *imperium proconsolare* ensured his con-

trol over all the major provinces and the army. In addition, he assumed the office of consul annually, although with a colleague of allegedly equal rank. In the year 23 BC he abdicated from this office and instead received the *tribunicia potestas*, the powers of a tribune of the people, which he could use to determine home policy. However, the real basis of his power lay not so much in these posts as in his influence on society. Augustus himself describes it in the *Res gestae*, an account of his deeds in which, at the end of his life, he summed up his own achievements for the benefit of posterity. He writes (*Res gestae* 34): 'Since that time I have outdone all others in influence and authority (*auctoritas*), but as to the power of office (*potestas*), I have never held more than the many who have been my colleagues in office.' He derived a large part of his *auctoritas* from the veneration in which his person was held, and which he very cleverly channelled. The nickname Augustus came from the religious sphere, and had hitherto been reserved for deities. Augustus avoided having himself worshipped as a god in his lifetime, in contrast to the current practice in the Greek kingdoms of the Hellenistic period (third to first centuries BC). Instead, he set up a cult to his personal patron deities, which very quickly spread among the population. The cities of the Greek east built temples to him, although he shared them with the goddess Roma.

As head of state, Augustus took on a number of tasks that had previously been in the hands of the magistrates, and were intended to ensure him the affection of the people. First there was the supervision of grain imports, which were of vital importance to the food supplies of the city of Rome. In addition, Augustus embarked on a mighty building programme embracing almost all the public squares, streets and temples of the city. At the end of his life he could boast that, where he had found a city of brick at the beginning of his reign, he left behind him a city of marble. Augustus had some of the buildings constructed himself, and members of his family and political adherents commissioned others. New and lavish settings for games were also built. A major project was the theatre that the *princeps* (emperor) dedicated to his dead son-in-law Marcellus. However, there was an unfortunate incident at the dedication ceremony, when the folding seat on which Augustus was about to take his place collapsed under him.

His supporter Lucius Cornelius Balbus built another stone theatre, and the able general Titus Statilius Taurus erected an amphitheatre – the first permanent building of its kind in Rome. Apparently, however, the important *munera* were still held in the Forum, probably because it could accommodate more spectators and, with the surrounding buildings, made a grander display. Augustus had the old place of public assembly, known as the *saepta*, converted by his general and son-in-law Marcus Vipsanius Agrippa into a magnifi-

6
**Roman theatre, Orange**
Early first century AD

Compared to the theatre at
Arles, the similar building in
Orange is in a much better state
of preservation, although no
major parts of the sculptural
decoration have been found.
The wall of the stage here
originally had a three-storey
pillared facade in front of it.
The prominent niche above the
central door was intended to
take a statue of the emperor.

cent complex with pillared marble halls, which could
also be used for gladiatorial contests and animal fights.
The summit of these activities was the placing of an
Egyptian obelisk on the *spina* (central barrier) of the
Circus Maximus.

Considerable expense on the games themselves, in
which Augustus far outdid his predecessor Caesar,
matched all this building activity. In the *Res gestae* (22)
he praises his own achievements as follows:

> Three times I held a gladiatorial spectacle in my own name
> and five times in the names of my sons or grandsons; in
> which spectacles some ten thousand men took part in
> combat. Twice in my own name and a third time in the
> name of my grandson, I provided a public display of
> athletes summoned from all parts. I held state games (*ludi*)
> four times in my own name and twenty-three times on
> behalf of other magistrates ... I have provided public
> spectacles of the hunting of wild beasts twenty-six times in
> my own name or that of my sons and grandsons, in the
> Circus or the Forum or the amphitheatres, in which some
> three thousand five hundred beasts have been killed.

In addition, there was a magnificent naval battle in a
lake specially dug for the purpose and measuring 500
by 360 metres, with thirty large ships and a large
number of smaller vessels on each side. Not counting
the slaves at the oars, 3,000 people in all fought on
this occasion alone. Like his predecessors Sulla and
Caesar, Augustus also founded games of his own that
took place annually and were intended to keep the
memory of his victories alive.

## THE IMPERIAL ROMAN PERIOD: THE JULIO-CLAUDIAN DYNASTY

As the first of the Roman emperors, Augustus had
secured and extended his dominance on the basis of
republican foundations. He had proceeded very cau-
tiously, and nominally ruled together with the senate.
His successors systematically built up their own power,
forcing back the representatives of the old aristocracy
even further.

All Roman emperors up to the death of Nero in AD
65 were of the Julio-Claudian dynasty, which started
with Augustus. During this period princely rule
became the accepted form of government. The relationship between the *princeps* and the people of Rome
also became established. The emperor and his advisers
learned how to assess and influence popular feeling in
this new political situation. The citizens might have
lost all influence in the daily business of politics, but
they still represented an essential factor within the city
of Rome, and one that could not be ignored. From the
time of Augustus onwards the identification of the individual with the state was linked to the person of the
emperor; the expectations of the *plebs* now related to
him, and no longer to the senate or the members of
various aristocratic families.

Augustus ruled as *princeps* from 27 BC to his death
in the year AD 14. During those forty-two years he consolidated a new form of government that at first had
been an experiment, and one that could have failed

had the head of state died prematurely. Many of the traditionally minded senatorial families were still in existence – enfeebled after the civil war, but still in possession of considerable influence. Only a carefully judged balance of power between emperor and senate managed to prevent the formation of a strong opposition, such as the opposition to Caesar that had arisen a few years earlier. Ultimately, it was the authority of Augustus that prevented any new clashes.

At the very beginning of his period of sole rule the *princeps* consistently endeavoured to establish a succession. To avoid tension in the senatorial ranks, that succession could not come from any of the aristocratic families. The potential inheritor of power received his legitimacy first and foremost from his membership of the family of Augustus. In addition, the rising man was to distinguish himself in political and military life, and hold all the offices of state, up to the consulate, in order to acquire authority of his own.

### Tiberius

When several contenders for the succession to Augustus had died, including his two grandsons Gaius and Lucius Caesar, he finally named as his heir his stepson Tiberius, whom he had adopted in the year AD 4. In his will he recommended the senate to accept this successor; at this point there was no precedent for the delegation of power in a princely state. Tiberius hesitated for a full month before he officially took up his new position. In the course of his reign it soon transpired that he did not have the knack of government. Like Augustus, he maintained what senatorial rights remained, but kept the making of all important decisions to himself. The classical sources describe him as solitary and unsociable. After twelve years he retired to Capri in AD 26 for the rest of his reign, while his representatives in the capital took the political decisions. The inhabitants of the city did not like his constant absence from Rome. In this situation there were bound to be actual or alleged conspiracies against the emperor, leading to a series of trials for high treason. The prefect of the Praetorian guard, Lucius Aelius Sejanus, who had married into the family of Tiberius, was the most prominent of those who lost their lives. In this atmosphere of distrust the *princeps* also had many innocent senators executed.

Tiberius had not given much thought to the inhabitants of Rome. He had no magnificent buildings constructed during his reign, and did not once hold games. On the contrary, he set upper limits to the wages of actors and the number of pairs of gladiators who might appear at a *munus*. Since his birthday fell during the period of the *ludi plebeii*, the organizers wanted to put on a particularly good programme in his honour by holding additional chariot-races, but the emperor rejected the idea, earning himself a reputation as a skinflint with all these unpopular measures. Since Tiberius very seldom attended the regular games, the

Romans hardly ever saw him, and the distance between *princeps* and people became even greater.

Able organizers tried to make capital out of these deficiencies by holding games at their own expense. They derived high profits from the entrance money, but saved whenever possible on the cost of the events themselves. This led to a catastrophe in AD 27, one that the historian Publius Cornelius Tacitus describes in his *Annales* (4, 62 f.) as the first event of that year.

At Fidenae, a place only 8 km north of Rome, the freedman Atilius had constructed an amphitheatre for gladiatorial contests that would bring in a good profit. However, as the businessman had to keep his expenses down in building the wooden arena, he had taken short cuts on both proper foundations and fixing the structure together. Because of its proximity to the capital and the economy measures adopted by Tiberius, the people of Rome flocked to Fidenae to enjoy a rare gladiatorial spectacle. The slapdash construction work was not up to this great crush of people. When the rows of seats were full the substructure collapsed, burying the spectators and those hoping to see the show who were just outside the amphitheatre. Tacitus gives the number of victims as 50,000 dead and severely injured. The senate investigated the disaster and passed a law making proper foundations compulsory for similar buildings. In addition, every organizer of such events had to show that he possessed a fortune of at least 400,000 sestertii (equivalent to the minimum assets of a senator). In this way it was hoped that speculators of doubtful repute could no longer earn money from such projects. The senate sent Atilius into exile.

### Caligula

Unpopular as Tiberius had been, on his death in AD 37 he left an established empire with its finances in good order. His great-nephew Gaius Julius Caesar, a great-grandson of Augustus, succeeded him as the only suitable candidate. He had spent his youth with his father Germanicus in the army camps on the Rhine, where to the amusement of the legionaries he often wore military boots (*caligae*) that were much too large for him – they earned him his nickname of Caligula, 'Little Boot'. Just twenty-five years old when he came to power, Caligula developed into a prime example of imperial megalomania. His political decisions were not very successful, but worst of all, he aroused the hostility of the senate and the members of his own family. The result was a number of conspiracies, followed by trials, which further decimated the ranks of those senatorial families into which Tiberius had already made inroads. In the four years of his reign Caligula squandered the huge fortune of 2.7 billion sestertii that his predecessor had left him. Among the main beneficiaries were the people of Rome, who after a lean period under Tiberius could at last enjoy state bonuses and brilliant games again. However, that pleasure did not last long, since the *princeps*, having frittered away his means, raised taxes to unprecedented levels, and did not shrink from imposing them on the poorer part of the population as well as the richer classes.

The scandalous deeds of Caligula were many – even affecting the games in which he enthusiastically took part. It would take too long to list all the infamous tales told of him, particularly since Roman historians undoubtedly exaggerated or invented some of them for the sake of effect. However, one characteristic and apparently authentic story is that the *princeps* himself performed as gladiator, charioteer, dancer and singer, if not so publicly as his later successor Nero. He was trained as a *thraex* (Thracian gladiator, see pp. 51–5), which was thought no disgrace, since most members of the high-ranking families of Rome had combat training. However, it is said that he transgressed all social conventions by actually appearing in the arena. At the theatre he sang along with the actors and imitated their gestures. Moreover, he was credited with having an affair with the actor Mnester.

He also drove publicly as a charioteer; racing was his great passion in life. His biographer Suetonius writes (*Caligula* 56):

> Caligula supported the Green faction with such ardour that he would often dine and spend the night in their stables and, on one occasion, gave the driver Eutychus presents worth 20,000 gold pieces. To prevent Incitatus, his favourite horse, from growing restive he always picketed the neighbourhood with troops on the day before the races, ordering them to enforce absolute silence. Incitatus owned a marble stable, an ivory stall, purple blankets, and a jewelled collar; also a house, furniture, and slaves – to provide suitable entertainment for guests whom Caligula invited in its name.

Caligula's whims were also directed against the members of the senate, whom he sought to humiliate in every possible way. Far from maintaining at least the appearance of a functioning Roman republic, he saw the senatorial body as a constant threat to his power. The senators reacted to the emperor's attacks on them with a number of conspiracies, the first of which ushered in a wave of executions when it was discovered. Finally, in January AD 42, an assassination attempt was made, and two high-ranking officers of the Praetorian guard murdered Caligula. The emperor was condemned to *damnatio memoriae*: his name was erased from all official records and inscriptions, and his portraits were destroyed – every memory of him was supposed to be obliterated.

## Claudius

If the senate had been able to decide on the choice of the next emperor, the history of the Roman empire would have taken a different course. Reeling from the shock of Caligula's reign, the consuls in office suggested that no new *princeps* should be installed, and that the republic in its old form ought to be restored instead. However, the majority of senators wanted a new emperor, although not of the Julio-Claudian dynasty. Even as the senate was sitting, a new force decided on the succession to the throne: a force that was to play an important part in the following period, the Praetorian guard. Augustus had stationed this troop in Rome to guarantee the safety of the emperor. The Praetorians were regarded as the elite of the Roman army, and in fact were the only part of it worth mentioning to be stationed in Italy; all other units were in the provinces. It was a bodyguard consisting of nine cohorts of 500 to 1,000 men, in all at least 4,500 soldiers, well trained and armed to the teeth. After the murder of Caligula this fighting force made his uncle Claudius the new emperor. The senate, who themselves depended on the ability of the cohorts of the Praetorian guard to police the city, had no objection. The new *princeps* bought the loyalty of his soldiers with the large sum of 15,000 sestertii each, in all at least 70 million sestertii.

Within a short time the new emperor succeeded in restoring order to the chaos left behind by his predecessor. He surrounded himself with advisers, each of whom took responsibility for certain areas of the administration, in modern terminology forming a kind of cabinet. The two freedmen Narcissus and Pallas had most influence. Unfortunately Claudius showed less acumen in the choice of his four wives. The amorous intrigues of the infamous Valeria Messalina did a great deal of damage to the reputation of the emperor, who was unaware of his wife's escapades for quite a long time. After Narcissus had succeeded in removing the threat she constituted, the choice of the *princeps* fell on his niece Julia Agrippina. She entirely dominated her husband and, as co-ruler with him, pursued the aim of acquiring power for the son of her first marriage, the future emperor Nero. To realize her ambitions, she finally had her husband poisoned in the year AD 54.

Claudius pursued consistent and successful policies both at home and abroad. He was realistic enough to meet the expectations of the people of Rome, whether in supplying the city with grain, constructing magnificent buildings or holding games, the number of which steadily rose under his rule. As a high point, he organized a naval battle on Lake Fucino. The occasion was an attempt to drain the lake through a canal over 5 km long, in order to create new and fruitful land (a project which, after several failures, was not realized until 1875). According to the historian Tacitus (*Annales* 12, 56), before the canal was opened 19,000 fighting men on board galleys performed in front of an enthusiastic crowd. The beginning of the spectacle proved embarrassing. The performers greeted the emperor with the words, 'Hail Caesar, we who are about to die salute you' (in fact recorded only in this one instance). Claudius gave a misleading reply which was taken by these candidates for death to imply the granting of

**7**
**Nero**
Reigned AD 54–68
Marble
British Museum, London,
GR 1805 7-3 246

This bust was adapted from
an original of about AD 60–65.
Nero was very conscious
of his outward appearance.
His full features were intended
to symbolize prosperity and
abundance. The hairstyle,
which would have been set
with curling tongs, marks a new
fashion of the time, and was
much copied.

The reality – so far as historians can judge today – was different. At the beginning of his rule in AD 54 the seventeen-year-old Nero was under the thumb of his mother Agrippina, who had been *de facto* co-ruler with Claudius. The first five years of his rule were considered happy. Great influence was exerted by the leader of the Praetorian guard, Sextus Afranius Burrus, and the philosopher Lucius Annaeus Seneca, who between them tried to make Nero into a capable *princeps*. Since the power-hungry Agrippina thus lost her own influence, there were tensions between mother and son, finally escalating to such an extent that in AD 59 they led to Agrippina's murder by the emperor. Nero withdrew more and more from the influence of his advisers (Burrus died in AD 62). His extravagant style of rule cost a great deal of money, and the inevitable happened: once again there were trials for high treason, taxes and duties rose, the currency was devalued, and the assets of private citizens were expropriated to fill the empty imperial coffers. In addition, there were the alleged sexual perversions of the head of state, and his un-Roman taste for poetry and song.

The classical historians agree that Nero was indeed trained in singing and in playing the lyre. He had summoned the famous musician Terpnus to his court to teach him. The emperor made his début in Naples, a city that was still more Greek than Roman at the time. According to Suetonius, during the performance an earthquake shook the theatre, but Nero took no notice – a story that is probably merely anecdotal. Finally he ventured to appear in Rome, and surrounded himself with a claque of 5,000 supporters ready to hail the *princeps* with all kinds of applause and expressions of approval. He also drove chariots himself; equestrian sports were regarded as his second greatest passion. So that he could appear in the capital itself, he founded the Neronian Games, which comprised the entire repertory of the ancient Greek examples, with chariot-racing, athletic contests and a singing competition. In AD 57 he built a wooden amphitheatre of unprecedented size in the Campus Martius for gladiatorial contests, but it burned down in the great conflagration of AD 64.

This fire completely devastated seven of the fourteen city quarters of Rome, leaving only rubble and ashes, and three more were partially destroyed. It began on the night of 18/19 July and raged for six days. Rumours were soon going around that the emperor himself had set the city ablaze to make room for new building projects. The claim cannot, of course, be proved either way today. The story that Nero sang an epic on the fall of Troy against the backdrop of the dying city will have sprung from the imagination of the people of Rome and its historians, but there is reliable evidence for the subsequent persecution of Christians, whom the emperor accused of starting the fire. They were also suspected of entertaining 'hatred for the entire human race' in general. This accusation, arising from the with-

instant pardon, and only dire threats could induce them to begin the fight. Then a silver triton rose from the water and blew the signal for the attack on its horn, and the massacre began. A huge audience watched the show from the surrounding mountains.

*Nero*
The last emperor of the family of Augustus is undoubtedly the most ambivalent character among the first Caesars of Rome. The popular image of Nero today has been shaped for good or ill by the novel *Quo Vadis* (1896) and the many film adaptations made of it, the version in which Peter Ustinov took the part of the emperor being the best known. The original novel by Henryk Sienkiewicz (1846–1916) is exciting and well worth reading, and combines source material from the accounts of such ancient historians as Tacitus and Suetonius with the lives of saints and with legends of the Christian martyrs who were suspected of arson after the fire of Rome, condemned to death and executed. The end product is a distorted picture of the period that has little in common with the actual historical facts (although that need not spoil a reader's enjoyment of the novel).

drawn lifestyle of the early Christians, led to all kinds of absurd speculations about secret rituals and criminal activities. Both charges could be punished by death according to Roman law of the time. *Damnatio ad bestias*, condemnation to being killed by wild beasts, was one of the usual sentences Roman judges were entitled to pass. However, Nero planned to make an unprecedented spectacle of these executions. He devised such perverse and sadistic methods of killing that even the hardened Romans felt sympathy for the tormented victims. Tacitus writes (*Annales* 15, 44): 'Hence, in spite of a guilt which had earned the most exemplary punishment, there arose a sentiment of pity, due to the impression that they were being sacrificed not for the welfare of the state but to the ferocity of a single man.'

Nero had a huge palace built on the site now available within Rome, including the Palatine hill and the slopes of the Caelian and Esquiline hills. In the hands of Greek architects and landscape gardeners, this area was turned into a Hellenistic complex of parkland with animal enclosures, pavilions, baths and dwellings all grouped around an artificial lake. A gilded bronze statue of the emperor stood in the pillared court at the entrance; it was 37 metres tall and showed him in the character of the sun god Sol. The magnificent banqueting halls were legendary: the central hall was crowned by a dome adorned with stars that revolved, imitating the constellations in their courses. When the work was finished, Nero, on seeing the palace, is said to have remarked that now at last he would begin to live like a man. He had completely transformed himself into a ruler on the model of a Greek god-king, losing all contact with the senate and the influential families of the city. A counter-stroke was not long in coming. In AD 65, under the leadership of Gaius Calpurnius Piso, influential members of the senate plotted to kill the emperor. His former tutor Seneca is said to have been part of the conspiracy. However, it failed, and the conspirators were executed or, like Seneca, forced to commit suicide.

In the following year Nero set out on a great journey to Greece, his principal aim being to take part in the great competitive events there. These were really held only every fourth year, but were staged at the emperor's insistence during his visit, with the result that some of them had to be held twice that year. He appeared in singing competitions (such a contest was specially added to the usual programme of the Olympic Games for him) and was at the starting line in several chariot-races. In Olympia he drove a team of ten horses which he could not control. Although he fell out of the chariot twice and failed to reach the finish, the well-instructed referee declared him the winner. Laden with prizes, he finally set off for home in the spring of AD 68. On his return, he dedicated over 1,800 victory wreaths to Apollo, god of the Muses, in his temple on the Palatine hill.

The Roman population had always looked indulgently on Nero's escapades – even in the years after his death he remained a popular ruler whose memory lingered long in the public mind. Rebellions by the governors of the provinces of Gaul, Spain and Africa, with whom the senate sided, finally led to his downfall. The future emperor Galba, legate in Spain, used a go-between to bribe the Praetorian guard. The senate thereupon declared Nero an enemy of the state, and he committed suicide. The last *princeps* of the Julio-Claudian dynasty died on 11 June AD 68.

## THE CRISIS OF SUCCESSION

With the suicide of Nero, the last descendant of Augustus died. The senate was in no position to resume authority and play an active part in Roman politics. Many of its members had discredited themselves as hangers-on of Nero. Bolder senators had been killed or sent into exile when their conspiracies failed. The throne was therefore available to those who commanded military power through their legions in the provinces. There were four successive emperors within a year, first Galba, next Otho, a former favourite of Nero's, and then Vitellius, commander of the legions stationed in Germania. But ultimately the winner of the prize was Vespasian (Titus Flavius Vespasianus), who was proclaimed emperor by the senate on 1 July AD 69. He came to power with the aid of the legions from the eastern part of the *imperium*.

Obviously there was no question of abandoning the system of princely rule after the end of the Augustan dynasty. The people had become used to that form of government: the emperors guaranteed a good supply of foodstuffs to the capital, as well as extravagant games and magnificent buildings – they had learnt their lesson since the time of Tiberius. The expense of providing these things had risen steadily. Vespasian and his successors drew their own conclusions and continued further along the same path, erecting the greatest monument in the city for the people of Rome: the Colosseum.

## THE FLAVIANS

The new ruler of Rome was not from the capital but from Rieti in the Sabine mountains north of Rome. Vespasian had grown up in Cosa, on the west coast of Italy, and came to the supreme office of state by way of a career in the army. As a military tribune under Tiberius, and a quaestor in the province of Crete and Cyrenaica, he rose to be praetor under Caligula. He commanded a legion during Claudius's conquest of Britain, and was made consul in AD 51 as a reward. Finally, he accompanied Nero on his journey to Greece, but fell from imperial favour when he dropped off to sleep during one of the emperor's song recitals. However, since the *princeps* thought highly of him, Vespasian was made

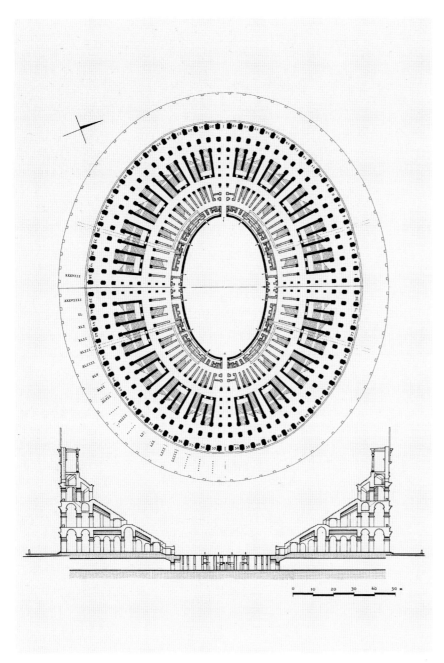

8

**Colosseum, Rome: ground plan**
Inaugurated AD 80

By modern calculations
up to 50,000 spectators could
be accommodated in the
Colosseum, and classical
sources give even higher figures.
The building of the huge
complex took about ten years.

been cleared up, and the civil war of AD 69 had led to further destruction. Vespasian adopted drastic measures to improve the state of the public budget: his thrift and his methods of collecting money were his only characteristics to attract adverse criticism from later biographers. He even taxed the public latrines. When his son, the future emperor Titus, said such a tax was not worthy of the dignity of the state, Vespasian held a handful of coins in front of Titus's face with the remark '*Non olet*' – 'Money does not stink'. He acted with similar pragmatism in foreign affairs; the administration of the provinces ran like clockwork during his reign.

A policy of the first importance was the utilization of the huge stretch of land Nero had claimed after the great fire for the building of his palace, the Golden House or *domus aurea*. Vespasian gave large parts of this area back to the citizens of Rome, and cleverly bound the people to him and his dynasty by erecting spectacular buildings on the site. First he completed the temple of the deified Claudius, which Nero had partially demolished because it lay on the site of the Golden House. He also built new baths, but the most striking of the buildings was a huge stone amphitheatre, the Colosseum.

Augustus himself had toyed with the idea of building such an amphitheatre for the people of Rome, but nothing practical came of it. Nero built a wooden amphitheatre on the Campus Martius, but it was destroyed in the great fire. The time was ripe for a permanent solution. Vespasian saw at once what prestige the construction of such a building would win him, and as the site of the arena he chose the lake that had been at the centre of Nero's palace gardens – a place in the very heart of the city, not outside its walls on the Campus Martius. The dimensions of this amphitheatre, the largest in Rome, are enormous; it measures 188 x 156 metres. The outer wall reached a height of 50 metres, and the tiers of seats could take 45,000 to 50,000 spectators by modern calculations; ancient sources even speak of 87,000 seats. The audience sat in an interior executed entirely in marble, its entrances adorned with reliefs, painting and stucco work. Building went on for about eight to ten years; when the Colosseum was inaugurated in AD 80, the attic storey on the top floor, with the pillared hall running around the building inside it, had not yet been completed.

Vespasian himself did not live to see the opening ceremony; he died in AD 79. His son Titus succeeded him on the throne, and the great event took place during the two years of his reign (AD 79–81). The games lasted a hundred days, and no fewer than 5,000 animals are said to have been killed in an animal fight on a single day. Gladiatorial casualties were higher than any ever known before. The people could take part in a free lottery: the emperor's servants threw hollow wooden balls into the audience, containing vouchers for clothes, food, cattle and even slaves. The

governor of Judaea in AD 67, with three legions under him to put down the Jewish revolt. Nero died during the fighting, and Vespasian ultimately emerged as victor in the struggle for his succession.

The new emperor had few links with the aristocracy of Rome. The senate had lost its own influence and accepted its new master, particularly since it could not oppose the military support upon which Vespasian could count. The first Flavian emperor was clever enough not to dwell unnecessarily on his superiority, but in view of the many tasks facing him as a result of the chaotic events of previous years he came to an accommodation with the senate. The state coffers were empty, short of the sum of 40 million sestertii that was necessary to get the state back on its feet. In Rome itself major building projects were waiting to be dealt with: the aftermath of the fire of AD 64 had not yet arena itself still had no subterranean structure when it was opened, so it was possible to flood it and stage a naval battle. The Colosseum was completed by Titus's successor, his brother Domitian.

## Domitian

Domitian had long been waiting for the opportunity to become *princeps* – there were rumours that he had a hand in his brother's death. His ambitions had been uncomfortably obvious even while Vespasian was emperor. In fact Domitian ruled very successfully and had the people on his side, although like so many of his predecessors he allowed the senate no independence. The imperial court was the power centre, and Domitian would give the senators no subsidiary role. After several plots against him, the emperor developed a morbid persecution complex. The last three years of his reign were a time of terror, when many senators and knights were executed for high treason. Finally one of the assassination attempts succeeded, and the last of the Flavians died in AD 96.

Domitian was noted for his clever policies, but most of all for his buildings. His most important project was a new palace on the Palatine hill to replace the Golden House of Nero, which had now been abandoned. Instead of an open parkland layout, he decided on a self-contained complex of buildings, with huge halls for holding audiences and state banquets. A great temple was built in honour of the Flavian dynasty, recording the family's claim to sovereignty and celebrating it as successor to the Julio-Claudian dynasty.

Domitian held games in honour of Jupiter Capitolinus on the Greek model, with athletic contests and singing competitions, and for the purpose he built a new stadium on the Campus Martius. Its ground plan remains to this day as the Piazza Navona, and it included an Odeion in which musical contests took place. The following account is from Suetonius (*Domitian*, 4):

> While presiding at these functions he wore buskins [half-boots], a purple Greek robe, and a gold crown engraved with the images of Jupiter, Juno, and Minerva; and at his side sat the Priest of Capitoline Jupiter and the Priest of the Deified Flavians, wearing the same costume as he did, except for crowns decorated with his image.

The appearance of the emperor at the games was associated with the cult of his person: he was the first ruler of Rome who insisted on being addressed as *dominus et deus* – lord and god.

Politically, Domitian set the seal on a practice that had been applied *de facto* by his predecessors long before: he claimed an imperial monopoly on the staging of great gladiatorial contests and other games. Even under Augustus, private men could only occasionally give *munera*. Domitian finally decreed that, apart from the state *ludi* and a *munus* organized by a quaestor, all such performances were to be the province of the emperor or his family. Since the state

9
**Colosseum, Rome**
Inaugurated AD 80

The outer facade, 50 metres high, remains one of the most striking sights in Rome. The attic storey still has the supports to take vertical wooden poles holding up sun awnings that would provide the spectators with shade. The complicated business of running the Colosseum was in the hands of the Roman marines.

games, too, were held in honour of the emperor, this important tool for influencing the people was now entirely in his hands. None of his successors departed from the practice.

## ADOPTIVE AND ANTONINE EMPERORS

On the death of Domitian the senate chose a candidate from among themselves, the former consul Nerva, who was already sixty-five. Everyone knew this was only a stop-gap measure. In fact Nerva died sixteen months later, but he had provided for a successor by adopting as his son the legate of the province of Germania, the future emperor Trajan. Trajan fulfilled the senate's expectations of him, and in his turn maintained the principle of adopting a successor, as did the emperors who followed him. In this way capable

25

**10**

**Commodus**
Reigned AD 180–92
Marble
Museum für Kunst und
Gewerbe, Hamburg,
1980.14/St.341

This portrait, with its full beard
and placid features, resembles
portraits of Marcus Aurelius.
Unlike his father, however,
Commodus followed no
philosophical ideology. He is
regarded as a prime example
of imperial megalomania, and
even appeared in the arena
as a gladiator himself.

politicians and military men rose to power. Trajan continued to pursue a policy of foreign expansion; he made war on the Dacians of the Danube area several times and took huge sums of money as booty, investing it not only in magnificent buildings and gifts of money to the citizens of Rome but also in games, a high point in the history of the institution.

On the occasion of his Dacian triumph in AD 107, there were festivities lasting several months in which 10,000 gladiators fought, and 11,000 animals were killed in *venationes*. Two years later, the games for the dedication of the Baths of Trajan lasted for 117 days, but were spread out from 4 June to 1 November, so that in fact they went on for almost five months, because regular feast days and days when the courts were sitting did not count. In all, the emperor offered the public over 8,000 gladiators and more than 10,000 wild beasts. In the year AD 113 there were extraordinarily magnificent *munera*, when over 2,000 gladiators faced each other. At this time the regular games lasted about four months. By way of comparison, during his very much longer reign Augustus had staged shows involving 10,000 gladiators in all.

Trajan's successors Hadrian, Antoninus Pius and Marcus Aurelius consolidated the empire and even withdrew from some of the conquered regions. During this long period of peace, prosperity increased in all provinces of the Roman empire, and Roman literature, art and architecture all flourished. Only in the last years of the reign of Marcus Aurelius did outside enemies again begin to threaten the empire. The Parthians forced Rome into a lengthy war in the east, which, however, the emperor managed to turn to his own advantage. In the course of this conflict there was a great plague epidemic which claimed many victims. Meanwhile, the Germanic tribes of the Quadi and Marcomanni on the Danube were threatening the frontiers of the empire. The emperor died during the war, and his son Commodus succeeded him.

Commodus was the first Roman *princeps* to be 'born in the purple', that is, as the son of a ruling emperor. His father had carefully prepared him to succeed: born in AD 161, he was given the title of Caesar as early as 166, and in 177, at the age of sixteen, he became co-ruler. On the death of Marcus Aurelius, Commodus himself was with the army at the front. He managed to conclude the war with an extremely favourable peace treaty, although it earned him accusations of giving way unnecessarily to the enemies of Rome.

*The people and the emperor*
Games and gladiatorial contests were still part of everyday life in Rome under Commodus. During his reign a remarkable event occurred, one that shows how the common people could intervene in the day-to-day policy of Rome through the circus, where the people of the city and the emperor met. Here the

crowd paid homage to their sovereign and demanded to be supplied with entertainment, but also took the opportunity of making political demands. Even under the first emperors there had been demonstrations of popular will in the theatres, but they were not as far-reaching as in the time of Commodus.

Commodus had surrounded himself with a number of advisers who occupied high administrative positions. The most important of them was Cleander, a freedman and the most influential of all those at the imperial court. He must have been an able politician, but he was also greedy for gain and made use of his influence to enrich himself. In this way he made many enemies who were merely waiting for the chance to overthrow him. The moment came in AD 190 when there was unrest among the population of the city because of a grain shortage; there was hardly any to be bought at all. The price of bread rose, and famine threatened. In this tense situation rumours spread that Cleander was hoarding grain himself to drive up the price and make a fortune. His opponents had probably invented these suspicions, but they led to a revolt in the Circus Maximus. In the words of the historian Cassius Dio (*Rhomaike historia* 52, 13, 3 f.):

> There was a horse-race on, and as the horses were about to contend for the seventh time, a crowd of children ran into the Circus, led by a tall maiden of grim aspect, who, because of what afterwards happened, was thought to have been a divinity. The children shouted in concert many bitter words, which the people took up and then began to bawl out every conceivable insult; and finally the throng leaped down and set out to find Commodus ... invoking many blessings on him and many curses on Cleander.

The people poured out into the streets of Rome, going along the Via Appia to a villa more than 6 km away, where Commodus was at the time. The crowd demanded Cleander's head. Commodus sent soldiers to drive the angry mob back to the city, but once there they lost control. The guards went over to the side of the agitators, and a street battle broke out. Only now did Commodus act to save his own skin: he had Cleander killed and handed the body to the mob, who mutilated it horribly.

This episode casts a significant light on conditions at the public games. A skilful agitator could easily manipulate the crowd, forcing the emperor to give in to the people's demands. On the other hand, such demonstrations were essential as a means of giving the citizens of Rome an opportunity of letting the emperor know what they wanted. Consequently, none of the Roman *principes* seriously considered putting an end to such expressions of opinion.

Commodus himself was a fanatical supporter of gladiatorial games. He had trained in all branches of the art, and even appeared in the arena himself in AD 193, when he wore the costume of Hercules and shot over a hundred exotic animals with arrows, in some cases giving his victims the death blow himself. He

12 (BELOW)
**Base of bowl with *retiarius***
Glass, fourth century AD
British Museum, London, MLA 1898.7-19.2

The broken base of this costly glass bowl from the late imperial period incorporates a blue disc decorated mainly in gold. It shows a net-fighting gladiator (*retiarius*) with his trident, dagger, arm-guard (*manica*) and shoulder-guard (*galerus*).

11
**Caracalla**
Reigned AD 211–17
Marble
Musei Capitolini, Rome, 2310

Under the emperors of the Severan dynasty, of whom Caracalla was the second, the Roman empire saw a final period of prosperity before the migrations of Germanic and Slavonic tribes, and economic problems at home, plunged it into severe crisis.

then fought with wooden weapons as a gladiator, and awarded himself a fee of a million sestertii for his performance. His contemporaries thought poorly of such performances, which could hardly be reconciled with the dignity of a *princeps*. Finally, he met the same fate as so many of his predecessors on the imperial throne: his enemies had him assassinated on the last night of the year AD 192.

## THE LATE IMPERIAL PERIOD AND THE END OF THE GAMES

After the death of Commodus, the Severus family held power for several decades. The emperors Septimius Severus, Caracalla, Elagabalus and Alexander Severus ruled until AD 235. Thereafter the purple changed hands quickly. The migrations of the Germanic and

Slavonic peoples were beginning; tribes from beyond the frontiers of the empire were in revolt, and involved the Romans in long wars that pushed the state into a deep economic and social crisis. Claimants to the throne were usually those generals who had the greatest military power and the most funds. Many of these 'soldier emperors' ruled for only a few months, and separate empires split away in Gaul and Britain. Finally, the emperor Diocletian succeeded in reviving the empire. He set up a system of government by four emperors, the tetrarchy. Two higher-ranking Augusti and two subordinate Caesares shared sovereignty between them. The provinces were given a new administrative structure, the currency was reformed, and the state fixed prices with a view to ending inflation. As long as the four rulers agreed with each other, the system worked, but the successors of Diocletian

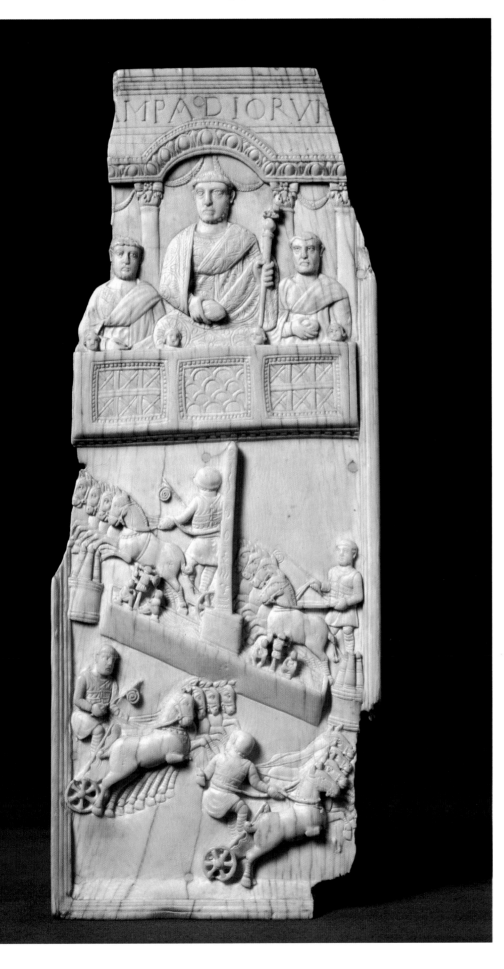

**13**
**Diptych of the Lampadii**
*c.* AD 430
Ivory
Musei Civici d'Arte e Storia di
Brescia, no. 4

Diptychs were hinged, two-
leaved tablets covered with a
layer of wax on the inside,
which could be written on with
a bronze stylus. In the late
fourth century AD it became
customary to inscribe the
content of important
documentary records on fine
ivory diptychs, which might, for
instance, be solemnly handed
to the consuls when they took
office. Diptychs were also
given as presents. A member of
the Lampadii family had the
diptych shown here prepared
on the occasion of games he
held in the circus. He himself is
enthroned in a box, flanked by
two companions, and is
holding a sceptre and the
*mappa*, the cloth with which he
would give the starting signal.
The four chariot teams
represent the four racing
stables, the Reds, Blues, Whites
and Greens (see p. 86).

**14**

**Circus contorniate**

Late fourth century AD

Bronze

Römisch-Germanisches
Museum der Stadt Köln, 69,2

Contorniates were medallions
rather than a form of currency
like coins. They often bore
portraits of popular emperors
of the past (Augustus or even
Nero) and scenes from the
games in the circus. It was
therefore thought for a long
time that they were used as
entry tokens for the games.
Today scholars assume that the
holders of games gave them
away as presents to the
spectators or as New Year gifts.
This contorniate from Cologne
shows the charioteer
Heliodromus in a *quadriga*
(four-horse chariot). The
goddess Victory is crowning
him to mark his success.

were soon at odds again. In the ensuing struggles the emperor Constantine won a decisive battle, in the name of Christ, over his rival Maxentius at the Milvian bridge in Rome.

Constantine made Christianity a religion tolerated by the state under the Edict of Milan in AD 313, thus ending a period of persecutions that had lasted for almost 300 years. He did not have himself baptized until he was on his deathbed, but he was the first emperor to pursue an active pro-Christian policy, and he built several lavishly furnished churches in Rome, Constantinople and the Holy Land. A 'new' religion was a good means of providing ideological backing for the political new start that was ushered in after the tetrarchy. Finally, the emperor moved the capital of the empire to the city of Byzantium on the Bosphorus, re-founding it under the name of Constantinople.

The victory of Christianity enabled its bishops and priests to campaign publicly against theatrical specta-cles. They had been criticizing these shows for cen-turies. Their attacks were chiefly directed against theatrical performances offering lewd and sometimes pornographic material, which in the eyes of Christian authors were a constant temptation to sin for the mem-bers of their congregations, and in AD 314 the Council of Arles excommunicated actors. At first criticism of the gladiatorial games took second place, but it led to Constantine's abolition in AD 325 of the custom whereby criminals could be condemned to gladiatorial training (*ad ludum*). To the modern way of thinking, the alternative does not seem much of an improve-ment, since the delinquents were sent instead to mines and stone quarries, and thus to certain death. But there were still gladiators; even Pope Damasius made use of their services, engaging a whole troop as his body-guard in AD 367. However, the end of the gladiatorial contests was now in sight. After the middle of the fourth century there are no records of any continuation of the *munera* in the eastern empire. They lasted longer in the western Mediterranean and Rome itself, until the emperor Honorius formally banned them in AD 404. After 650 years men no longer fought each other to the death to entertain a pleasure-seeking crowd. None of the later civilizations of Europe tried to revive the terrible practice.

Chariot-racing and *venationes* continued to be very popular even under the Christian emperors. The offi-cial prohibition of heathen religions and cults by the emperor Theodosius did not affect them. In an edict of AD 380 the emperor decreed that all his subjects were to be of the same religious faith, and the edict was given binding form (and is valid to this day) at the Council of Constantinople the following year. Since people still went on worshipping in heathen temples, he issued a decree in 391 forbidding attendance at temples and sacrifices, and in the next year he banned all heathen ceremonies of every kind.

This was a crucial moment for the games, since most of them were held in honour of heathen gods and began with sacrifices. Apparently performances did carry on, but without religious rituals. Chariot-racing flourished again under the Byzantine emperors, and continued to be popular until well into the Middle Ages. The hippodrome in Constantinople, next to the imperial palace, resembled the Circus Maximus in Rome under the heathen *principes*. Obelisks and stat-ues adorned its *spina*, the people urged their teams on, and there were bloody revolts that concluded in the circus. Not until the crusaders captured Constantino-ple in AD 1204 did the great age of chariot-racing come to an end.

# Familia Gladiatoria:
# The Heroes of the Amphitheatre

The victorious gladiator, a fighting machine made of muscle and gleaming metal, proudly sets his foot on his adversary's neck. He holds his short sword in his right hand, ready to give the death blow. His head, concealed by a huge visored helmet, is turned expectantly up to the auditorium, where sentence of life or death will be pronounced. The defeated man, a youth of girlish beauty, naked but for his loincloth, writhes beneath his conqueror's brutal tread and holds his right hand up in a helpless plea for his life. In a movement echoing his own the Vestal Virgins on the podium, Fury-like in appearance, thrust their arms forward as they deliver their unanimous verdict: thumbs down, death to the defeated.

The Vestals' fatal gesture gives the famous painting by Jean-Léon Gérôme (fig. 15), the central scene of which is described above, its title of *Pollice Verso* ('thumbs turned'), which, however, Gérôme mistakenly interpreted as meaning thumbs down when in reality thumbs were turned up to confirm the death sentence. The picture, painted in 1872 and a major work of historicism, very effectively unites all the elements of gladiatorial combats as they feature in the popular imagination: the gigantic dimensions and monumental decoration of the amphitheatre, the emperor in his box, cynically manipulating the masses, the audience avid for sensation and relishing its apparent power, the antagonists in the arena delivered up to the vagaries of victory and death. The combination of voyeurism with a sense of moral superiority is certainly a specifically nineteenth-century ingredient, but we should not be so sure about the baroque splendour, bizarre exoticism and sadism inherent in the scene. Gérôme may have captured the atmosphere of the amphitheatre more realistically than many purists would like to think.

As usual with artists of his period, Gérôme did careful research into the subjects of his paintings. His depiction of the architecture of the Colosseum is based on drawings accurately reconstructing its appearance, and the armour worn by the gladiators follows the design of originals found in Pompeii. The painter also turned to written sources to complement the archaeological material, but as so often this procedure created more confusion than clarity, a methodological problem to which reference will be made at greater length later. Without going into detail here, it must first be said that, faithfully as the victorious gladiator's armour is depicted, it is not properly assembled. Most important of all, except for the sword, not a single item corresponds to the armour one might expect to see worn by the *contraretiarius* or *secutor* (pursuer), and the situation presented here shows that the man is indeed a gladiator of that type, for the defeated gladiator is undoubtedly a *retiarius* ('net fighter'): his typical weapons, the net and trident, are lying on the sand beside him.

Even today we do not have a much better idea than Gérôme and his contemporaries of the armaments and fighting techniques of the gladiators. Indeed, the painter saw more correctly than most modern interpreters in one respect, for he assumes that the original helmets and other items of armour found in Pompeii were genuine fighting equipment, whereas it is usually claimed that the Pompeian artefacts were merely parade armaments. No full scholarly study of this armour has yet been published.

The following pages will look at the practical aspects of those Roman competitive sports to which gladiatorial combat was central. Since 1997 the author and the Rheinisches Landesmuseum in Trier have been working on a research project to reconstruct and test gladiatorial arms and armour (cf. fig. 16). As research into military history has shown repeatedly in recent years, experimental archaeology is an essential aid to the study of weapons and fighting techniques. The present author is preparing a publication on this subject entitled *Das Spiel mit dem Tod – Roms Gladiatoren im Experiment* ('Playing with Death – Experimenting with the Gladiators of Rome').

## THE ORGANIZATION AND TRAINING OF GLADIATORS

Gladiatorial combat was not invented by the Romans, but Rome developed all the essential features of the system, bringing it to the state of perfection it had reached around the beginning of the present era. It can therefore be correctly considered a specifically Roman form of competitive sport – if such a euphemism may be used as a general term for the disciplines discussed below.

At first gladiatorial combat was only a matter of a few prisoners of war or slaves facing each other in contests staged at the funerals of distinguished Romans. In the course of the second and first centuries BC, however, these warlike spectacles assumed such dimensions that they required a great deal of organization. Gladiatorial schools (*ludi*) were set up, each run

15
***Pollice Verso***
Jean-Léon Gérôme
1872
Oil on canvas
Phoenix Art Museum,
museum purchase

by a *lanista*, a private entrepreneur who acquired suitable men by purchase or recruitment, trained them and then hired them out to interested parties. The gladiators, whose ranks now also included condemned criminals and quite a number of volunteers (*auctorati*), lived in barracks and were subject to a strict discipline. Their trainers aimed to achieve maximum physical fitness through a well-balanced diet, constant hard

training and careful medical attention. The training itself was entrusted to *doctores* and *magistri*, most of them probably former gladiators.

The gladiators practised in a small arena, using blunt weapons generally made of wood. They trained first with a post (*palus*) as opponent (this was also the normal method in the army), and later with another gladiator. The upper ranks of the paramilitary gladiato-

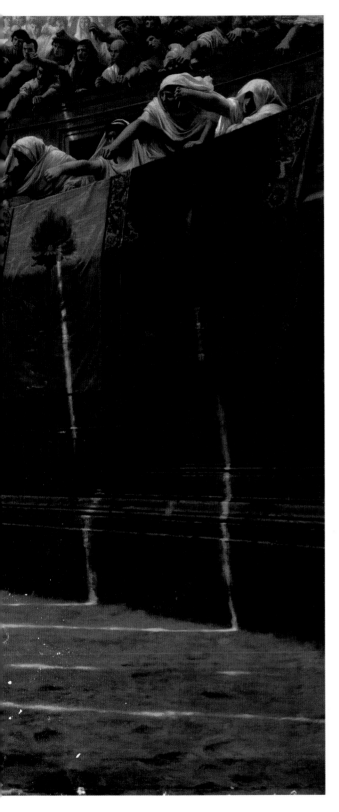

the highest distinction of all, the laurel wreath. Information of this kind appears on programmes of the games, on graffiti showing pairs of fighters, and on the tombstones of gladiators.

The members of a gladiatorial school formed a *familia gladiatoria*, usually called after the owner. In most public contests members of the same gladiatorial 'family' fought each other, so that if a duel ended in death it was a man's own comrade who had to deliver the fatal blow. But sometimes several schools would take part in a large spectacle, and gladiatorial companies also went on tour.

When gladiatorial combats came under state control with the establishment of the empire, the private schools continued in existence, but great imperial *ludi* were also set up, managed by officials of knightly rank (*procuratores*). From the late first century AD onwards there were no less than four imperial *ludi* in Rome, the most important being the *ludus magnus* beside the Flavian Amphitheatre (the Colosseum). An underground passage linked it directly to the arena in the amphitheatre, so that the gladiators could reach the scene of their combat without being seen by the public.

16
**Victorious *murmillo* with palm branch**
Reconstruction: Marcus Junkelmann/Rheinisches Landesmuseum Trier

rial hierarchy were called after these training posts: each category of gladiators had its own *palus primus*, *palus secundus* and so forth. Naturally the status and market value of a gladiator depended on his success in the arena. Careful records were kept of the number of fights a gladiator had behind him, how often he had won, how often he had left the arena defeated or after a fight ending in a draw, and how often he had gained

**17**
**Colosseum, Rome**
Inaugurated AD 80

A view of the interior of this
vast amphitheatre shows
corridors and rooms on two
storeys beneath the floor
of the arena, which consisted
of wooden staging covered
with sand.

## THE ARENA

The first public appearances of gladiators in the city of
Rome were in the Forum Boarium in the third century
BC. Soon the scene of their performances was moved to
the Forum Romanum, where it remained until the
building of the Colosseum in the second half of the first
century AD. The arena in the Forum Romanum lay
between the Basilica Aemilia and the Basilica Sempro-
nia, and was elliptical in shape to suit the rectangular
ground plan of the space available. It must have measured about 60 x 35 metres. In the second century BC a
wooden, amphitheatre-like structure was raised around
the arena and served as the model for the stone
amphitheatres of the late republican period, built in
the first century AD in both Italy and the Roman
colonies.

During the imperial period (particularly in the
second century AD) amphitheatres were erected in
many parts of the empire, frequently modelled on the

magnificent architecture of the Colosseum. Jean-
Claude Golvin has listed 186 proven amphitheatres
throughout the empire. During the imperial period,
however, gladiatorial contests and animal fights were
also held in venues that were something between a
theatre and an amphitheatre. In Gaul, for instance, certain buildings combined the semi-circular form of the
theatrical auditorium (*cavea*) with the elliptical arena
of the amphitheatre, while in the Hellenistic east,
where there were only a few genuine amphitheatres,
most such performances were held in ordinary stadiums and theatres, adapted for this additional purpose
by the addition of a few extra features such as a raised
*podium* as protection against the wild beasts.

Gladiatorial contests took place in the forums until
there was a general move towards the building of permanent amphitheatres. The larger arenas measured in
general 65–80 x 35–50 metres. The gladiatorial fights
themselves, for the most part duels on foot, did not
really need such a large arena, but the spectacles as a
whole also comprised impressive mass appearances
such as the procession opening the show (*pompa*), and
these required more space. Moreover, during the imperial period animal hunts and animal fights (*venationes*),
originally held in the circus, were moved to the
amphitheatres.

As the name suggests, the arena (from *harena*,
'sand') was a sandy surface on which the performers
could move unimpeded. In many of the amphitheatres
of the imperial period the arena stood not on solid
ground but on wooden staging above a complex of
underground rooms and passages, the *hypogeum* (cf.
fig. 17). The *hypogeum* contained rooms for storing
scenery and props, dressing rooms, and ways into the
arena for the gladiators, the wild beasts and the auxil-
iary staff, as well as lifts which could bring the performers, human and animal alike, up into the arena to
good dramatic effect, surprising the audience. Besides
the underground complexes, a circle of rooms called
*carceres*, partly opening into the arena, ran behind the
high wall of the *podium* which surrounded the arena
itself, and sometimes there was also a gallery running
around the inside of the building. In amphitheatres
without underground rooms all the technical equipment, cages and weaponry had to be stored in the
*carceres* and the ground-floor passages linking them.

In a few amphitheatres (for instance Verona, Mérida
and probably the Colosseum before the building of the
*hypogeum* by the emperor Domitian) large basins of
water were dug in the arena. These basins were covered for normal performances, but could be made
available when required for special events in the programme, for instance the hunting of aquatic creatures
such as crocodiles and hippopotamuses, or for mythological tableaux and ballets featuring bathing nymphs
or Nereids. However, these basins were much too
small to stage naval battles (*naumachiae*) and would
accommodate at most only small boats and model

ships. The frequent assumption that the whole arena could be flooded for the performance of naval battles cannot be correct. The great *naumachiae* of which records have come down to us were staged not in the amphitheatres, but on artificial or natural lakes of very much larger size. For mythological spectacles, hunts and staged executions landscapes with rocks, trees and buildings were constructed in the arena to create as perfect an illusion as possible.

Special precautions had to be taken to ensure the safety of the spectators. The *podium* wall, 2.2 to 4 metres high, surrounded the arena, but big cats can jump so high that the *podium* alone was not sufficient protection. The enclosure was made higher at such performances by nets stretching up above the wall. A common alternative was to drive posts into the arena 2 to 4 metres in front of the *podium*, and then stretch nets between them to prevent the wild beasts from even reaching the foot of the wall. This measure had the additional advantage of ensuring that none of the acts worth seeing took place in a blind spot directly behind the *podium*, depriving some of the spectators of their view.

There was potential danger from the gladiators themselves as well as the wild animals, as the revolt led by Spartacus had shown (p. 129). As a result, prisoners and condemned criminals were strictly supervised and had sharp-edged weapons handed to them only in the arena. Volunteer gladiators, on the other hand, seem to have been regarded as no threat. As the finds in the gladiatorial barracks of Pompeii show, they were not disarmed or kept in confinement, or indeed screened off from the public in any other way.

Additional protection from potential attack by wild beasts or gladiators was provided by the large number of soldiers posted in the amphitheatre. Apart from the incidents of 59 BC in Pompeii, which led to a ten-year closure of the amphitheatre, very few records have come down to us of vandalism or hooliganism of the kind familiar from modern football. The race-going crowd in the circus, and more particularly the audiences at theatrical performances, seem to have been far more inclined to violence than fans of the shows in the amphitheatre.

There was certainly no lack of explosive potential in the amphitheatre. Although there were no organized associations of supporters like those for the Blues, Greens, Reds and Whites whose teams of charioteers raced in the circus (p. 86), popular gladiators had hordes of fanatical followers. The spectators gave loyal support not only to individual heroes of the arena but to certain categories of gladiators. The first and second centuries AD saw passionate altercations between the supporters of gladiators fighting with the large shield (*scutum*) and gladiators who fought with the small shield (*parma*), known respectively as *scutarii* and *parmularii*. The differences between these categories will be studied below.

## GLADIATORIAL CATEGORIES – TO THE TIME OF AUGUSTUS

Our ideas of the appearance and swordsmanship of gladiators are based on the conditions prevailing in the first to third centuries AD, the period from which most of the written accounts, pictorial depictions and original weapons date. However, it would be quite wrong to graft these notions on to the preceding republican era, since a rapid and fundamental change in the equipment and classification of gladiators seems to have occurred around the beginning of the imperial period. In many respects it was Augustus who gave the gladiatorial system, like so much else, its final form.

Naturally the reorganization of gladiatorial contests in the early imperial period did not entail a complete break with the past. Rather, it was a deliberate process of selection from the existing diversity of methods, and of continued development of those elements that had now been clearly defined and standardized. The meagre nature of the source material makes it far more difficult to perceive the traditions on which these reforms rested than to recognize the results.

Frescoes in Oscan and Lucanian tombs of the fourth century BC found in Paestum, and generally regarded as the earliest representations of gladiators, show pairs of fighting men armed with spears and lances. Some wear tunics, others only loincloths, and a few are completely naked. All have magnificent helmets in the southern Graeco-Italian tradition familiar to us from many tombs of the period. The originals are always made of sheet bronze. The large, round, convex shields are similar to those used by Greek hoplites (heavily armed soldiers). Both men involved in these combats are armed in the same way, and their equipment is identical with that shown in pictorial depictions of a clearly warlike character. After the fourth century BC this pictorial tradition breaks off, and so do the finds of bronze armour, for under Roman influence the custom of burying weapons as grave goods was abandoned, and the remarkably sparse remains of Roman art of the third and second centuries BC mean that there are almost no pictorial representations from that period at all.

A change came in the late republican period. A whole series of reliefs dating from the first century BC comes from the funerary monuments of municipal officials who had featured as the holders of games (*editores muneris*) and on the occasion commissioned depictions of scenes from the gladiatorial contests. Most of the gladiators are shown naked except for a loincloth (*subligaculum*) held in place by a broad metal belt (*balteus*). Such belts, consisting of a long strip of bronze with a leather lining and fastened by hooks, are in an old southern Italian tradition. Many of the gladiators wear greaves (shin-guards) to above the knee (*ocreae*).

The majority of helmets shown belong to a late Hel-

18
**Helmet**
First century BC
Bronze
Museum für Kunst und
Gewerbe Hamburg, 1917.173

Soldiers and gladiators alike
wore helmets of this shape.
Unfortunately both the cheek-
guards, which were movable
and fitted on hinges, are
missing from this otherwise
well-preserved example now
in Hamburg.

lenistic hybrid type combining elements of the Boeotian helmet, with its broad folded or curved brim, and
the Attic helmet, with its forehead peak curving back
to lateral volutes, a metal crest (not always present)
and broad cheek-guards. Several reliefs of this period
show that such helmets were also worn by the Roman
army. The Hamburg Museum für Kunst und Gewerbe
has the best-preserved example of this type (fig. 18). It
probably comes from south Italy, and cannot be definitely identified as either a military or a gladiatorial
helmet, since there was still no clear distinction
between the equipment of soldiers and gladiators in
the pre-Augustan period.

The shield (*scutum*) was generally large and tall;
some examples were rectangular, some oval or a
blunted oval in shape, with a rib (*spina*) running
down their length. Any round shields still in use were
very much smaller than the old hoplite shields, and
were either convex or had concentric circular ribs and
channels.

A few depictions show body armour either in the

form of a coat of scale armour (*lorica squamata*) or a
rectangular breastplate fastened by straps crossing
each other and buckled at the back (*pectorale, cardiophylax, spongia*). The latter, abbreviated form of body
armour appears in a relief from the Tiber, probably of
the Augustan period (fig. 21). It goes back to an old Etr-
usco-Italian tradition that the evidence shows was current in the Roman army until the second century BC.
The lower right arm and hand were protected by a
long glove (*manica*) held together by a network
of straps, obviously modelled on the boxing glove
(*caestus*).

Among offensive equipment, the lance and spear
now fell into disuse, and the principal weapon was a
sword of medium length with a broad, straight blade, a
rib down the back and a sharp point, the famous *gladius hispanensis* used by the Roman army since the late
third century BC, which gave its name to the word
'gladiator' itself. In addition there were very short
swords with straight or curved blades.

Roman authors have left us a whole series of names

for the various gladiatorial categories (*armaturae*) of this period, but it is difficult to correlate them with the pictorial depictions we have. The *samnis* or Samnite is the category most frequently mentioned, a word deriving from the powerful Italian Samnite tribal league in Campania with which the Romans waged long and eventful wars in the fourth and third centuries BC. This would agree with the assumed Campanian origin of gladiatorial contests. The Samnite was a heavily armed man with a helmet (probably of the kind with a brim and crest), a large shield (*scutum*), a sword and probably a greave on the left leg. This category disappears in the early imperial period. The *murmillo* and *secutor* (see below, pp. 48 and 61) probably derived from the *samnis*.

Two other categories also drew their names from enemy tribes, the *gallus* (Gaul) and the *thraex* (Thracian; cf. fig. 19). As with the Samnites, the first representatives of these types must have been captured Celtic and Thracian warriors who were made to fight with their own kind of armour and in their own way, and then gradually developed into standardized gladiatorial categories. Our ideas of the appearance of the *galli* can only be suppositions, since it is impossible to identify them in any detailed descriptions or pictorial depictions. This category, too, failed to survive the reforms of the early imperial period, unlike the *thraeces*, who were to remain very popular until gladiatorial contests finally came to an end. The early *thraeces* wore Attic crested helmets and a pair of greaves, and carried a small rectangular shield and a short, curved sword (*sica*).

The predecessors of two further categories of gladiators in the imperial period can be identified on late republican and Augustan reliefs with a high degree of probability: these were the *equites* and the *provocatores*. Although described as horsemen, the *equites* are mostly shown on foot, not because they did not really have horses – several depictions of the imperial period show them mounted – but because artists generally showed the decisive closing phase of the fight. The *equites* seem to have opened their fights on horseback, using a lance, but then dismounted (unless they were thrown off the horse first) to end the duel on foot, fighting with a sword. *Equites* can be recognized by the combination of a brimmed helmet without a crest and a medium-sized round shield (*parma equestris*), a traditional item of armour carried by the republican cavalry, and also by the fact that they wore no greaves and did not fight naked to the waist. While later depictions show these horsemen wearing tunics, in the early reliefs they were protected by scale armour. Another characteristic of the *equites* is that they always fought against men similarly equipped, never against another gladiatorial category. In this respect, with very few exceptions, they resembled only the *provocatores* among gladiators of the imperial period.

The earliest and best depiction of *provocatores* is on

the relief found in the Tiber between Rome and Ostia, which can be dated to the Augustan period (fig. 21). On the left, the relief shows two gladiators of the same type, each wearing a heavily folded loincloth with a broad metal belt; a greave to above the knee on the left leg; a *manica* (arm-guard), shown here in particular detail on the lower right arm; a *cardiophylax* (partial breastplate); and a helmet with a large horizontal neck-guard, broad cheek-guards, ornamentation resembling eyebrows on the forehead, and feathers at the sides but no crest or plume. The medium-sized shields are of the blunted oval type with a *spina* (a rib down the length of the shield), and the weapon used is a short sword with a straight blade.

The helmet deserves special attention, since this is

the oldest representation of what is known as the Weisenau ('Imperial Gallic') type, a new development of the Augustan period combining Celtic and Roman features. What the two gladiators are wearing was also the latest model of Roman army helmet. The feathers at the sides, frequently found on military helmets of the same period, were in a central and southern Italian tradition going back for centuries, and the sockets to hold them are found on countless original examples. In gladiatorial equipment they appear not only on the helmets of the *provocatores* but on those of most other categories as well, frequently together with a central *crista* (plume of horsehair or feathers). Apart from the helmet, the breastplate buckled over the chest is the most distinctive feature of the armour of the *provocatores*. The one worn by the gladiator on the left of the relief is in the form of an *aegis* (the bib-shaped breastplate of Minerva) and adorned with a Gorgon's head. Only the buckle at the back of the breastplate worn by the gladiator on the right is in view.

A gladiator from a different category is shown to the

19

**Two lamps with gladiators**
First century AD
Pottery
Antikensammlung, Staatliche Museen zu Berlin, 31291 (left), 31292

Depictions of gladiators were prominent among the many subjects from everyday life used by lamp-makers to decorate their products. They took pains to show gladiatorial equipment in such detail that the category of the fighters can be identified. These lamps show two Thracians, or *thraeces*, one standing at ease, the other ready to attack.

**20**

**Lamp with gladiatorial equipment**

First century AD

Pottery

British Museum, London, GR 1856.12-26.414

Possibly intended to represent the arms and armour of a pair of gladiators, the equipment shown on this lamp said to be from Pozzuoli includes helmets, swords, shields and greaves.

**21**

**Relief with gladiators**

30–10 BC

Marble

Museo Nazionale Romano alla Terme di Diocleziano, Rome, 126119

This large and fine relief comes from a tomb. Since the inscriptions record the names of the gladiators and the results of their fights, the relief must refer to a particular event, perhaps the *munera* held in honour of the occupant of the tomb on his death.

right of these two men. He has no breastplate, and his helmet is adorned with a crest-shaped plume of horsehair. Since the relief has suffered some damage we cannot see whether he was wearing greaves, but if so they must have been short, ending below the knee. He has let his *gladius* (sword) drop from his hand in token of surrender, and it is dangling from a loop. The blunted oval or oblong shield is similar to that of the *provocatores*. All that is visible of his opponent is his much smaller rectangular shield, but it almost certainly identifies him as a *thraex*. In that case we are looking at the classic match of a *thraex* against a *murmillo*, which would agree with the equipment of the defeated gladiator. As a *murmillo* he would have worn a short greave on his left leg, no longer visible because of the damage to the relief.

There are several inscriptions on the top border of this relief giving information about the men depicted and their fates. The name of the gladiator on the left is lost, but what remains of the inscription, 'IVL VVV' (in full: '*Iulianus pugnarum V, coronarum V, vicit*'), tells us that he belonged to the *ludus iulianus*, a gladiatorial school founded in Capua by Julius Caesar and thus one of the most prominent *ludi* of the early imperial period. In addition, the inscription notes that this was his fifth fight, and that he had won such clear victories in all five as to be awarded the laurel wreath given for outstanding feats of arms (only the palm branch went to every victor, while the wreath was a special distinction and merited separate mention on monuments). He has also won the fight shown on the relief (*vicit*). The defeat of his opponent is indicated by the fact that the man's shield is resting on the ground and his right arm is raised, both of them typical gestures made by a gladiator signalling his surrender. The name of the loser (Clemens) and the fact that he was discharged from the arena alive after surrendering ('M', for *missus*) have been preserved. Of the defeated *murmillo* to his right, we are told that he too left the arena alive, but died afterwards of his wounds, as indicated by the theta sign (*theta nigrum*) behind the man, standing for the Greek word *thanatos* (death).

This relief illustrates the transition from the old to the new gladiatorial system. A brand new type of helmet appears, but it still lacks the characteristic feature of gladiatorial helmets of the imperial period, the visor covering the face, which seems to have been introduced in the late Augustan period, very soon after the relief was carved.

## FIGHTING WEAPONS OR PARADE ARMOUR?

Archaeological finds are of great importance in the reconstruction of arms and armour. They are far more reliable than written texts and pictorial depictions, and above all they provide information about the materials used in armaments and the technology of making them. Over 75 per cent of all equipment that is clearly

gladiatorial, and on which material has been published, comes from the site of a single find. The armour was excavated in 1766/7 in the gladiatorial barracks at Pompeii, but the methods of the period mean that the circumstances of the find are inadequately recorded. Some pieces have now been lost, and what survives, with the exception of items given to Napoleon Bonaparte as First Consul in 1802 and now in the Louvre, are in the National Archaeological Museum of Naples. Including the items in the Louvre, the armour and defensive weapons in the find comprise fifteen com-

plete helmets (in one case with the visor missing), six single greaves of the short type, one single greave of medium size, five pairs of greaves of the long type, three shoulder-guards, a small round shield and several fragments.

The great majority of the items found at Pompeii (for instance, eleven of the fifteen helmets) are lavishly embossed with ornamental and figural decoration. As a result, the ornamented armour from Pompeii has been interpreted by most scholars as purely parade equipment, worn in the procession (*pompa*) with

which gladiatorial contests began, but not during the fights themselves. This theory has occasionally been questioned, but classification of the finds as parade armour has remained generally accepted to the present day. What, then, are the arguments for and against the use of this ornamented armour in the actual fighting?

The parade armour theory rests on the following assertions: first, that these lavishly embossed ornamental items were too expensive to be exposed to possible damage. It is also claimed that the surfaces bearing reliefs were too vulnerable to stand up to serious

blows. The fact that the equipment shows no traces of damage inflicted in hand-to-hand fighting is seen as further proof that it was purely parade equipment. Finally, the armour itself, particularly the helmets, is said to be much too heavy to be worn in a fight.

However, there are counter-arguments: first, extravagance was in the very nature of gladiatorial contests. The *munera* (games) were a violent spectacle, a dramatic display and not least a demonstration of equipment. The gladiators were expected to present as imposing a picture as possible, and shining metal armour was the best way of achieving such an effect. If a piece was occasionally damaged, that was the least of the expenses a *munus* might be expected to entail. In addition, the danger of really serious damage to the equipment was not as great as it may appear at first sight. Given materials of the same thickness, a piece of embossed metal is not weaker but in fact stronger than a similar piece with a smooth surface. For one thing the embossing thickens the material, and for another the embossed profile is a particularly stable curved structure. The bowls of the Pompeian gladiatorial helmets are generally made of sheet bronze (only one is made of iron) that is 1–3 mm thick, with an average thickness of around 1.5 mm. The visor gratings have an average thickness of 1.8 mm. All edges are faced with metal three or four times as thick as the bowl of the helmet. In comparison, the bowls of military helmets of the same period are on average 1 mm thick, and thus clearly weaker than gladiatorial helmets. One can hardly imagine the Romans making more massive helmets than for their soldiers if those helmets were not seriously intended to be worn in combat. For pure parade purposes thin sheet metal would have been good enough, and would have made it considerably easier to carry out the embossing without detracting from the attractive appearance of the helmet.

Heavy cut-and-thrust weapons were not used in the arena, nor were the throwing and thrusting spears particularly powerful. Swords were short and light, and when used to slash could injure only unprotected parts of the body. Stabbing was the most usual method of striking, in particular with short swords and daggers. Experiments have shown that the bowls of replica helmets made to the thickness of the originals suffer only slight and barely perceptible denting even when struck a direct blow at a right angle. The sole exception is the effect of the trident wielded with both hands by a *retiarius*, which could strike with terrible force. It is not surprising that the helmet of the *secutor*, the opponent of the *retiarius*, was even thicker than the helmets worn by other gladiators. Moreover, all three *secutor* helmets found in Pompeii are plain and smooth, so that the points of the trident could not catch in the embossed work, but would slip off the metal instead.

Since the weapons supplied to the gladiators could do no serious damage to the massively constructed helmets, let alone penetrate them, the men will have been careful not to target their opponents' heads in fighting – it would have been a mere waste of strength to do so. Thrusts at the visor grating, however, were probably fairly common because they would act as an irritant. If a helmet did get scratched it could certainly have been repaired easily enough in the armourer's workshop, so it is not surprising that the extant helmets and greaves, with one possible exception, show no traces of damage from weapons, or at least not to the naked eye. The exception is a *provocator* helmet with a crescent-shaped piece of bronze riveted to its bowl, perhaps as a repair. Moreover, only a very few military helmets, which are preserved in much greater numbers, bear marks that can be identified with any degree of probability as those left by weapons.

The complete gladiatorial helmets found in Pompeii weigh between 3.3 and 6.8 kg, with an average weight of 4 kg. This is about double the weight of a normal infantry helmet of the first century AD. However, military helmets and gladiatorial helmets were worn in very different circumstances. The infantryman not only had to wear his helmet when fighting – perhaps for hours on end – but also when he was on the march, and he also had to carry an extensive amount of other equipment. In battle readiness – that is to say, without his marching pack, which weighed at least 20 kg – the legionary of the early imperial period still had at least 25 kg of clothing, equipment and weapons about his person. By way of contrast, the entire weight of arms and armour for even the heavyweight gladiatorial categories was clearly less than 20 kg, despite the double weight of the helmet. Above all, the gladiator, a trained professional fighter who entered the arena rested and in top form, put on his helmet at a precise moment in time and could take it off again after the fight, which seldom lasted more than ten to fifteen minutes. We had no problems at all when experimenting with

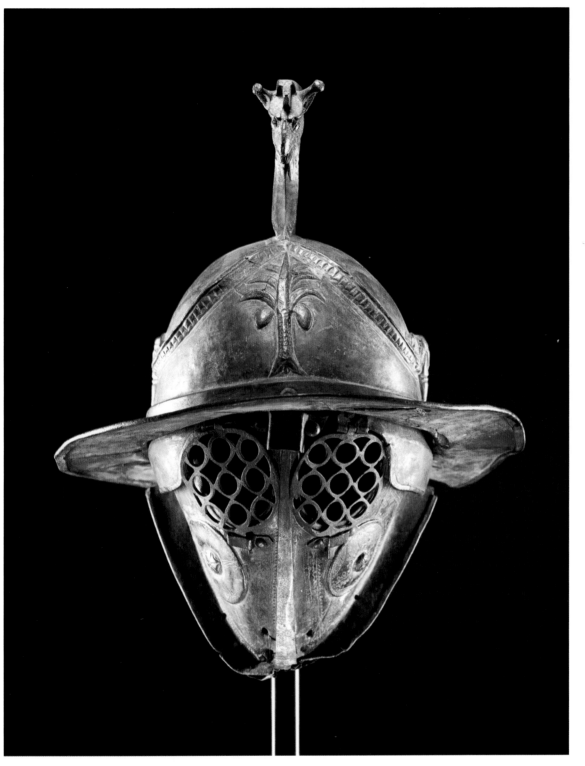

23
**Gladiator's helmet**
First century AD
Bronze
Museo Archeologico
Nazionale di Napoli, 5649

This helmet for a *thraex*
comes from the gladiatorial
barracks of Pompeii, one of
the cities buried during the
eruption of Vesuvius in AD 79.
The embossed ornamentation
showing the palm of victory
over the forehead and the
lances and round shields on
the cheek-guards refers to
events in the arena.

reconstructions of helmets weighing between 3.3 and 4.5 kg. The weight on the head is nothing like as uncomfortable as one might imagine from simply picking up the helmet. In addition, the gladiatorial helmets were well balanced, and by comparison with many other face-covering helmets they impeded vision and breathing only very slightly. The exception, however, was the helmet worn by the *secutor*, which completely covered the face except for two small eyeholes measuring a bare 3 cm in diameter (cf. fig. 22). This was

necessary, since the thin prongs of the trident that was his enemy's principal weapon would easily have penetrated a visor grating, but it did make that type of helmet very uncomfortable, and severely limited the wearer's field of vision.

Two other facts suggest that the helmets and other arms and armour from Pompeii were normal gladiatorial weapons for fighting in the arena: first, all the items agree with contemporary depictions, and can be conclusively assigned to definite categories of gladiators.

The great tomb relief from Pompeii (fig. 34) even shows the embossed work on the helmets and greaves of the fighting gladiators. Second, they are perfectly practicable in size and function, which in view of the complicated construction of the visors would have entailed unnecessary expense in a piece of armour worn purely for show.

The Pompeian helmets can now be placed in the history of the development of the gladiatorial helmet. Most have broad brims and can be traced directly back to the Boeotian and Attic military and gladiatorial helmets of the late republican era. The outline of the brim comes in two variants. The earlier type, to which the Naples helmet (figs 23 and 47) belongs, has a horizontal brim like a hat. In the second variant (fig. 24) the brim curves up like a roof over the forehead, and bends sharply at both sides before merging with the horizontal side and back parts. It can thus cover rather more of the back of the neck. This was a transitional stage before the final phase of development, not yet present in the Pompeian finds, but represented by a helmet in Berlin (location of find unknown). In this type the bowl went vertically down over the neck, ending in a broad, extensive neck-guard; the helmet no longer has any real brim, but the curve above the visor grating extends well down vertically, framing the very high grating as if between a pair of blinkers (fig. 25).

The visor developed in step with the construction of the brim. It was made in two movable hinged halves, showing that it derived from the cheek-guards of the earlier models, now so greatly enlarged that their vertical inner edges met in the middle to cover the whole face. These inner edges had narrow extensions at the top, with their ends fixed in a small container at the centre of the forehead area. When the visor was closed the ends extended further into this container, fastening the upper part of the two halves of the visor. At the lower end, chin straps threaded through internal eyelets were tied together, and the visor was then firmly closed. A strip of soldered metal allowed one half of the visor to overlap the other, covering the narrow gap where they met. It should be emphasized that the halves of the visor closed in the middle and opened out sideways (cf. figs 23, 24); they were not opened and closed by being pushed up or down, as in late mediaeval and early modern helmets.

The lower parts of the visor halves had outward-projecting rims to guard the throat. Special measures

were taken to protect the very vulnerable hinges from weapons. Two transverse rectangular pieces of metal were riveted under the brim in the area of the temples, to cover the hinges. It is possible that gladiators aimed deliberately at this one weak point in the construction of the helmet, hoping to break the visor open. The main effect of the metal guards over the hinges, however, was that the two halves of the visor could open only far enough for the wearer to take the helmet off and put it on again, without letting the upper ends of the two halves slip out of the container above the forehead.

In the early stage of development vision was through small, round eyeholes. These holes were very soon enlarged to a diameter of about 8 cm (cf. fig. 26). As in all the helmets of this kind from Pompeii, they could be protected by removable disc-shaped gratings.

In helmets with curved brims a horizontal grating replaced the eyeholes and discs, and constituted the whole upper part of the visor (fig. 27). The two halves of the visor now consisted of two separate parts joined by a flexible peg and socket connection: the top part was the grating and the lower part the closed chin and cheek-guard. The rim of the grating was straight inside and at the lower end, and curved outside and at the top, so as to fit the curve of the brim exactly. At the top a peg-shaped extension could be pushed into a slit in the brim and fastened with a pin, fixing the grating in place. Another peg at the lower end was pushed loosely into a horizontal groove on

**25**
**Gladiator**
**First to second century** AD
**Bronze**
British Museum, London,
PRB 1888.7-19.97

This figurine shows a heavily armed *murmillo* or *thraex*, wearing loincloth, protective waist-belt and guards for his shins and sword-arm. The sword and shield are broken away. His elaborate helmet has a tall crest and side plume, and the visor grating is of the developed, high-arched type.

**24** (LEFT) **Gladiator's helmet**
Bronze, first century AD
British Museum, London, GR 1946.5-14.1

Helmet of a *murmillo*, with the distinctive high angular crest, broad brim and bulbous visor with eye gratings. Above the brim is a bust of Hercules.

**26**
**Head of a gladiator**
First century AD
Tufa
Museo Archeologico di Verona,
29514

This life-size head comes from the amphitheatre in Verona. It was probably part of the decoration of the building. The broad brim and crest of the helmet have been destroyed, making it impossible to determine what type of helmet it was.

27
**Helmet visor**
First century AD
Bronze
British Museum, London,
GR 1857.10-13.3

A two-piece visor grating for
the type of helmet depicted
on the figurine in Fig. [N5].
The fine ivy-leaf decoration
of the border is deceptive: the
grating is made of thick bronze
and combines strength and
protection with maximum
visibility.

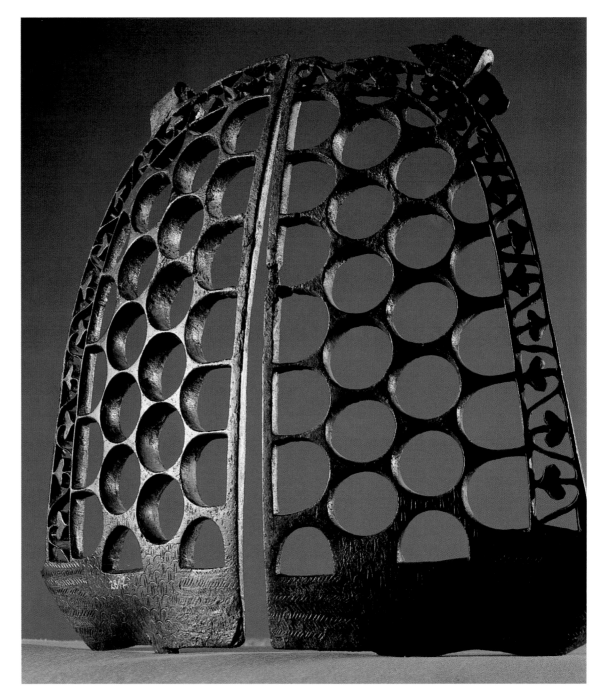

the lower part of the helmet, so that it could slip back and forth in the groove when the helmet was opened or closed. The visor of the Berlin helmet is made in this way, but the grating is now considerably higher and occupies the larger part of the surface of the visor.

The brimmed helmets from Pompeii all have high crests soldered to the top of the bowl. In form, they can be identified as belonging to two different categories of gladiators. Six of the helmets have crests with an angular outline, rising vertically in a straight line from the back of the neck, and bending forward at an angle of 90 degrees at their highest point. From here the crest runs on in a straight horizontal line to the front, where it shows a concave indentation.

Such helmets were worn by the *murmillones*. The other three helmets have curved crests in the shape of the upper part of a crescent, with the head of a griffin made in the round fitted to the top, a feature clearly indicating, as many pictorial depictions confirm, that the three helmets belong to the *thraex* category (figs 23, 47). With the exception of the *secutor* helmets, all the helmets found in Pompeii have two sockets at the sides of the metal of the cap to hold feathers.

The *secutor* helmets, as already discussed, are specially adapted to the particular difficulty of fighting *retiarii*. The size of the eyeholes is much reduced (to 3 cm). There is no brim or tall crest, so that the helmet offers no hold for the net and trident. Instead, the helmet has a low, rounded crest like a crescent directly placed over it. The bowl ends in a narrow downward-sloping guard at the back of the neck.

To conclude this section, let us look at the helmet from the National Museum in Naples, on display in the exhibition (figs 23 and 47). It has a horizontal brim, and a visor with eyeholes and disc gratings. Helmets of this kind are shown in the tomb relief from Pompeii (fig. 34), which dates from the second quarter of the first century AD. The curved crest and griffin's head on top of the bowl show that it was the helmet of a *thraex*. The bowl, as in all helmets of this kind, has a gable-shaped area over the forehead and volutes at the sides. The front of the gable shows a depiction of a palm tree, probably in reference to the palm branch awarded to a victorious gladiator. Both halves of the visor are decorated below the eyeholes with round shields of the *parma equestris* type, and two crossed lances behind them. In spite of this ornamentation it cannot be the helmet of an *eques*, since these helmets, though of this kind, did not have a crest and protome in the shape of a griffin on top. The surface of the helmet must have been partly tin-plated to emphasize the embossed features and produce the contrasting effect of gold (the plain bronze) and silver (the plated parts) so popular among the Romans. A removable plume of large feathers could be fixed to the top of the crest.

## GLADIATORIAL CATEGORIES – THE IMPERIAL PERIOD

The visored helmet was a distinctive item of gladiatorial equipment in the imperial period (cf. figs 25, 29). It gave the professional fighter a threateningly anonymous appearance. It is true that from Augustan times helmets covering the face were also sometimes worn in the army, particularly by the cavalry, but their anthropomorphic masks gave them a completely different character. The visored helmet in one form or another was worn by all categories of gladiators, with the sole exception of the *retiarius*, who was an innovation of the first century AD and fought bareheaded.

Besides the relatively few pieces of armour that have been preserved, sources available to us include a large number of pictorial depictions: stone sculptures, mostly from tombs; small terracotta or bronze figures;

28

**Gladiator's helmet**
First century AD
Bronze, tinned
British Museum, London,
PRB 1966.6-5.1

The remains of tinning on the surface of this helmet from Hawkedon, Suffolk, show that when originally used it would have had a shiny silver appearance. Damage includes loss of the visor, but study of the surviving rivet holes suggests its appearance would have been similar to that of one of the helmets from Pompeii. The Hawkedon helmet is one of the best pieces of evidence for gladiatorial combat in Roman Britain.

29 *Murmillo*

First to second century AD

Terracotta

Museum für Kunst und
Gewerbe Hamburg,
1999.83a–b

A large number of terracotta
statuettes of gladiators have
been preserved. In some
examples, like this *murmillo*,
it is possible to take off the
separately made helmet and
see the gladiator's face.

30 (BELOW)

**Bowl with gladiators**

Second century AD

Pottery, samian ware

Historisches Museum der Pfalz,
Speyer, Sl.Gr.168

Like pottery lamps, decorated
bowls were made from
negative moulds. This kind of
pottery is now known as *terra
sigillata* or samian ware from its
bright red glaze, and there were
major centres of production in
Italy, the Germanic provinces,
Gaul and North Africa. This
bowl was made at Rheinzabern
and has reliefs showing fighting
between *retiarii* and *secutores*.

31 (BELOW)  **Lamp with a *hoplomachus***

Pottery, first century AD

Museum für Kunst und Gewerbe Hamburg, 1906.27

The gladiator is raising his shield in the attitude of a victor. Despite
its small size, this finely worked relief shows every detail of his
equipment. The hole beside the figure was used to fill the lamp,
and the pictorial surface is concave so that no oil would be spilt in
the process. Such lamps were mass-produced in negative moulds.

epigraphs – inscriptions on tombstones, the programmes of performances, graffiti and similar records.

Before looking at the gladiatorial categories individ-
ually, it will be useful to make some observations
about the armaments of gladiators in general during
the imperial period. It is obvious at once that parts of
the body were protected or left unprotected in very different ways. While the head, face and throat were rendered almost invulnerable by the large metal helmet,
the extremities of men in the various categories were
partially protected in different ways by wrappings of
organic substances (leather, quilted linen) or metal
guards, the latter principally in the form of bronze
greaves. The torso, however, remained enticingly
unprotected, except in the case of the breastplate of
the *provocatores*. With the exception of the tunic-clad
*equites*, all categories exposed their naked chests to
the weapons of their opponents. The only piece of
clothing was an elaborately draped loincloth (*subligaculum*), held in place by the broad bronze belt mentioned above (or in late antiquity by the *cingulum* of
ring-shaped buckles). In the second and third centuries
BC broad sashes, probably of leather, might also be
worn under the belt.

This cleverly devised system of partial protection,
especially of the extremities, indicates that the style of
swordsmanship was subject to precise rules for the var-

miniature reliefs on oil lamps and vessels made of *terra
sigillata* (cf. figs 30 and 31); mosaics; and frescoes. The
two last kinds of depictions are particularly illuminat-
ing, since they show the colours of the arms and
armour. But if we are to assign these depictions and
the extant equipment to distinct categories of gladiators, we must return to the written records, particularly

ious gladiatorial categories. The complete armour for the head, particularly the face, with the good protection given to the right arm (the left arm was in any case covered by the shield) and to the lower legs, show that the intention was to avoid chance hits which would disable a man quickly, thus detracting from the drama and duration of the fights. Anyone who has ever tried fighting with shield and sword will know that an unprotected sword arm is very soon black and blue and running with blood, not so much from the opponent's weapon as from colliding with the edge of your own shield and his. The thickly padded *manicae* worn by gladiators were ideally suited to obviating this danger and encouraging an aggressive style of swordsmanship.

The baring of the upper torso (cf. fig. 32) presents

greater problems. It has nothing to do with the nudity of Greek athletes, regarded as so suspect in Rome. The genitals were always covered with a loincloth in the old Italian and Roman tradition. It was in the very nature of the gladiatorial system that fighters were ready to die, and demonstrated that readiness by baring their torsos. If the fighters had been entirely unprotected, the outcome would have been either a brief, unskilled bloodbath or an excessively cautious, boring fighting style. The juxtaposition of armed and unarmed parts of the body controlled the use of weapons and created the conditions for dynamic and skilful swordsmanship. Nor must we forget the visual stimulation of seeing muscular bodies in vigorous exertion, defying death and injury.

The protective wrappings for arms and legs were

almost always, as mentioned above, made of organic materials, leather and stout linen, the latter usually lined. *Manicae* (arm-guards) of metal scale armour or chain-mail were not worn regularly until late antiquity. At first they protected only the hand and lower arm, and consisted of a long glove covered by densely interlocking pieces of leather or broad, overlapping straps. Then sleeve pieces made of horizontally quilted linen seem increasingly to have replaced leather wrappings. Thick straps could reinforce weak areas, and also served to fix pieces of armour to the arm. Like the boxing gloves of the time, the *manicae* in their fully developed form reached to the armpits, and sometimes shoulder-caps of leather or metal were added. The gloves were always of the mitten type, as a rule covering only the outside of the hand and thumb, and were fixed to the fingers with leather loops. If necessary, the hand could be slipped out of the loops to leave the glove dangling.

The wrappings and padded tubes (*fasciae*) for leg protection developed in just the same way, and were worn with short leather gaiters covering the lower calves, the ankles and the backs of the feet. They also provided a good lining for the heavy greaves, for otherwise the lower edges of the greaves would have put very uncomfortable pressure on the unprotected tops of the feet. Such gaiters were often worn without additional wrappings. However, gladiators probably very seldom wore sandals or other footwear, since open shoes are not suitable for wear on sand. Broad leather straps firmly tied around the legs below the knee were very common. It seems to have been thought that their constricting effect would provide short-term stimulation of the muscles, and perhaps protection for the sinews.

The following descriptions of gladiatorial categories in the imperial period allow us to identify some 99 per cent of extant depictions showing fighters of various types, a fact that illustrates the extraordinary degree of standardization in the gladiatorial system throughout the entire period from the first to the fourth centuries AD. Nor can any significant differences be observed between the different parts of the empire, although occasional variations confined to certain regions do occur.

*Eques*

The *equites* (plural of *eques*, 'horseman'), who fought only against other gladiators of their own kind, have been discussed above (p. 37). In the imperial period they were clothed in a voluminous sleeveless *tunica* of various different colours, with *clavi* (two vertical stripes of another colour woven into the fabric). The tunic was belted at the waist and ended a hand's breadth above the knees (cf. fig. 33). The *equites* wore short gaiters on their legs, and sometimes wrappings on the lower legs, but never greaves. They also had the usual *manica* on the right arm, and a visored helmet

32
**Lamp with a *murmillo* and a *thraex***
First century AD
Pottery
Römisch-Germanisches
Museum der Stadt Köln, Lü 663

The *murmillo*, standing on the left, has just lost his shield and is now exposed to his adversary's attack. The scene apparently shows the closing phase of the fight, which will presumably end with the victory of the *thraex*.

33

**Two *equites***

Reconstruction: Marcus
Junkelmann/Rheinisches
Landesmuseum Trier

According to Isidore of Seville (*Origines*, 18, 53 ff.), the *equites* rode white horses and were the first pair to feature on the programme of fights. On the Pompeian tomb relief (fig. 34) the horses of the *equites* are shown above left being led by assistants in the entry procession (*pompa*). Other assistants, further to the right, are carrying the horsemen's helmets and round shields. The middle section of the relief shows the *equites* fighting on foot, and they do indeed constitute the opening pair (far left). The duel is over: the loser, probably wounded, is lying on the ground, while the victor triumphantly raises his shield and awaits the verdict of the public and the *editor* (fig. 36). A scene in the mosaic cycle from Zliten near Leptis Magna in North Africa (fig. 35), which is variously dated from the late first to the third centuries AD, also shows *equites*, again on foot in the crucial final stage of the fight. A whole series of other reliefs and mosaics confirms Isidore's statement that the horsemen were the first pair to fight, but their correct identification was long prevented by the fact that they are almost exclusively shown on foot.

*Murmillo*

The *murmillo* (or *myrmillo*) seems to have derived his name from a Greek term for a fish. This has led to his

34

**Relief with gladiators**

AD 20–50

Marble

Museo Archeologico
Nazionale di Napoli, 6704

without a crest. Two decorative feathers were often worn in the sockets at the side of the bowl, but there was never a central plume (cf. frontispiece). The shield was the traditional *parma equestris*, the medium-sized round shield of the knightly cavalry with its concentrically shaped surface. These shields, with a diameter about 60 cm, seem to have been made of thick compressed leather. The weapons were a lance (*hasta*) 2–2.5 metres long, with a leaf-shaped point, and a medium-length sword with a straight blade (*gladius*). Carrying a total weight of 10–12 kg in arms and armour, the *eques* was one of the more lightly armed categories.

frequent confusion with the *contraretiarius* or *secutor*, the opponent of the gladiator with the net. The *murmillo* fought a man bearing a small shield, the *thraex* or *hoplomachus* (cf. fig. 37). He has very often been equated with the latter, who was in fact one of his standard adversaries. Finally, the term *samnis*, which does not occur after the Augustan period, has also been applied to the *murmillo*. He may in fact have been descended from the *samnis*, but in the imperial period the term is an anachronism.

Like all the following categories of gladiators, the *murmillo* fought with his torso bare. Besides the loincloth (*subligaculum*) and belt (*balteus*), he wore the

35 (BELOW) **Mosaic with gladiators: detail of** *equites*
*c.* AD 200 (?); Archaeological Museum, Tripoli

This is part of a large mosaic from a Roman country villa near Zliten in Libya, showing not only gladiatorial contests but also animal hunts (*venationes*) and executions in the arena (cf. fig. 83).

manica on his right arm, a gaiter on his right leg, and very thick wrappings covering the tops of his feet and looking almost like a plaster cast. A very short greave, with an indentation for the padding at the top of the feet, was fitted over these wrappings by means of several straps threaded through pairs of eyelets. Five such greaves, often wrongly thought to be arm-guards, have survived from Pompeii (fig. 38), and there is one greave, of unknown provenance, which matches the *murmillo* helmet now in Berlin. These greaves each weigh about 1 kg.

The brimmed helmet has the angular crest described above, on which a plume of feathers or more frequently horsehair could be placed. There were also single feathers in the lateral sockets.

The shield (*scutum*) was a tall oblong, curved like the section of a cylinder. In size and construction it corresponded to the *scuta* of the army infantry in use at the same time. It was made of a kind of plywood and covered with leather, at least on the outside. The outer edges were reinforced with narrow strips of bronze, and there was a vertical wooden reinforcement in the middle (*spina*) shaped like an ear of barley or, more usually, a convex semi-globular boss made of bronze or iron (*umbo*). A circle was cut out of the shield behind the *spina* or *umbo*, and the transverse central grip ran through this hole. The shields were brightly painted with ornamental or figural motifs. As finds from military camps show, their average height was a good 100 cm and their breadth about 65–70 cm.

On many of the depictions from both military and gladiatorial contexts, the shields appear rather smaller, but we have a fairly clear indication of the size of a *murmillo* shield in the dimensions of the greaves. The function of the greaves required the lower edge of the shield and the upper edge of the greaves to overlap by at least 10 cm when the fighter was standing in his basic position, left shoulder and left foot forward,

36 (ABOVE)
**Relief with gladiators:**
**detail of** *equites*
AD 20–50
Marble
Museo Archeologico
Nazionale di Napoli, 6704

37
***Murmillo* (left) and** *thraex*
*Reconstruction*: Marcus
Junkelmann/Rheinisches
Landesmuseum Trier

shield raised to mouth level (an attitude shown in countless pictorial depictions of legionaries and gladiators; cf. fig 16). Only this overlap ensured that the aggressively advanced left leg of the *murmillo* would be protected from both his adversary's weapon and collision with the lower edge of his own shield. For this purpose the shield had to be at least 100 cm tall, depending on the height of the man carrying it. Reconstructed shields of such shape and dimensions weigh 6–8 kg. They give excellent protection and their weight can also be employed offensively, but of course their active use calls for considerable force.

The *murmillo* had only one weapon of attack, a

49

**38**
**Greave**
First century AD
Bronze
Musée du Louvre, Paris,
BR 1143

This short greave, found in
Pompeii, was part of the
armour of a *murmillo*.
The embossed relief shows
a goddess between acanthus
tendrils. She may be the
goddess of love, Venus,
regarded as the lover of Mars,
the god of war, and thus
particularly popular among
soldiers. Generals such as
Sulla and Pompey also
venerated her.

40 (BELOW)
**Lamp with a *murmillo* and a *thraex***
Pottery, first century AD
Historisches Museum der Pfalz, Speyer, RHG B1/13

**39**
**Dagger**
First century AD
Iron blade, bone hilt
Museo Archeologico
Nazionale di Napoli, 5681

41 (RIGHT)
**Mosaic with gladiators: detail
of a *thraex* and a *murmillo***
c. AD 200 (?)
Archaeological Museum,
Tripoli

50

short to medium-length sword with a broad, straight blade, a *gladius*, and here again there is a direct parallel with the weapons of the army infantry. These swords, 40–50 cm long, were primarily for thrusting, although they could slash to some effect when attacking unprotected parts of the body.

In later depictions the *gladii* often appear as short as daggers. Very short swords of the Greek type, more like daggers, were in fact found in the gladiatorial barracks of Pompeii (fig. 39). The blades, barely 30 cm long and with a very sharp point, are rhomboid in cross-section. Weapons of this kind could be used by various different categories of gladiators, but were probably most typical of the *hoplomachi* and the *retiarii*.

The total weight of arms and armour for a *murmillo* was 16–18 kg, the large shield being easily the heaviest item. The *murmillo* was thus one of the heavyweight gladiatorial categories, like his opponents. The *murmillo* never fought one of his own kind. His most frequent adversary was the *thraex* (cf. fig. 40), followed by the *hoplomachus*. In fact the pitting of a *murmillo* against a *thraex* may be regarded as the standard pairing in the first century AD, and not until the second and third centuries did the most frequent combination become *retiarius* against *secutor*.

The second group on the central section of the great Pompeian frieze (fig. 34) shows a *murmillo* (left) who has been fighting a *thraex*. The former has just won, and is standing in an attitude of lordly composure, sword raised, beside the referee. The defeated *thraex*, seen from the rear, kneels on the ground, tended by no fewer than five arena assistants (*harenarii* or *ministri*). He has lost his helmet, but can be clearly recognized by his quilted leg wrappings and two long greaves; one of the *harenarii* is holding the small rectangular shield that puts his identity as a *thraex* beyond all doubt.

The Zliten mosaic (fig. 41) shows two similar gladiators still in action. The *thraex*, forced on to the defensive, is on the left, while the *murmillo*, left leg forward, is trying to get a thrust in above the edge of his opponent's shield.

### Thraex and hoplomachus

The *thraex* (or *thrax*, meaning Thracian, cf. fig. 42) is often confused with the *hoplomachus*, since they shared a number of pieces of equipment in common – the quilted leg wrappings, two high greaves and a brimmed helmet with a tall crescent-shaped crest – and they also fought the same adversary, the *murmillo*. However, the *thraex* was clearly distinct from the *hoplomachus* in the rectangular, almost square shape of his small shield (*parmula*) – the shield of the *hoplomachus* was round – the griffin's head on the crest of the helmet, and his weapon of attack: a curved short sword instead of a straight short sword and lance.

The reason for the heavy armouring of the legs of gladiators who carried small shields was naturally the

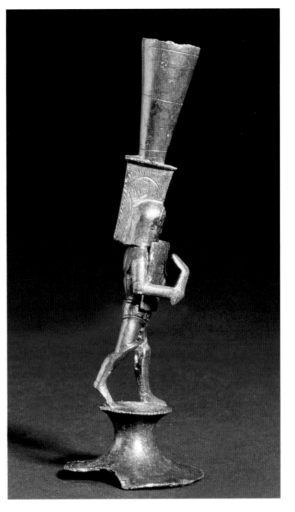

42

**Candlestick in the form of a *thraex***

Second century AD
Bronze
Römerhaus Walheim, on permanent loan from the Württembergisches Landesmuseum Stuttgart, R 80 W 1244

43

**Gladiator combat**

First to second century AD
Terracotta
British Museum, London, GR 1907.5-18.4

The distinctive small shields of this pair of gladiators show that the duel is between two heavily armed combatants, a *hoplomachus* and a *thraex*.

**44**
**Gladiator combat**
First century AD
Terracotta, glazed
British Museum, London,
GR 1856.12-26.592

One figure has broken away.
The remaining combatant is a
*thraex* with the characteristic
crested helmet and high
greaves.

**45**
***Murmillo* (left) and**
***hoplomachus***
Reconstruction: Marcus
Junkelmann/Rheinisches
Landesmuseum Trier

fixed to the legs. Long, close-fitting trousers rather like tights were worn under the greaves. Above the knee, most depictions show horizontal wrappings or padding up to the hips, disappearing under the *subligaculum* (cf. fig. 51). Some frescoes show that such trousers could be ornamented with embroidery, an indication that they were normally made of textile materials, probably linen with a sturdy lining and stitched to create a quilted effect. The trousers ended in the usual gaiters, particularly important here to mitigate the pressure of the heavy greaves. Experiments have shown that when worn with well-fitting padded trousers these greaves are not felt to be an impediment, despite their length and great weight.

On his right arm the *thraex* wore the usual *manica*, and on his head a brimmed helmet with a crescent-shaped crest and the famous griffin's head (fig. 47). The griffin was the companion of Nemesis, goddess of fate, an avenging figure of judgement. Many amphitheatres had small shrines dedicated to Nemesis. The crest could be adorned with a *crista* (plume) of feathers, and the helmet could have single feathers at the sides, but the *thraeces* do not seem to have worn horsehair plumes.

The small shield (*parmula*) resembled a scaled-down form of the *scutum*. It was rectangular, almost square and strongly convex. The material will again have been plywood covered with leather. Its dimensions can be assessed from pictorial depictions as about 60 x 55 cm. The shield of the *thraex* usually had no boss. It must therefore have had a stirrup-shaped handhold projecting from the back of its surface, probably running vertically. The weight of such a shield was about 3 kg.

The typical weapon of attack for the *thraex* was a very short curved sword, almost like a dagger (known as *sica* or, less commonly, *falx*). The blade had a smooth, regular curve, but in the imperial period a variant with a bent blade often also occurred. A wooden practice *sica* found in the Augustan legionary camp at Oberaden has a 'blade' 34 cm long. The *sica* was a weapon used solely for thrusting.

The standard opponent of the *thraex* was the *murmillo*, but occasionally epigraphic sources and pictorial depictions mention or show fights between two gladiators bearing small shields: *thraex* against *hoplomachus*. Both categories were of the heavily armed type, with arms and armour weighing 17–18 kg. As described above, in his basic equipment (close-fitting trousers and *subligaculum*, a pair of long greaves and the *manica*) the *hoplomachus* was exactly like the *thraex*, and is therefore frequently confused with him. His helmet too was similar, but the crest had no protome in the shape of a griffin.

The very small shield borne by the *hoplomachus* was always circular and very convex. It was made entirely from strong sheet bronze. A surviving richly decorated example from Pompeii (fig. 48) has a diameter of 37 cm, and the convex curve measures 5 cm at its deepest. With a thickness of metal measuring 1.42

fact that the *parmula* protected only the lower torso. The *thraex* and *hoplomachus* therefore wore a pair of very high greaves reaching to mid-thigh, with ornamentation in the knee area (fig. 46). The metal was of the same thickness as for short greaves, and they weighed 2.2–2.5 kg. These greaves too had eyelets to take straps, arranged in pairs and enabling them to be

46
**Greaves**
First century AD
Bronze
Museo Archeologico Nazionale
di Napoli, 5645, 5647

This pair of greaves comes from
the Pompeian gladiatorial
barracks. The decoration
consists of embossed figures
and engraved ornamentation in
the form of tendrils. The greave
on the right shows Neptune,
god of the sea, holding a trident
and a sea serpent, while that on
the left depicts Jupiter, father of
the gods, with a lance and bolt
of lightning.

**47** (LEFT)  **Gladiator's helmet**

Bronze, first century AD

Museo Archeologico Nazionale di Napoli, 5649

This *thraex* helmet comes from the gladiatorial barracks in Pompeii (cf. fig. 23). The crescent-shaped crest bears a griffin's head cast in solid metal.

**48** (RIGHT)  **Round shield**

Bronze inlaid with copper and silver, first century AD

Museo Archeologico Nazionale di Napoli, 5669

The coloured ornamentation must have looked even more magnificent when the bronze still had its original shine. The medallion at the centre of the shield, surrounded by laurel wreaths, shows the Gorgon Medusa, whose glance, according to legend, could turn any living creature to stone. Such round shields were carried by *hoplomachi*.

**49** (BELOW)  **Finial in the form of a *thraex***

Bronze, first to second century AD

British Museum, London, GR 1919.6-20.4

This small but detailed figure of a victorious *thraex* has greaves, an arm-guard (*manica*) and a small rectangular shield resting on the ground at his side. Clearly visible on the flamboyant crested helmet is the two-piece visor grating.

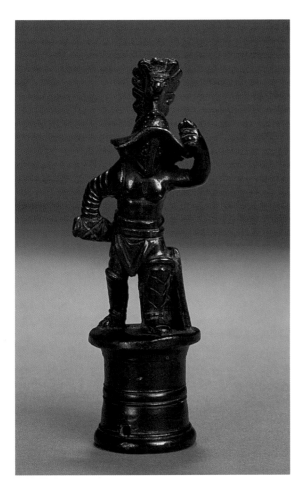

mm, the shield weighs 1.6 kg. The form, with its border area set on a slant to the main body, makes this specimen look like a small-scale descendant of the classic Greek hoplite shield. In most depictions the shield of the *hoplomachus* looks considerably thicker and is almost semi-globular, and it does not have the border area mentioned above.

The specimen from Pompeii also resembles the hoplite shield in having a broad strip of bronze fixed to the centre at the back, forming a kind of stirrup through which the bearer passed his lower arm to grasp a leather loop fitted to the border area. This way of carrying a shield must have been in general use, judging by the depictions. It also enabled the *hoplomachus* to hold his second weapon, a long dagger, in his left hand at the same time. If he lost his first weapon, the thrusting lance, and moved the dagger to his right hand, he could hold the shield by the central stirrup.

Both the round, convex bronze shield and the weapons – lance and dagger or short sword – are very reminiscent of the Greek hoplites, which may also explain the origin of the Greek name of this type of gladiator (*hoplon* means weapon in general but a hoplite's shield in particular, and *machein* means to fight).

The usual opponent of the *hoplomachus* was the *murmillo*, but in exceptional cases he might fight the *thraex*. By pitting the *murmillo*, armed like a legionary,

50
**Gladiator's shield**
Bronze, first to second century AD
British Museum, London, GR 1772.3-3.141

A small shield of the type used by the heavily
armed *hoplomachus* gladiators.

52 (ABOVE) **Mosaic with gladiators:
detail of a *hoplomachus* and a *murmillo***
*c.* AD 200
Archaeological Museum, Tripoli

51 (LEFT) **Relief with gladiators:
detail of a *hoplomachus* and a *murmillo***
Marble, AD 20–50
Museo Archeologico Nazionale di Napoli, 6704

against the *thraex* armed in the Thracian style or the *hoplomachus* with his Greek equipment, the games in the amphitheatre mimicked the opposition between Roman soldiers and their various non-Italian enemies.

The group on the extreme right of the central section of the Pompeii tomb relief (fig. 51) shows the closing phase of a fight between a *hoplomachus* (left) and a *murmillo*. The latter is in retreat, his shield already on the ground, and his sword thrust has missed the head of the *hoplomachus*, who is thrusting his own dagger into his opponent's chest. The Zliten mosaic (fig. 52) shows the *hoplomachus* leaning on his lance in victory. The *murmillo*, bleeding profusely from a wound in his shoulder or arm, has dropped his shield and is raising his left hand, forefinger outstretched, as a sign of surrender. Another pairing shows what is obviously a victorious *hoplomachus* with lowered lance; damage to this area of the depiction leaves only the legs of his opponent on the ground still visible.

### Provocator

This category, which has attracted little attention, was described in detail above, on p. 37. To sum up the basic facts again: *provocatores* usually fought other men in their own category, wore the *subligaculum* and *manica* (loincloth and arm-guard), and had a half-length greave on the left leg, a rectangular breastplate (or in the later imperial period it might be crescent-shaped), a visored helmet without crest or brim, a curved rectangular shield with a *spina* (rib or spine) or a boss, and a sword with a straight blade. The shield

53

***Provocator***

Reconstruction: Marcus Junkelmann/Rheinisches Landesmuseum Trier

54 (FAR LEFT)

**Relief with a *provocator***

Third century AD
Marble
Antikensammlung, Staatliche Museen zu Berlin, SK 794

The gladiator is surrounded by victory wreaths won in the course of his career.

55 (LEFT)

**Relief with gladiators**

Third century AD
Marble
Antikensammlung, Staatliche Museen zu Berlin, SK 964

An inscription gives the names of the gladiators: Asteropaios, most probably a *murmillo*, is defeating the *thraex* Drakon. Both men have lost their shields at this deciding phase of the fight. This relief and that shown in fig. 54 were part of a parapet from Ephesus.

56
**Funerary relief of a *retiarius***
Third century AD
Marble
Museum of London, 3378

The relief shows the *retiarius* armed with trident, dagger and shoulder-guard. Only his net is missing.

was probably rather smaller than the shields of the *murmillones*, since the left greave came higher, to just above the knee. With arms and armour weighing 14–15 kg, the *provocatores* (cf. fig. 53) can be regarded as a middleweight category.

The central group of gladiators on the Pompeian monument (fig. 34) consists of *provocatores*. The victor on the left is turning his breastplate to the viewer; it is ornamented with a Gorgon's head on a background with a pattern of scales.

A relief of the third century AD (fig. 54), possibly from Ephesus, shows the late form of *provocator* equipment, very often found in the east of the empire. The helmet comes down further over the back of the neck and at the sides, and ends in a broad, downward-slanting neck-guard. The breastplate is crescent-shaped.

### Retiarius

The *retiarius*, who fought with a net (from *rete* – net), is the easiest of all the gladiatorial types to identify. As he wore no helmet or greaves, did not carry a shield, and had the *manica* on his left arm instead of his right, he can be distinguished from all other gladiators at first sight. Other features peculiar to him were the *galerus* (or *spongia*), the tall metal guard on his left shoulder, and his weapons of net and trident (cf. fig. 56).

The *retiarius* was an entirely new category introduced in the early imperial period. The large cycles of reliefs from Pompeii (fig. 34) and Chieti, both dating from the first half of the first century AD, show neither the *retiarius* nor his adversary, the *secutor*. This pairing seems to have gained favour only around the middle of the century, becoming steadily more popular in the following centuries, up to the very end of the gladiatorial games.

With his equipment, clearly derived from the sphere of the sea, the *retiarius* did not fit at all well into the generally military context from which the other categories originated. The sources give no indication of the reasons for this development, and we can hardly guess at them now. The system of pitting gladiators armed very differently against each other was widespread in general during the imperial period. There are only a few exceptional pairings of men similarly armed, in particular the *equites* and *provocatores*. The system was exaggerated to a positively bizarre degree when the almost entirely unprotected *retiarius* with his fisherman's equipment was matched against the heavily armed *murmillo* turned *secutor*. As practical experiments have shown, the combination could produce exciting fights full of incident.

The *retiarius* was naked except for the *subligaculum* (loincloth), gaiters, and the *manica* (arm-guard) on his left arm, ending in the tall *galerus* (shoulder-guard). Some depictions show him wearing a light tunic leaving the right shoulder bare instead of a loincloth. The *galerus* was a piece of sheet bronze that covered the outer area of the gladiator's upper arm and shoulder

and was fixed to the top of the *manica*. A guard turning strongly outwards rose vertically 12–13 cm above the shoulder. If the *retiarius* put his left shoulder forward he could duck down behind this shoulder-guard, thus protecting his head to some extent from his opponent's weapon. The outward curve of the guard was important, since otherwise his head could have collided with it during violent movement. Three such pieces of armour were preserved in Pompeii (fig. 58). They are 30–35 cm in length, and about the same breadth at their widest point. The weight of each is 1.1–1.2 kg.

In late antiquity the *retiarius* sometimes seems to have fought without a *galerus*, at least in the eastern part of the empire. In such cases he wore a chain-mail metal *manica* instead, covering a large part of his shoulder and upper chest.

The net, the weapon from which this gladiator derived his name, is shown on very few depictions. To judge by those that do exist, it was a round, wide-meshed throwing net (and therefore also called a *iaculum*) with a diameter of about 3 metres. Experimental tests, and comparison with the throwing nets used in fishing, suggest that the edge of the net carried lead weights. A handled ewer from Rheinzabern (fig. 59) clearly illustrates the throwing technique. The *retiarius* held the folded net in his right hand and prepared for

57

***Retiarius***

First to second century AD
Bronze
British Museum, London,
GR 1873.8-20.53

This little figurine shows both the developed chest musculature of the gladiator and some of the distinctive equipment of the retiarius: loin cloth (*subligaculum*) with broad belt, long-handled trident (the forked end now missing) and metal shoulder-guard (*galerus*).

**58** (ABOVE)

***Galerus***

First century AD

Bronze

Musée du Louvre, Paris,
BR 1142

The tall shoulder-guard
(*galerus*) offered the head of the
*retiarius* some protection from
his adversary's attack. Here a
medallion with the picture of
Hercules adorns its otherwise
smooth metal surface. The
demi-god was particularly
popular with gladiators because
of his superhuman strength and
famous deeds.

**59** (ABOVE RIGHT)

**Flask with a *retiarius***

Second century AD

Pottery, samian ware

Historisches Museum der Pfalz,
Speyer, S.L.F.St.VII

A *retiarius* prepares to throw
his net. His adversary, a *secutor*,
is shown on the other side.

an underarm cast, while wielding his other two
weapons, the trident and a long dagger, in his left
hand. He kept the trident prongs held down to prevent
entangling the net in them. The throwing of the net
does not often seem to have decided a fight. The *secutor* would naturally do his best to prevent his opponent from picking the net up from the ground again
and trying a second throw, so that sooner or later the
*retiarius* would be restricted to the use of his trident
and dagger.

The three-pronged trident, about the height of a man
and known as the *fuscina* (or sometimes *tridens*), was
undoubtedly the main weapon of a *retiarius*. After
losing his net he would hold the trident in both hands.
Its handle could now be used to parry blows, as in
fighting with staves, and he could strike with either
side of it. The prongs of the trident could also be used
to parry blows or to exert a levering effect on the other
gladiator's sword or the edges of his shield and helmet.
Not for nothing did the opponent of the *retiarius* wear
a completely smooth, rounded helmet, for the force of
the trident when wielded with both hands was terrible.
The *retiarius* is often shown stabbing at his adversary's
legs below the man's shield, and a thrust at the helmet
from above was also common. The prongs could not
actually penetrate the thick metal, but there was a

danger that the point of one of them might pierce
through an eyehole, with horrible consequences. The
*secutor* ducked down behind his shield or lowered his
head when attacked in this way, thus depriving himself
of a good view and allowing his agile opponent the
advantage.

The *retiarius* held his third weapon, a long, straight
dagger (*pugio*), in his left hand. He used it when he
had taken his opponent by surprise, jumping at him
from a favourable angle and throwing him to the
ground. The *retiarius* had at all costs to avoid close
combat at the distance usual in a swordfight, for
here he was hopelessly inferior to his heavily armed
opponent.

With arms and armour weighing in all 7–8 kg
(including the 2–3 kg net), the *retiarius* was the most
lightly armed of the *armaturae* (gladiatorial categories)
of the time. He always fought the *secutor*. In a variant
of this pairing for which several depictions provide evidence, the *retiarius* was pitted against two *secutores* at
once. Although outnumbered, he made up for this disadvantage by standing on a raised platform or bridge
(*pons*) with two short flights of steps leading up to it. In
addition to his usual weapons, he had a supply of
apple-sized round stones stacked up in a pyramid,
which he could throw at his opponents before and

while they tried climbing up to his platform, another good example of the skill of the Romans in devising clever ways of giving an equal chance even to adversaries of very different kinds.

The names of the platform (*pons*, 'bridge') and of the gladiators who fought on it (*pontarii*) suggest that it was sometimes constructed above water. There were already basins of water in some arenas, and in others a small-scale version could be improvised with the aid of wooden tubs. Perhaps versions of the fight staged in this way suggest the possible origin of the mysterious pairing of 'fish' and 'fisherman' (i.e. *murmillo* and *retiarius*).

### Secutor

The *secutor* (pursuer) or *contraretiarius* was a variety of the *murmillo* (cf. fig. 60) specially developed to fight the *retiarius*. The equipment of *murmillo* and *secutor* differed only in the shape of their helmets, described above (*secutor*, p. 41). Apart from the practical considerations dictating the specific design of the *secutor* helmet, the visual effect could also have played a part. The smooth surface, rounded, streamlined shape, small eyeholes and fin-like crest give the helmet the

look of a fish's head, suiting the role of the opposing gladiator, a 'fisherman' with a net and trident.

The bronze figurine of a *secutor* from Arles (fig. 62) has a helmet with a movable visor. The original construction of the visor would have been too complicated for a small statuette, and consequently the craftsman fitted a visor that could be pushed back in

the same way as those of the closed helmets of the fifteenth to seventeenth centuries. The terracotta figurine of a *thraex* from an unknown location (fig. 63) also allows a view of the gladiator's bare head. In this case the whole helmet can be taken off, again in contravention of the way in which real gladiatorial helmets functioned.

The usual tactics of the *secutor* were to try closing in on his adversary's body with his shield held in front of him. The other man would naturally try to avoid close combat, and if necessary would retreat, waiting for an opportunity to take his pursuer by surprise and then use his net or trident. The *secutor* also had to be very careful when attacking, particularly as his sight and hearing were severely affected by the complete closure of the helmet, except for its small eyeholes. He also had to husband his strength carefully, for if a fight went on for a long time the weight of his armour and the

61 (ABOVE)
**Finial in the form of a *secutor*'s helmet**
First to third century AD
Bronze
British Museum, London,
GR 1873.8-20.169

This decorative terminal shows the distinctive features of a *secutor* helmet: a heavy visored front with smooth surface, low, rounded crest and small eye holes.

60 (ABOVE LEFT)
***Secutor*** (left) and ***retiarius***
Reconstruction: Marcus Junkelmann/Rheinisches Landesmuseum Trier

61

reduced air supply would make him tire more quickly than his lightly armed, bare-headed opponent.

Some of the sculptural depictions from the east of the empire show a special form of *secutor* armour. The gladiator has the usual helmet and short greaves on both legs, but no shield. Instead he wears a long coat of scale armour and holds in his left hand a curious item, a blade shaped like a chopping knife with a short central handle leading to a tubular arm-guard. This instrument must have been used to parry the net and trident.

## OTHER CATEGORIES

The following paragraphs comprise comments on a few other gladiatorial categories for which the information to be gleaned from the sources is inadequate in one way or another. Either there is good written evidence but no clear depictions, or we have pictorial depictions but no name for the category shown.

*Essedarius* ('war-chariot fighter'): this is a category known after the middle of the first century AD from a great many inscriptions. The name derives from *essedum*, the light two-wheeled chariot of the Celts. The *essedarii* normally seem to have fought each other. As there are no pictorial depictions, we have no further information about their equipment and manner of fighting. It has been suggested with good reason that a certain type of sword-fighter armed with a curved oval shield and brimless helmet, who always fought against his own kind, may be identified as the *essedarius*. These couples always fought on foot, and there is no sign in pictorial depictions of the war chariot that gave the *essedarius* his name. It is possible, however, to imagine the *essedarii* making a spectacular appearance as they stormed into the arena in their chariots, but then getting out to fight on foot, as Homer's heroes often did. Perhaps the expensive chariots were abandoned over the course of time, but the term itself was retained. This explanation would have the advantage of allowing us to connect a gladiatorial type that is relatively often mentioned with a hitherto unidentified pair of gladiators, but there is no positive proof.

*Dimachaerus* (fighter with two swords or daggers): the written accounts we have of this category are very few and far from clear, and there is no definite pictorial documentation.

*Crupellarius*: a term mentioned by Tacitus (*Annales* 3, 43–6) for a category of Gallo-Roman gladiators who were so heavily armed that in battle with Roman soldiers during a civil war, when they were thrown to the ground by their enemies, their armour had to be hacked off with picks.

*Paegniarius*: this category, according to the written sources, was not intended to perform in serious fighting with sharp-edged weapons. Its task was to entertain

the audience with burlesque duels during the intervals, particularly the long interval in the middle of the day. The fourth pair from the left on the great Pompeian relief (fig. 34 and detail, fig. 64) consists of two fighters during one of these intervals. They seem to have neither helmets nor shields, and no weapons of attack are visible. They wear wrappings to halfway up their legs, and the head (preserved in the case of only one of the men) also seems to have some kind of wrapping round it. These figures may be *paegniarii*.

*Laquerarius*: many scholars equate the *paegniarius* described above with the *laquerarius*, while others see the *laquerarius* as a variety of *retiarius* carrying a kind of lasso (derived from the Latin *laqueus*, 'noose') instead of the net.

*Sagittarius* (archer): there are a few written mentions of this category, but they are not at all clear. Pictorial

63 (ABOVE)
***Murmillo* (left) and *thraex***
Second century AD
Terracotta
Württembergisches
Landesmuseum Stuttgart,
Antikensammlung, Arch. 65/6
(Swords restored)

62 (OPPOSITE)
***Secutor***
Second century AD
Bronze
Musée de l'Arles Antique,
FAN 92. 00. 1371

(See fig. 22.)

63

depictions show such men with oriental reflexive bows, pointed helmets and scale armour. Presentation of this gladiatorial category in the amphitheatre must have entailed great risks for the public, in view of the long range of such bows (about 200 metres), since shots could easily have missed their aim or ricocheted. Very special security measures would have had to be taken.

64

**Relief with gladiators: detail of gladiator and assistants**

AD 20–50

Marble

Museo Archeologico Nazionale di Napoli, 6704

There is controversy over the identification of this gladiatorial category.

## PREPARATIONS FOR THE FIGHTING

The gladiatorial contests were the culmination of the programme of the *munera*, the games originally held by private citizens. In the imperial period *venationes* (animal hunts or animal fights) and the execution of criminals (*noxii*), not previously part of the *munera*, also became part of the spectacle. Animal hunts were held in the morning; executions, athletic contests, ballets and comic interludes generally took place in the mid-day interval; and the conclusion and high point of the programme came with the gladiatorial contests in the afternoon. A *munus* usually lasted several days.

While in the early days of the games only a few pairs of gladiators fought, in the late republican period

(the first century BC) their number increased to such an extent that several laws had to be passed in an attempt to keep the ruinously extravagant competition between holders of *munera* within justifiable limits. In the imperial period the number of gladiators performing in a *munus* could vary enormously. For various special occasions some of the emperors arranged huge shows lasting days or weeks, in which hundreds or even thousands of pairs fought. Much of the information provided by Roman historians, who were often anxious to emphasize the munificence of a 'good' emperor or the wastefulness of a 'bad' one, may be distrusted, since they could have exaggerated for both these reasons. However, when Augustus himself states in his account of his achievements that in the course of eight great *munera* he sent 10,000 gladiators in all into the arena, we may take his word for it, since his contemporaries could have checked his statement.

Such mammoth spectacles were very rare, even in Rome. At *munera* in the smaller cities of Italy, about which we are very well informed from announcements and programmes that have been preserved, it was usual for between twenty and fifty pairs to appear, that is to say forty to one hundred gladiators. On a single day of a *munus* the average number was twelve to thirteen pairs.

The preparation and staging of a *munus* followed an established pattern in the imperial period. Once the *editor* (the holder of the games) had come to an agreement with the *lanista* (the private entrepreneur who supplied the programme), he would draw the attention of the public to the forthcoming event by having *edicta muneris* displayed on easily accessible walls. The many surviving examples, particularly in Pompeii, show that these *edicta* were painted on the walls in attractive script by professional scribes specializing in posters. They usually contained the following information: the occasion of the *munus* (generally in honour of the emperor); the name of the *editor*; the number of pairs of gladiators appearing (*gladiatorum paria*) and/or the name of their company (*familia gladiatoria*); any additional events on the programme (*venatio, athletae, noxii* – animal hunts, athletic contests, executions); any measures to be taken for the comfort of the spectators (the provision of *vela*, or sun awnings, and *sparsiones*, the spraying of perfumed water); the location of the show; and the day or days of the performance.

One or two days before the opening of the *munus* the fighters were introduced in some public place such as the town forum. The evening before the show a banquet (*cena libera*) was held for all performers; it was also open to the public, who thus had another opportunity to take a look at the gladiators.

At this point the *libellus munerarius*, a detailed programme listing the pairs in order of their appearance, was available to provide further information. After the names of the performers, who had mostly adopted stage names such as Pugnax (the pugnacious one),

Tigris (tiger), Hermes (in the god's capacity as the guide of souls) or Columbus (dove), it listed the number of their fights and victories to date. Before this *libellus* could appear, the *compositio*, the pairing of the fighters, had to be decided, a task undertaken by the *editor*, no doubt with the advice of the *lanista* and the *doctores* (trainers).

The show itself opened with a solemn procession (*pompa*). The upper section of the Pompeian tomb relief (fig. 34) shows scenes from this festive procession, led by the two lictors, officers of the holder of the games, who bear visible witness to his political and social rank (fig. 65). They wear the toga, the official ceremonial garment of a Roman citizen. In their left hands they hold the *fasces*, a bundle of sticks enclosing an axe, carried over the shoulder and symbolizing the power of their office, and in their right hands they carry staves, here missing because of damage to the relief. The lictors are followed by three *tubicenes*, trumpeters. Four men follow carrying a *ferculum* on their shoulders (fig. 66). This was a platform on which statues were carried in procession, usually depicting such deities of victory or warfare as Victory, Hercules, Mars and Nemesis, but here the figures of two smiths are crouching on the *ferculum*. These men will have been the armourers who provided the gladiators with their equipment. The next two figures carry a writing tablet (*tabella*) and a palm branch. The tablets were for the information of the audience, and the palm branch was intended to honour the victors. Then comes a Roman in festive garments, no doubt the *editor* in person. He is turning to his six assistants, who are carrying the gladiators' shields and helmets. A seventh is holding an object that cannot now be identified, and then comes another player of a wind instrument, this time a *lituus*, a short, curved trumpet. The rear is brought up by two more assistants leading the horses ridden by the mounted gladiators (*equites*).

The group comprising the *editor* and armour-bearers on the relief is frequently taken to show the *probatio armorum*, the checking of weapons before the fights began, as described by the authors of classical antiquity. It applied to offensive weapons, and was intended to ensure that they really were sharp and pointed, and the gladiators could not fake anything. But in fact the relief shows exclusively defensive weapons – shields and helmets – which did not need to be checked in this way. The scene should therefore be interpreted as part of the procession itself, with the gladiators' showy helmets and shields borne before them in the fashion of a medieval tournament. This practice also had the advantage of providing a view of the faces and bodies that would later be covered by visors and large shields. The gladiators themselves are not shown participating in the *pompa* on the relief, but the whole of its main area is devoted to them.

Music was a feature not only of the procession but of the fighting itself, which was accompanied by the

**65**
**Relief with gladiators: detail of lictors and trumpeters**
AD 20–50
Marble
Museo Archeologico Nazionale di Napoli, 6704

The upper right-hand corner shows the stylized depiction of a *velum*, the sun awning that protected visitors to the amphitheatre from the heat. The availability of this luxury is often mentioned in the surviving announcements of forthcoming *munera*.

**66**
**Relief with gladiators: detail of *ferculum* with armourers**
AD 20–50
Marble
Museo Archeologico Nazionale di Napoli, 6704

**67**
**Trumpet**
Fourth to third century BC
Bronze
British Museum, London,
GR 1839.11-9.46d

The curved Roman trumpet (*cornu*) developed from early instruments like this. The strident sounds of trumpets and water-organs were used to heighten the drama of events in the amphitheatre, in particular to signal key stages in gladiatorial combats.

68

**Mosaic with gladiators: detail
of musicians with a water
organ and wind instruments**
*c.* AD 200 (?)
Archaeological Museum,
Tripoli

69

**Lamp in the form
of a water organ**
Late second to early third
century AD
Pottery
British Museum, London,
GR 1965.10-11.1

The seated organist (head now
missing) plays the *hydraulis*, an
organ powered by water and
compressed air.

## THE CONDUCT OF GLADIATORIAL CONTESTS

The introduction to the gladiatorial contests consisted of a *prolusio* (prelude). The various pairs fought with blunted weapons, giving a foretaste of their skill. This phase helped to warm the fighters up and get the public into the right mood for the spectacle to follow. The *arma lusoria* (mock weapons) used at this point were probably the same wooden weapons (*rudes*) as those employed in training.

After the *prolusio* the 'sharp iron' (*ferra acuta*) was brought in and checked during the *probatio armorum*. Now the gladiators fought each other in the pairings drawn up by the *editor*. The mounted gladiators always began the performance, but there does not seem to have been a set order of appearance for the other categories.

Normally, the gladiators fought only in pairs, as shown in pictorial depictions (cf. fig. 70) and as enumerated in lists and programmes (*gladiatorum paria*). An exception was the fight for the 'bridge' between a *retiarius* and two *secutores*. Mass fights between whole troops of gladiators (*gregatim*) are occasionally mentioned in the sources, but they must have been held only at very large *munera*. Such mass fights were probably re-enactments of mythological or historical battles, like the naval battles (*naumachiae*) staged on water. But only second-class gladiators would have fought in these events, perhaps men condemned to death rather than professional fighters.

In the *compositio*, or composition of the pairs, care usually seems to have been taken to match fighters of equal ability with each other. Tried and tested *veterani* were seldom pitted against beginners (*tirones* – recruits), but there were exceptions. A talented and ambitious beginner could be very dangerous to a veteran, as various inscriptions make clear. For instance, a graffito from Pompeii records a fight between the *murmillo* Marcus Attilius, a *tiro* making his first appearance, and the *thraex* Hilarus from the Neronian *ludus*, a veteran who had already won fourteen victories (fig. 71). Attilius won the duel, and the defeated Hilarus left the arena alive (*missus*). The surprise victor obviously had natural talent. A few centimetres away another graffito (endpapers) shows his next fight against the *thraex* Lucius Raecius Felix, who had fought twelve times and won victory wreaths in all twelve fights. He, too, was defeated and discharged from the arena alive.

There were *praecones* (heralds or announcers), but it was impossible for a single speaker to make himself heard by spectators in the top tiers of seats in a large amphitheatre. Information must have been provided on large inscribed tablets (*tabellae*), one of which is shown on the Pompeian tomb relief. On the entry of a gladiator a *tabella* was probably carried before him, giving his name and the list of his successes.

A fresco from the *podium* of the Pompeian amphitheatre, now extant only in a copy, shows two

sound of various different instruments. Military brass instruments, the *cornu* (large coiled circular horn; fig. 67), *tuba* (long straight trumpet) and *lituus* (short trumpet, curving up in front), had always been dominant in the arena, but the *tibia* (double shawm) was also played and seems to have given the signal for the separate duels to begin. The *hydraulis* or water organ (figs 68, 69), was added in the first century AD and in time came to be a typical instrument associated with fighting in the amphitheatre. The Zliten mosaic (fig. 68) shows this organ, played with the accompaniment of brass instruments.

antagonists, a *murmillo* and a *hoplomachus*, facing each other. They are armed except for their helmets, which, like their offensive weapons, are held ready for them by assistants crouching on the ground. The *hoplomachus* is challenging his opponent by playing a melody on the *cornu* (horn). No doubt gladiators frequently tried to impress their adversaries and the audience with such theatrical gestures before the beginning of a duel. A referee (*summa rudis*) in a voluminous tunic stands between the gladiators, easily recognizable by his long stick (*rudis*).

## RULES AND REFEREES

The referees were very important characters in the arena. They usually seem to have officiated in twos, the principal referee (*summa rudis*) with an assistant (*secunda rudis*) standing beside him. The fight was not a wild exchange of blows, but a skilful duel that observed strict rules (*dictata, leges pugnandi*). Unfortunately very little is known of the details. In certain kinds of fights lines were marked on the ground with white chalk (*lineae albae*) and the fighters had to keep between them. In the case of contraventions of the rules or incidents that put a gladiator at a disadvantage through no fault of his own (for instance if a part of his armour fell off), the referee would interrupt the fight, and the combatants then went back to their starting positions. While there were no rounds, as in modern pugilism, if the duel went on for a very long time the referee could order a break (*diludium*). An interval of this kind is shown on the Pompeian tomb relief (fig. 34, centre right, and detail, fig. 64), where two gladiators are being tended by assistants (*harenarii, ministri*), who are massaging them and serving drinks. Slight wounds could also be treated. However, if the fighters showed indiscipline or a lack of attacking spirit the referee made ruthless use of his stick. In really bad cases assistants were sent in with whips, torches and red-hot irons, but such occurrences were almost entirely confined to third-class performances when the duels were between amateurs condemned to death rather than professional gladiators.

Well-trained swordsmen had a wide repertory of moves – lunging, parrying and feinting – which were appreciated by a knowledgeable audience. Fencing techniques were not like those of the present day, since the weapons were completely different. The swords were so short that blades can have crossed only in exceptional cases. A man would attack and defend principally with his shield, impeding his opponent with it, forcing him back, tempting him forward, feigning an attack to provoke a wrong reaction, or striking horizontally with the lower edge of the shield. The sword would be held back behind the cover of the shield so that the gladiator could thrust straight at his target in a surprise move. Cuts were very much less common than thrusts. In the closing phase of a fight

the opponents quite often fought at very close quarters, wrestling as they writhed on the ground.

There was no set time limit to the fights; they went on until victory was decided. No points were scored. Draws were relatively rare: if two gladiators had fought for a very long time with outstanding style and courage, and neither seemed to have the upper hand, the ovations of the spectators might show that they were willing to dispense with a decision. The opponents could then both leave the arena undefeated, *stantes missi* (dismissed standing), as the technical term had it.

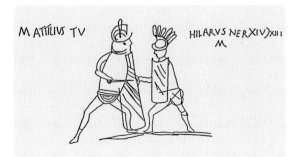

**70**
**Drinking flask with a *retiarius* (right) and a *secutor***
Second to third century AD
Pottery
Römisch-Germanisches
Museum der Stadt Köln, 79,15

The palm branch awarded to the victor at the end of the fight can be seen between the two gladiators.

**71**
**Graffito of a *murmillo* and a *thraex***
Drawing after an original in Pompeii
*c.* AD 60

The *murmillo* Attilius defeats the *thraex* Hilarus.

Normally, however, there were clear winners and losers. The simplest form of decision came when one of the gladiators was so severely wounded that he died or was unable to go on fighting. This is clearly the case with the *hoplomachus* and *murmillo* on the extreme right of the central area in the Pompeian frieze (fig. 51). It was much more usual, however, for one of the swordsmen to be forced to capitulate by wounds or

**72**
**Mosaic with gladiators: detail of a *retiarius* and a *secutor***
*c.* AD 200 (?)
Archaeological Museum, Tripoli

exhaustion, as with the three pairs on the left of the same relief (fig. 34). The loser showed that he admitted defeat by throwing his shield or trident to the ground, or lowering it and raising one hand with forefinger outstretched. On the Zliten mosaic the *retiarius* wounded in the leg is adopting this attitude (fig. 72). Now the referee would intervene dramatically by coming between the fighters and preventing the victor from making any further attack on his defenceless opponent, if necessary seizing his sword arm, as in the case of the victorious *eques* in the first pair on the same mosaic (fig. 35).

But what distinguishes gladiatorial contests from all other forms of competitive sport between two opponents, however risky, is the fact that the matter was still not decided with the capitulation of the loser, over whose head the sword of Damocles still hung in the form of possible execution by the victor. The decision on the loser's fate lay with the *editor*, but as a general rule he went along with the feeling of the audience. If the loser had shown courage and fought fairly, giving in only when the situation was hopeless, he could hope for the sympathy of the spectators, who would wave the hems of their togas or cloaks and cry '*missum!*' or '*mitte!*' The *editor* then gave a signal to the referee to discharge the defeated gladiator from the arena alive.

However, if for one reason or another the audience was not happy with the loser's performance, they would then demand his death by turning their thumbs up (*pollice verso*) – contrary to the popular modern misconception that thumbs down meant death – and

crying '*iugula!*' (kill him). In this case it was expected that at least in death the loser would give an *exemplum virtutis*, a good example of manly conduct. If his strength still permitted he would kneel before his opponent, arms clasped behind his back or, in a touching gesture, he might embrace the legs of the man standing over him, voluntarily offering himself up for the death blow. He did not remove his helmet so that – unless he was a *retiarius* – his face was hidden, no doubt making it easier for the victor to do his dreadful duty. One function of the visored helmet, and it is not to be underestimated, must have been that it depersonalized the wearer, making him an uncannily threatening and anonymous fighting machine, against which aggression could be exerted with far fewer inhibitions than if a man were fighting an opponent whose uncovered face constantly identified him as a familiar brother in arms. At the moment when the loser was killed, or 'took the iron' (*ferrum recipere* was the technical term), the audience shouted '*habet!*' (He has it!), an exclamation that also accompanied every decisive hit.

The moment of truth when a gladiator delivered himself up to the mercy or condemnation of the audience, their freedom to decide on his life or death, and the carrying out of that decision must have been the high point of a *munus*. Even if it did not always materialize, the bloody end in which every fight might conclude gave gladiatorial contests a darkly heroic aura that is absent from such a sport as boxing, for all its brutal aspects.

When a gladiator died in the arena he was taken away on a covered stretcher and placed in the *spoliarium*, the mortuary, where his throat was cut as a matter of routine, to prevent any rigging of the outcome that might have left him alive. He was then undressed and prepared for burial. Certainly he was never dragged out of the arena by a hook, like a common criminal, as many writers state. That was the fate of the *noxii*, criminals executed in the arena. Several stretchers ready for use are shown on the Zliten mosaic. It is not at all sure whether the fallen gladiators were accompanied by arena staff costumed as the gods of the underworld (such as Mercury in his capacity as the conductor of human souls, *Dis Pater*), as we are told by the Christian apologist Tertullian (AD 156–220), who constantly emphasized the links between paganism and public spectacles. At least, there is no pictorial depiction of such a custom. Many gladiators had proper funerals, as a number of funerary inscriptions prove.

The wounded – victors and losers alike – received the best possible medical treatment. A tried and tested gladiator had very considerable market value, and neither the *lanista* nor the *editor* wanted to suffer unnecessary losses. The latter had to pay the entrepreneur a much higher sum for a dead or permanently disabled gladiator than the basic fee due if a fighter survived his duel without severe injury.

After the fight the victor ascended a flight of steps to the *editor*'s platform to receive his prizes. These regularly consisted of a palm branch (*palma*) and a considerable sum of money (*praemium*), the exact amount depending on the gladiator's ranking. For particularly outstanding achievement he might also be awarded the coveted laurel wreath (*corona*) and other gifts. In the later imperial period the wreath seems to have been awarded as routinely as the palm branch. The money prize was the gladiator's own property, whether he was a free man or a slave. A very special distinction was the wooden sword (*rudis*) handed to a swordsman as a sign that he was now released from his obligation to fight in the arena. This award, too, cost the *editor* dear, for he had to provide the *lanista* with an equally good gladiator as a replacement. When the victor had received his prizes he would run a lap of honour round the arena, waving the palm branch.

## CHANCES OF SURVIVAL

The question of course arises as to how many fights ended in the death of the loser and how many with the *missio* (discharge). Due to a lack of comprehensive statistics, no precise answer can be given. We may also conclude that circumstances changed a good deal over the centuries. Information is scantiest for the republican period, but written records convey the impression that fights often did have a fatal outcome. The *munera* were above all a vehicle of the struggle for political power between rival noblemen, who tried to outdo one another in the voters' estimation by putting on shows with large numbers of participants. To appear generous in the eyes of the ordinary people, the *editores* could hardly avoid extravagance in shedding the blood of gladiators. Juvenal (*c.* AD 58–140) gave striking expression to these pressures: '*Munera nunc edunt et, verso pollice vulgus cum iubet, occidunt populariter*' (3, 36 f.), 'Today they hold shows, and win applause by slaying with a turn of the thumb whomsoever the mob bids them slay.'

The basic situation did not change in the imperial period, but there were some mitigating circumstances. First, there was less pressure on holders of the games to present a high political profile, and second, the imperial ideology was based on a sense of mission combined with certain more humane tendencies. Augustus regulated the scale and practice of the *munera*, and above all he prohibited fights *sine missione*, contests in which the release of the loser with his life seems to have been ruled out from the start. In the first century AD, for which the sources are particularly good, fights seem to have had a fatal outcome less often than in any other century before or afterwards. In the later imperial period, however, the chances of a gladiator's survival again declined, a development accompanying a tendency towards brutal

severity which can also be observed in the military and judicial systems of the epoch.

Georges Ville, who has studied the subject in more detail than any other scholar, has analysed the known results of a hundred duels of the first century AD. Nineteen of the two hundred gladiators involved died in these fights. That means that a swordsman entering the arena had a good 9:1 chance of survival. The prospects were 4:1 for the loser, although it is not clear how many of those who perished died fighting, how many died later of their wounds, and how many were killed in the arena when the appeal for *missio* had been turned down.

For the second and third centuries AD we do not have as much unambiguous source material, but there is enough information to confirm a steeply rising death rate. Ville estimates that in the third century AD every other fight ended in the death of one of the partici-

73

**Gladiator**

First to second century AD
Bone or ivory
British Museum, London,
PRB 1899.10-10.1

A small carving, found at Lexden, Colchester, showing a victorious *murmillo*. Naked but for a loincloth and reinforced belt, he is armed with a large visored helmet, a short sword, a curved rectangular shield, metal greaves to protect the legs and a padded guard on his sword arm. Appropriately, a scene of gladiatorial combat is carved in miniature on the shield.

**74**

**Flask with a *venator***

Third century AD

Pottery

Römisch-Germanisches
Museum der Stadt Köln, KL 441

The upper picture shows a
*venator* wrestling an animal
to the ground. The inscription
under the victory wreath runs
*taurisc[us] nika* – may Tauriscus
win.

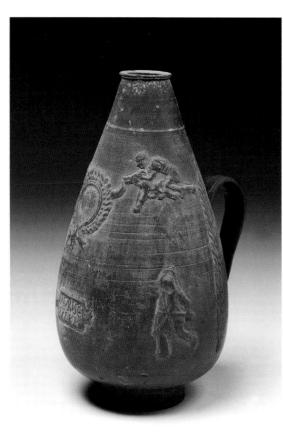

**75**

**Relief with an ape as
charioteer**

Second century AD

Marble

Museo Nazionale Romano alla
Terme di Diocleziano, Rome,
496

A trained ape drives a chariot
drawn by two camels. The
realistically reproduced
crouching attitude of the
'charioteer' is in deliberate
contrast to the upright, tense
physical posture of his human
counterparts.

pants. That is to say, at the beginning of their duels
gladiators had a 3:1 chance of survival, but the losers
must reckon on a 50 per cent probability of death. This
change may perhaps be interpreted as showing that in
the early imperial period the *missio* was the norm and
only performances that might be described as far
below average were punished with death, but that in
the late imperial period the killing of the loser became
the rule, and the *missio* was now a distinction awarded
for an above average performance.

The next question to arise is that of a gladiator's
long-term life expectancy. It seems that a normal professional swordsman did not have to count on very frequent appearances in the arena. There are even
records of gladiators complaining that they were
obliged to spend the best years of their lives in idleness
because of the few *munera* held. If we assume that a

gladiator had an average of three fights a year, then
purely statistically, even in the less savage first century
AD, he could expect to be killed in the fourth year of
his career at the latest. Like all such calculations, however, averages say nothing about an individual's fate.
By far the majority of gladiators were overtaken by disaster at the very outset of their careers. The more fights
a swordsman had behind him, the better his chances
of survival.

There were several reasons for this. First, the early
fights constituted a kind of selection process in which
only the fittest survived. Second, a gladiator's experi-
ence, self-confidence and prestige increased with
every contest. The reputation that preceded an 'invin-
cible' swordsman was undoubtedly calculated to
intimidate many of his opponents so much that the
duel was as good as decided from the start. And finally,
a famous champion had a large body of supporters
who would not let him down even in the case of an
occasional defeat. As a result, the veteran who had
won many fights had far better chances of the *missio*
than an unknown and only average gladiator. This
helps to explain the fact that there were swordsmen
who could chalk up 60, 80, 88, 107, 125 and even
150 victories on their tombstones. Such numbers also
show that top gladiators made many more appearances a year than the average calculated above.

According to the tombstones, gladiators in the first
century AD reached an average age of twenty-seven,
which means that the gladiator had no worse a life
expectancy than any normal citizen of the time. However, the tombstones undoubtedly reflect the fate only
of the more successful members of the profession. The
great mass of beginners who died before they could
achieve fame and be given a relatively expensive
burial have only occasionally left any record behind
them in the form of an inscription. Most gladiators
must certainly have died a violent death at the age of
eighteen to twenty-five.

## ANIMAL HUNTS

The term *venatio* (hunt) embraced a whole series of
very diverse performances that had in common only
the appearance in the arena of wild animals (*bestiae*).
They ranged from the mere presentation of exotic
species and shows with trained performing animals (cf.
fig. 75), through the hunting of game and fights
between professional *venatores* and dangerous beasts,
to the execution of criminals condemned to die as
*damnati ad bestias*, wrongdoers who were thrown
defenceless to the wild animals.

The *venationes* originated during the Punic Wars,
when the Romans took elephants and other exotic animals as loot for the first time. They were put on show
during triumphal processions. If their numbers were
excessive, the organizers of these events disposed of
them by using them in hunts and fights full of special

effects. During the republican period the *venationes* became part of the *ludi*, and usually took place in the Circus Maximus. At the beginning of the imperial period they then became a regular component of the *munera*, and performance was transferred to the amphitheatre. They were on the morning programme.

The huntsmen and animal fighters (*venatores*), like the gladiators, were recruited from among prisoners of war, slaves, condemned criminals and volunteers. In prestige and pay they were clearly inferior to gladiators. The *venatores* were assisted by the lower-ranking *bestiarii*, who had to look after the animals and provoke them with whips and torches during the performance.

Augustan reliefs, and several terracotta reliefs of the first half of the first century AD modelled on them (fig. 81), show *venatores* appearing in the Circus Maximus with armaments – metal helmets, loincloths, greaves, swords and some type of sword – exactly like those of contemporary gladiators. After the middle of the first century AD such armed animal fighters no longer appear. The *venatores* now, like ordinary hunters, wear only the *tunica* and short or knee-length leg wrappings (*fasciae crurales*), and their weapon is the hunting spear (*venabulum*). These lightly armed *venatores* must

also have been far more usual in the first half of the century than armed men fighting with sword and shield, in particular if they were fighting not big cats or bears but less dangerous animals. The two *venatores* depicted in the lower section of the Pompeian gladiatorial relief (fig. 34) also wear only *tunica* and wrappings. One is fighting a bull with his spear, and the other is in combat with a boar. On the right there are three *bestiarii* (fig. 77), one of them thrown to the ground by an attacking bear.

In the course of the second century AD the *venatores* acquired knee-breeches and very broad belts in addition to the leg wrappings, and sometimes even wore small, decorated breastplates. In the following century their clothing was again reduced to the *tunica*, in which the *venatores* on the Zliten mosaic appear (fig. 83). Shields lying on the ground show that they still sometimes used this defensive weapon.

We have far less information about the organization of the *venationes* than of the gladiatorial contests. The *venatores* hunted relatively harmless game such as deer, ostriches and wild asses on horseback or on foot, using both throwing spears and hunting spears. In these hunts the *venator* could do no more than demonstrate his skill in the use of his weapons.

77 (ABOVE)
**Relief with gladiators: detail of *bestiarii***
AD 20–50
Marble
Museo Archeologico Nazionale di Napoli, 6704

76 (ABOVE LEFT)
**Lion and *venator***
First century AD
Jet
Historisches Museum der Pfalz, Speyer, HM 1927/35

The lion has thrown a *venator* armed with shield and sword to the ground.

78
**Relief with tauromachy (bull wrestling)**
Second century AD
Marble
Ashmolean Museum, Oxford, Michaelis 136

**79**

**Lamp with bull-leaping**

Late second to early third century AD

Pottery

British Museum, London, GR 1814.7-4.151

A man, perhaps an acrobat, vaults over the horns of a charging bull using a long pole.

More dangerous was the discipline of the *taurocentae*, who performed a kind of rodeo. A relief probably from Smyrna (fig. 78) shows several of them riding up to bulls to seize them by the horns from behind and at the same moment swing themselves off their horses and on to the backs of the bulls. The purpose of this manoeuvre, performed unarmed, was to throw the bull to the ground, as the second *taurocenta* from the right has already succeeded in doing.

Even greater risks were run by those *venatores* who practised what was undoubtedly the most popular variant of *venatio*, combat on foot with a large and dangerous beast of prey, usually a lion, tiger, leopard or bear. After the arming of *venatores* like gladiators had gone out of fashion, they too fought almost exclusively with spears, in particular the hunting spear held in both hands. It seems that the custom of the *missio* also applied to these conflicts. If the man fighting the beast thought he had done enough or if he was rendered incapable of going on by injury or exhaustion, he could ask to be discharged from the arena. If his request was refused, he then had to fight the next animal. In contrast to modern bull-fighting, the animal itself was sometimes granted the *missio*. There were famous lions who had killed a whole series of *venatores* during their careers. With black humour, a par-

**80**

**Relief with lion and gladiator**

First or second century AD

Marble

British Museum, London, GR 1873.5-5.1

Only the right half of this relief from Ephesus has survived. It appears to depict the second and fourth stages of a fight between a *venator* and a lion. The Greek inscription may be translated: 'Second [fight] … fourth [fight]. He was taken away for burial.'

**81**

**Relief fragment with *venatio***

First to second century AD

Terracotta

British Museum, London, GR 1866.4-12.13

Part of a scene showing an animal hunt (*venatio*): the huntsman (*venator*), distracted by another animal, is unaware of the attacking lioness to his right.

ticular efficient she-bear was given the name of Innocentia (innocence). But in most cases there is no doubt that the man was the victor.

However, the imbalance of odds was nowhere near as great as in modern Spanish bull-fighting. According to admittedly incomplete statistics, 398 men died between 1747 and 1962 in the official corridas. Of these men, only 51 were full matadors, while 153 probationary matadors, 132 bandilleros, 60 picadores and two clowns lost their lives. Such figures also confirm statistics cited for the present state of the sport, in which experienced bullfighters are considered to have much better chances of survival than newcomers.

Another variety of *venatio* consisted of pitting animal against animal (cf. fig. 82). Dogs, as the companions of the *venatores*, were principally used to hunt normal game. However, they could feature without human partners, matched with one kind of animal or another. But above all the Romans loved to see large and dangerous animals fighting each other. As these creatures by no means always showed the requisite fighting spirit they were often chained together. The Zliten mosaic (fig. 83) shows a bear and a bull fighting in this way.

Finally, mention must be made of the executions carried out in the context of the *venationes*, usually as

82
**Two lamps with fighting animals**
First century AD
Pottery
Antikensammlung, Staatliche Museen zu Berlin, TC 6315.89 (left), Misc. 8856

part of the mid-day programme. *Noxii*, prisoners condemned to a shameful death, were handed over by the authorities to *editores*, with the stipulation that their punishment was to be carried out at a *munus* within a certain set time. Various methods of execution were applied in the arena, many of them staged as grotesque and horrific dramatic productions, usually of a mythological character.

Condemnation *ad bestias*, together with crucifixion and burning alive, was regarded as the most severe

83
**Mosaic with gladiators: detail of *damnatio ad bestias***
*c.* AD 200 (?)
Archaeological Museum, Tripoli

form of death penalty to which a Roman judge could condemn a criminal. The *noxii* had not the slightest chance. Naked except for a small loincloth, unarmed, and in most cases also bound, they were exposed to the big cats. The two upper sections of a relief from Smyrna (fig. 136) show the criminals in procession. Driven in by a *bestiarius* (assistant), who seems to be wearing some kind of protective clothing, they had to enter the arena two by two, each pair bound together by a rope around their necks. In some similar depictions the condemned carry small tablets (*tabellae*), presumably giving the reasons for their punishment. The Zliten mosaic (fig. 83) shows the full horror of the fate that awaited the *damnati ad bestias*. Two men are bound to stakes, each on a small, two-wheeled chariot, as leopards attack them. A *bestiarius* wielding a whip is driving another criminal towards a lion.

The corpses of the executed *noxii* were usually thrown into the Tiber or some other river. At the amphitheatre in Trier, countless remains from meagre and perfunctory interments have recently been found. Many of the graves contained mutilated corpses or merely separate body parts. As some of the skeletons are those of women, these will not be the burials of gladiators, but they may be the remains of *noxii*.

## THE *NAUMACHIAE*

Romans of the imperial period had a marked inclination for taking theatrical spectacles to extremes that mingled illusion and reality in a distinctly bizarre fashion. Among the most striking manifestations of this preference are the *naumachiae*, mock naval battles, staged at enormous expense. They were too large to be performed in the arena, and demanded their own settings. Some arenas did have large basins of water where miniature ships could be manoeuvred, but these were only Lilliputian performances compared to the great *naumachiae* in which dozens of full-sized warships and thousands of oarsmen and warriors took part. The largest of these shows was held by Claudius on Lake Fucino, a natural lake in the Abruzzi. No less than 19,000 condemned prisoners are said to have manned the ships. On this occasion the men hailed Claudius with the words '*Ave Caesar, morituri te salutamus!*'

(Hail Caesar, we who are about to die salute you!), as reported by Suetonius, *Claudius* 21, 6. However, there are no records proving that this famous remark was ever uttered by gladiators in the amphitheatre.

Most *naumachiae* were held in Rome itself on artificial lakes, also described as *naumachiae* or *stagna*. The largest of these complexes was built by Augustus in the southern part of present-day Trastevere. It was elliptical in shape and measured 536 x 357 metres. There was an island 100 metres in diameter in the middle. Since no unambiguous depiction of a *naumachia* exists, we must rely on conjecture. The lake was made large enough to allow the use of genuine war galleys, at least of the smaller-sized classes. When Augustus staged a version of the sea battle of Salamis (which took place in 480 BC), in all thirty triremes and biremes (ships with three and two banks of oars respectively) went into battle. One trireme was about 35 metres long, and with its oars out had a breadth of 10 metres and a draught of 1.2 metres. The crew consisted of about 150 oarsmen and 80 marines.

The Romans liked to give their *naumachiae* some historical theme; the re-enactment of famous battles that has become so popular in modern times can therefore be considered a Roman invention. To heighten suspense, however, the outcome of the fighting remained open in *naumachiae*, independently of their historical models. In the 'Battle of Salamis', for instance, the result did reflect the original battle of 480 BC, when the Greeks defeated the Persians; not so with the naval battle of Syracuse (424 BC) staged by the emperor Titus: it was won by the 'Athenians', who historically had been the losers. Excitement was therefore more important than historical accuracy, and the Romans may even have relished this ironic playing with the facts. A similar approach was taken to mythological subjects when, for instance, a *damnatus* miming Orpheus was torn to pieces by the beasts despite (or because of?) his supposedly captivating song. However, there were limits to this mingling of reality, fantasy and chance: no Roman defeat could ever be contemplated. This was certainly one of the reasons why subjects from Greek and Middle Eastern history were always chosen for *naumachiae*, but never themes from the past of Rome itself.

# Greek Athletics in Rome:
# Boxing, Wrestling and the Pancration

The sports of boxing, wrestling and the pancration (a form of no-holds-barred wrestling) bring us to the sphere of Greek athletics, the Olympic *agones*. Scholars have long regarded them as late introductions, which were always felt by the Romans to be foreign and never really integrated into the traditional Roman festival games of the *ludi* and *munera*. It has been claimed that the first athletic competition in the city of Rome did not take place until 186 BC, and then obviously with only moderate success, since there were very few further events of the kind until the end of the republican period. It is also said that only philhellenic emperors like Nero and Domitian tried introducing Greek athletics into their own games in Rome in the first century AD – again without lasting success.

This view requires some emendation. The Romans had regularly practised many athletic disciplines – running, wrestling and in particular boxing – ever since the late regal period of the sixth century BC, probably under the influence of their Etruscan neighbours. Together with chariot-racing and the performances of the *desultores* (acrobatic riders), they were an established feature of the *ludi circenses*. They were regarded as Roman sports and enjoyed great popularity. The chief novelty of the games in the year 186 BC had been the appearance of professional Greek athletes, and on that occasion the programme also included other forms of competition not previously practised by the Romans, in particular the Olympic pentathlon, a light athletics event comprising the five sports of running, wrestling, jumping, javelin and discus throwing. However, the majority of the Roman public did not really take to athletic performances of this kind.

We are told that the Romans were particularly ill at ease with the complete nudity that was part of Greek athletics, but it seems that the writers who inform us of this aversion were trying to present an ideological contrast between ancient Roman virtue and modern Greek decadence. Originally, Etruscan and Roman sportsmen no doubt wore a loincloth, like the Greeks of the Homeric age. There are still occasional depictions of Roman boxers wearing loincloths in the imperial period, but nudity seems to have become the norm in Italy quite early.

As for the technical aspects of athletics, the Etruscans and Romans were undoubtedly under strong Greek influence from an early period, for both heavy and light athletic disciplines had attained a degree of perfection in the classical period that made them an example to all who practised similar forms of sporting activity. This influence is evident in the fact that the terminology for these sports was largely of Greek origin, whereas the reverse was true of gladiatorial contests – and, contrary to a common misconception, the Greeks were by no means too noble and sensitive to enjoy that extreme form of combat sport. Gladiatorial contests and animal hunts were very popular in the Hellenistic east, where the Latin terminology became established in Greek form.

The classic setting for athletic contests was the stadium. Like the other sporting venues of the Greeks, their stadiums were laid out with a minimum of architectural extravagance. While the Romans derived the monumental circus from the Greek hippodrome, and the amphitheatre was their own invention, there was almost no large-scale architectural development of the stadium as a separate sporting location in the west of the empire, very much in contrast to the Greek-speaking east. The one major exception in the west was the Stadium Domitiani, now the Piazza Navona in Rome. During the *ludi* both athletic contests and horse-racing took place in the circus, and wooden stadiums were built for special events. In the imperial period, moreover, athletic contests were often an additional part of the programme of the *munera* in the amphitheatre.

Our knowledge of the fighting techniques of heavy athletic disciplines comes chiefly from pictorial depictions and incidental comments in literary texts: very little of the once extensive specialist literature has survived. The most important extant document is a treatise written by Philostratus in the second/third century AD.

## BOXING

Boxing (*pugilatus*) was easily the most popular form of heavy athletic contest among the Romans. According to the authors of classical antiquity, it was considered the most rigorous and dangerous discipline of all, and regularly led to severe injuries. No doubt this aspect contributed a good deal to the sport's attractions for a public used to indulging itself with gladiatorial contests. It is not surprising, then, that in the course of the imperial period boxing was deliberately made more brutal by the introduction of increasingly hard gloves. A similar tendency can be observed in the gladiatorial games of the same time.

Like all performers in public sporting events, the

**84**
**Relief with boxer**
First century AD
Terracotta
British Museum, London,
GR 1805.7-3.390

A statue of a victorious boxer
is shown in this scene in a
*palaistra*, the place where
boxers and wrestlers trained.
He holds a palm-branch and a
winner's ribbon, and a boxing
glove is bound to his left fist
and forearm.

century, but assumed its present form in the United States. As with the sport in classical antiquity, the modern boxer may use only his fists, and nothing approaching wrestling (a clinch) is allowed, nor is kicking. Classical depictions showing either clinches or kicking are not scenes from a boxing match but illustrate the pancration, which is described in more detail below. Another point in common between ancient and modern boxing is the wearing of special gloves, but the gloves of classical antiquity are so different to those today that they also provide the main distinguishing feature between the sport then and now.

The thickly padded modern boxing glove has two functions: first, it is intended to protect the wearer's fist, which may be injured if it strikes a hard target such as the arms and in particular the head of the opponent. The bone structure of the hand is very complex, and is hardly protected at all by any cushioning of muscle or fat. Even thick modern gloves cannot prevent about a third of all injuries in boxing matches from being to the hands. The second function of the glove is to soften the blow for the boxer's opponent, reducing his own risk of injury.

The Greek boxing glove developed from long straps that the boxer wound around his fists and lower arms in a complicated system. Around 400 BC a broad knuckleduster was added, sharp-edged and consisting of several layers of thick leather. It was worn over the lower joints of the fingers, omitting the thumb, and was fixed to the interwoven leather beneath it with thin straps. This system was soon replaced by a glove all in one piece, which was considerably easier to put on and take off. This new boxing glove left the fingertips free and was open on the inside. It also covered most of the lower arm and ended in a broad fur cuff, probably the lining of the glove turned inside out at the top. A firmly fastened wrapping of leather straps enclosed the glove, giving it stability. A projecting bulge on the back of the hand immediately behind the knuckleduster was intended to prevent it from shifting position. This was the classic form of Greek boxing glove, and was adopted by the Romans. The marble statue of a boxer from Sorrento (figs 87 and 88) and the hand of a bronze statue from Verona (fig. 89) show the structure of the glove (*caestus*) in detail.

As with the gladiatorial *manica*, there was a tendency for the *caestus* worn by boxers to be elongated in the course of the imperial period into something more like a sleeve reaching up to the armpit. At the same time the leather knuckleduster was replaced in many *caestus* by a semi-cylindrical bronze reinforcement, from which spikes or a shovel-shaped device with a jagged edge projected in the direction of the adversary. Although there are no references to it in the ancient sources, it is commonly thought that this semi-cylinder and its projections were made of metal, which would have changed the *caestus* into a real and murderous weapon. This has led to the conclusion that this

boxers were professional fighters, legally and socially outside the ranks of Roman citizens. No doubt members of the social élite who admired the ideals of Greek culture, including Greek athletics, did practise boxing and other sports, but as distinguished amateurs. To appear in public would have been degrading, in contrast to the situation in archaic and classical Greece, where athletics had been the province of the upper classes. However, a tendency towards professionalization became perceptible among the Greeks themselves in the late classical and Hellenistic periods, particularly in the heavy athletics disciplines.

In spite of their low social standing, successful boxers could win great sporting prestige, and it was reflected in high prize money. The aura of heroism surrounding gladiatorial contests was of course absent from boxing. The death of a man's opponent was not the aim, although fights often did end in death because of the severe injuries inflicted. Damage to the head and face meant permanent disfigurement, which again helped to deprive boxing of the macabre eroticism of the gladiatorial contest.

Wrestling and boxing are the two forms of classical combat sport where the existence of modern versions allows us to make useful comparisons. Modern boxing developed in England in the course of the nineteenth

85
**Bust of a boxer**
Third century AD
Marble
Antikensammlung, Staatliche
Museen zu Berlin, SK 465

Only a few marble portraits of
boxers have been preserved,
and they are all from the
eastern provinces of the Roman
empire. Originally part of a
statue, this kind of portrait used
to adorn sporting venues or
theatres. The characteristic
hairstyle was partly a matter of
practical considerations: in the
pancration, where no gloves
were worn, an opponent could
get no grip on the very short
hair in front. It was worn longer
at the back of the head, in a
small pigtail.

86
**Boxing glove**
First to second century AD
Terracotta
British Museum, London,
GR 1814.7-4.1021

This fragment of a statuette
shows the forearm of a boxer.
His glove (*caestus*) is of the
normal Roman type, with long
straps and reinforced knuckleduster.

87 (RIGHT)
**Victorious boxer: detail of
glove, with some modern
restoration**
Mid-first century BC
Marble
Museo Archeologico Nazionale
di Napoli, 119917

88 (OPPOSITE)
**Victorious boxer**
Mid-first century BC
Marble
Museo Archeologico Nazionale
di Napoli, 119917

The sprig of olive in the young
athlete's hair shows that he has
won a boxing match. The
signature on the plinth is that
of the sculptor Koblanos of
Aphrodisias in Asia Minor. He
based this figure on classical
Greek models of the fifth and
fourth centuries BC, and the
head therefore lacks the realism
of later portraits of boxers (see
figs 85 and 93). A small herm in
the likeness of Hercules stands
beside the athlete; this was a
symbol of the gymnasium, the
place where athletes trained.

kind of *caestus* began to be used by gladiators and not
athletes.

Hugh M. Lee disagrees with this usual view that due
to their brutality Roman boxing matches became gladiatorial combats. He thinks that the *caestus* never was
a gladiatorial weapon – in this respect he is undoubtedly right – and that it was no more dangerous than
the traditional form of boxing glove. In his opinion the
semi-cylinder was made of leather and was held inside
the fist. This stabilized the fingers and gave protection
to the palm when stopping a punch with the open
hand. The 'spikes' were just the fingers wrapped in
leather.

The Hamburg Museum für Kunst und Gewerbe is,
however, in possession of a metal *caestus* reinforcement (fig. 89). It covers the outside of the hand in the
knuckle area and the lower joints of the fingers, and
was held on the inside by a transverse piece that
served as a grip. From the depictions we can assume
that the surface was covered with fur, which would
soften the effect and make the object primarily into a
defensive device. In this case the projections cannot be
explained as either fingers or spikes. Whatever the
answer, the murderous character of the Roman *caestus*
should, I think, not be exaggerated.

The differences with the modern boxing glove are
obvious. Then, as now, the glove fulfilled its defensive
function well. However, the thick modern glove is
considerably wider, allowing the boxer to entrench

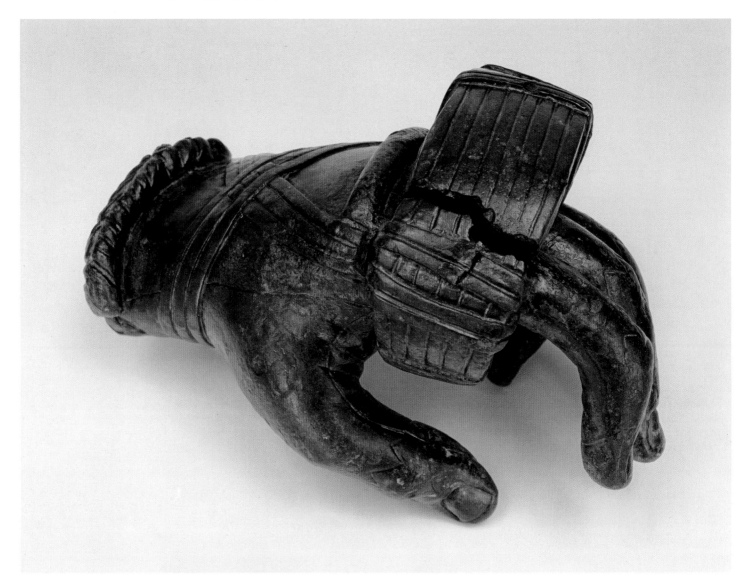

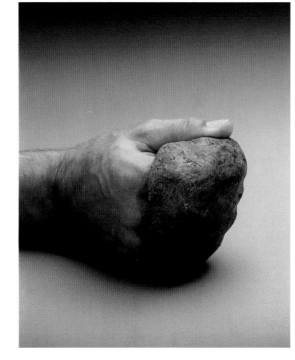

**89**

**Hand with a *caestus***

First century AD

Bronze

Museo Archeologico di Verona, 22092

This bronze hand originally belonged to a life-size statue. Since the glove did not enclose the whole hand, and was made of soft leather except for the knuckleduster, the boxer could not only punch but also use his open hand for defence and for certain attacking techniques.

**90**

***Caestus***

Second to third century AD

Bronze

Museum für Kunst und Gewerbe Hamburg, 1997.356

himself behind his raised gloves, and even if the force of an opponent's punch flings the boxer's own fists against his head, the soft glove means that the outcome is not fatal. The boxer of classical antiquity could not adopt such a defensive position; the *caestus* was too narrow and too hard. The length of the padded sleeve, however, allowed Greek and Roman boxers a defensive technique unavailable to modern boxers: the bent arm could be held either diagonally to shield the face or vertically to protect both the face and the top of the head. The boxer thus covered himself with his lower arm and not his fists.

So far as the offensive effect of the glove on a boxer's opponent is concerned, the contrast between the ancient *caestus* and the modern boxing glove could not be greater. Far from softening the blow, in many models of the imperial period the *caestus* was designed to increase its force. As a result, injuries were undoubtedly far more frequent and severe in classical antiquity than today, and several other features also contributed to the greater ferocity of the Graeco-Roman boxing match.

91

**Two African boxers**

Second or first century BC

Terracotta

British Museum, London,

GR 1852.4-11.1, 2

The potter has captured well the fighting technique of Graeco-Roman boxers, with the left leg advanced, a leading left fist and a much more open stance than that adopted by boxers today. The older, balding, boxer is staggering back from an upper cut.

As in all varieties of combat sports in ancient times, there was no time limit to the length of the fight, which went on until it reached a definite result. Since no points were awarded, a match could end only with a knockout or the capitulation of one of the boxers. There were no rounds, so that the boxer could not rely on regular breaks to recover from a bad round. It is likely that if the fight went on for a long time both boxers would come to some kind of mutual understanding, and with the referee's consent would pause to get their breath back, but that was not something they could count on.

There was absolutely no question of a break if only one of the boxers needed it, while the other was still in full possession of his strength and naturally wanted to press on without compunction, forcing a decision. Even if his opponent was on the floor he could continue attacking with blows from above – usually in the form of the direct downward punches to the skull that are banned today – until the loser admitted defeat or was quite unable to fight any longer.

There was no division into classes of different weights. The opposing pairs were decided by all the

92
**Hydria with a boxer**
Fourth century BC
Pottery
Antikensammlung, Staatliche
Museen zu Berlin, F 3037

This vessel, of the form known
as a hydria, shows a boxer
apparently prancing on the spot
in a typically pugnacious
attitude. His right arm is bent,
ready to punch, and his left arm
is stretched out in defence. The
depiction of the leather straps
around his fists and lower arms
is stylized, so the shape of the
glove cannot be reconstructed.
Knuckledusters were not yet in
use at the time when this vase
was made.

boxers drawing lots, a procedure that naturally favoured big, strong men. However, a boxer with a less impressive physique could sometimes make up for it by greater agility, for this was a very fast-moving form of sporting contest involving intensive legwork. Movement was not restricted by the confined ring that, together with the large, soft glove, gives modern boxing its specific quality. Consequently there was no danger of being driven into a corner and involved in an exchange of blows if a man preferred to avoid it. Ancient boxing could thus develop a wide-ranging, elegant mobility.

The opponents first faced each other standing upright, with arms bent and held forward. The raised fists were at head height, but kept a considerable way from the body. It was usual for a right-hander to adopt a characteristic orthodox stance with the left foot forward, the legs wide apart, and the left fist in front. The right arm was bent rather more sharply, and the fist was therefore taken further back, ready to deal a sudden blow. The torso was completely exposed in a stance of this kind, and we need only compare it with the much narrower stance adopted by the modern boxer with arms bent close to the body to see that a different kind of guard was required. It is clear that in ancient boxing the head was the exclusive target of attack; body blows occurred only by chance and may even have been against the rules, although there is uncertainty on that point.

The boxer could move from the position described above to various forms of both attack and defence. The left hand held out in front of him warded off his opponent, impeding his advance, since the other man would have to strike sideways past it, and the surface of the hand could stop the other man's punches before they achieved their full force. The use of the open hand held well in front of the body is very characteristic of the open boxing technique of antiquity, which was almost a kind of fencing with the fists.

> Defensive moves could exploit both the heavy, hard armour on the fist and the fur lining of the sleeve on the lower arm, which softened the effect of a blow. If a boxer of antiquity wanted to make full use of the advantage offered by this glove, hoping to tire a vigorously attacking opponent so that he could create a favourable situation for his own attacking move, he had to keep the other man's attack at a distance. Powerful, lightning footwork with little skips or jumps was essential to keep him just far enough away to be unable to get in a blow to the head, but not so far that, in view of his inability to land a punch he would decide to go on the defensive himself and conserve his strength. (Rudolph 1965, p. 20)

Ducking was not an effective method of defence, since the hard gloves did not allow a man to cover his head well in that position. On the other hand it was usual for him to tempt his opponent to land a blow in thin air by swiftly withdrawing his head or dodging aside.

The basic stance in defence, one arm stretched out with the hand open, the other bent diagonally or vertically in front of the face, allowed a boxer to move swiftly on to the attack by using the bent arm to deal a mighty punch, striking diagonally outward in the first case and directly from above in the second. Another defensive-offensive stance was borrowed from the typical attitude of the *sagittarius*, or archer. The boxer held

93
**Bust of a boxer**
Second to third century AD
Bronze
British Museum, London,
GR 1814.7-4.989

This bronze counterweight from some scales is made in the form of a portrait bust with the characteristic features of a professional boxer, notably the cauliflower ears and broken nose.

his arm back as if bending a bow so that his fist was at head height. This was a good position for a swift straight punch. Sometimes the 'ram tactic' (*aries*) was used to break an opponent's cover. Bending forward, one lower arm held protectively in front of his face or over his head, the other held beside the head in the *sagittarius* position, simultaneously guarding himself and ready to strike, the attacker would get under his opponent's defence and try to land a straight punch with his *sagittarius* arm.

Heavy downward punches and straight punches were obviously preferred in ancient boxing to hooks and swings, as we can deduce from the mechanisms of the wide-open arm position and the fact that the boxers usually kept each other at a distance. Punches were aimed mainly at the chin, the ear area and the top of the skull, parts of the head where a man could be knocked out at once if a hit was scored with great force, or alternatively at the nose, mouth and eye area, where the effect could wear him down in the long term.

Since no protection was worn, broken noses and jaws, knocked-out teeth and concussion of varying degrees of severity must have been the order of the day, not to mention bruising, lacerations, cauliflower ears and swollen eyes. If *caestus* reinforced with metal were used, the danger of broken bones or even a fractured skull increased dramatically.

Even today boxing is a sport involving many injuries, but the incidence of fatalities is surprisingly low by comparison with many other kinds of sports usually regarded as far less violent. The number of deaths caused by boxing recorded world-wide between 1945 and 1979 were 335, almost all of them as a result of brain damage. In the United States the death rate among 1,000 active boxers was 0.13 per cent. In the very tough sport of American football the figure was 0.3 per cent, and among professional jockeys as high as 12 per cent, over ninety times as great as the figure for boxers. As a result of regulations and precautionary measures, fatal injuries in boxing are now relatively rare. The people of classical antiquity saw no reason to take such precautions, and in addition medicine then was far less efficient than it is now. In such circumstances the number of fatalities in ancient boxing must have been incomparably higher than it is today, even though it certainly cannot compare with the death rate among gladiators. However, in the absence of statistical records no more precise details can be established.

## WRESTLING

Wrestling (*luctatio*) was the only combat sport of antiquity where the result did not normally depend on the

**94**

**Two wrestlers**
Third century BC
Bronze
Römisch-Germanisches
Museum der Stadt Köln, 44,107

The bearded pancratiast is just about to win the fight; his opponent has lost his firm footing and can no longer use his arms. The bearded victor has the features of Hercules, and the loser may represent the giant Antaios. The complex structure of this group is drawn from scenes at real pancration matches. The relative position of the bodies can be worked out only if the sculpture is viewed from different angles. Groups of wrestlers and pancratiasts of this kind were made in Alexandria, the capital of Hellenistic Egypt. In some cases the faces of victors have the features not of a god but of one of the rulers of the Ptolemaic dynasty.

loser's surrender or inability to go on fighting; the match was decided when one man had been thrown to the ground three times. Since wrestling was a sport depending entirely on strength and skill, using no aids of any kind and allowing no blows, kicks or thrusts, it should be regarded as by far the least dangerous of all the heavy athletics disciplines.

The wrestlers of classical antiquity fought from a standing position. The two opponents grappled with each other and tried to induce a fall, particularly through using lever-holds. As soon as one of them succeeded, the fight was stopped, and the two men returned to their initial positions for the next round. Fighting on the ground was not allowed, nor were throttle-holds or twisting the joints.

As in boxing, there was no division into classes by weight, so this relatively static method of fighting gave the heavier wrestler a clear advantage. Speed and skill could not compensate much for obvious superiority in weight and power. Consequently, the harmless sport of wrestling was regarded by spectators as the least interesting of the three heavy athletics disciplines.

## THE PANCRATION

The pancration – an all-in athletic contest – was late in gaining acceptance by the Romans, unlike boxing and wrestling. It combined features of both in a kind of free-style fighting with considerably fewer rules than those of the two disciplines themselves. Since no gloves were worn, in spite of its considerable brutality the pancration must be regarded as a less dangerous form of combat sport than boxing.

In the pancration the entire body of a man's opponent was a legitimate target for any kind of attack. The combatants could strike with the open hand or the clenched fist, kick and thrust with feet and knees, or attempt to throttle one another or dislocate limbs. Only biting and eye-gouging were forbidden. The fight consisted of phases that alternated between boxing and wrestling. The wrestling phases differed from wrestling proper in that the fight continued on the ground, and was not decided when one man succeeded in throwing his opponent. Consequently swings and throttle-holds were more commonly used in the pancration than the lever-holds typical of ordinary wrestling. A position on the ground even offered certain advantages when a man was fighting a standing opponent, and was voluntarily assumed by one or other of the adversaries in many phases of the fight. A man could make very effective use of his legs, in particular, from a supine position. The diversity of fighting methods made the pancration a form of heavy athletic combat for which it was very difficult to train, but one that offered a spectacle of great variety to the audience.

As in boxing, the result was decided by a knockout or by the surrender of one man, and the pancratiasts had particularly powerful means of breaking their opponents' fighting spirit in the form of throttle-holds and lever-holds.

# On the Starting Line with Ben Hur: Chariot-Racing in the Circus Maximus

**95**

**Lamp with chariot-racing in the Circus Maximus**

Second to early third century AD

Pottery

British Museum, London, GR 1814 7-4 106

The lamp-maker has skilfully condensed the whole event into a small space. Around the edge are shown the starting gates and the crowds in the stands, as well as the lap-counter, obelisk and turning posts of the central barrier, while in the centre the four-horse chariots of the four factions (Reds, Blues, Whites and Greens) race round the track.

Few images are conjured up as vividly and automatically by the words 'Ancient Rome' as that of chariot-racing in the circus arena. The novel *Ben Hur* and its various screen versions must be held responsible, particularly the film made by William Wyler in 1959. The eight minutes and twenty seconds devoted by Wyler to the chariot-race have helped to form our picture of the Roman world to an extent equalled in the twentieth century only by the *Asterix* strip-cartoon books. It seems justifiable, then, to take the race presented in the 1959 film of *Ben Hur* as the starting point of this chapter, looking at it point by point and comparing the popular idea of a Roman chariot-race in the circus with the facts as they can be gleaned from the sources.

While I shall be mentioning the many errors in the film version, I do not intend it as niggling criticism of one of the classic scenes of cinematic history. Although there are a number of inaccuracies, the film as a whole thrillingly conveys the character and atmosphere, one might even say the quintessence, of such a sporting event, in a way that scholarly attention to detail could never have done on its own.

## CHARIOTEERS AND CIRCUS FACTIONS

There are nine teams at the start of the race in William Wyler's film version of *Ben Hur*, an improbable number for a Roman chariot-race during the imperial period. Horses and charioteers were entered by the great circus factions (*factiones*) – racing clubs or racing associations would be a better term – and although there was state support, the officials organizing the races had to dip deep into their own pockets. There were four factions, the two main groups of the Blues (*veneti*) and the Greens (*prasini*), and the two subsidiary factions of the Reds (*russati*) and the Whites (*albati*). Accordingly, the number of participants could always be divided by four, each faction having one, two or three teams on the starting line, so that there could be four, eight, or more usually twelve teams running in all.

It may be objected that the race in *Ben Hur* is held not in Italy or one of the western provinces of the empire, but in either Antioch in the Hellenistic east (in Lew Wallace's original novel of 1880) or Jerusalem (in the 1959 film version). And it is true that only in the west of the empire was racing in the early imperial period dominated by the circus factions, which apparently did not become the norm in the east until the

fourth century AD. At the time of *Ben Hur*, under the rule of Augustus and Tiberius, chariot-racing in the east of the empire still followed the Greek tradition: the owners of teams sent them into the arena without involving any large, well-established associations. Most owners engaged professional charioteers, but some drove their own chariots. In marked contrast to the situation in Rome, persons of rank and fortune in the Hellenistic east were not disqualified from taking part in the racing themselves, or indeed from joining in other public sporting events. Since there were no factions, and as yet no permanent circuses with starting boxes limited to twelve on the Roman pattern, any number of vehicles could have been on the starting line in the east.

However, the film version anachronistically shows a perfectly built circus in the Roman manner, not a more or less improvised Greek hippodrome. Consequently the race itself must be assumed to be in the Roman style, too, as suggested not least by the appearance of the provincial governor Pontius Pilate as holder of the games. But whether the race itself was run in the Greek or Roman manner, the personal participation of the Roman tribune Messala in a public spectacle of this nature is absolutely unthinkable. It would have ruined the man's military and public career, not to mention his position in society, quite apart from the fact that the governor would have forbidden his subordinate to indulge in such an escapade for pragmatic political reasons: if Messala won, his victory would have displeased the local population of the province, and if he lost they could have shown undesirable elation at his defeat. The appearance in the arena of his adversary Ben Hur is not much more convincing. He could indeed have taken part in the racing as a member of the Judaeo-Hellenistic upper class, but not as the adopted son of a Roman admiral.

So who really were the *aurigae*, the Roman charioteers? Generally they were slaves or freedmen, but in spite of their low social status, they could win fame

alty of the public was in general to the factions rather than the individual charioteers. This fanatical partisanship, more marked in chariot-racing than in any other sport of classical antiquity, was regarded with particular disfavour by critics of the time:

> If they were attracted by the speed of the horses or the drivers' skill one could account for it, but in fact it is the racing-colours they really support and care about, and if the colours were to be changed in mid-course during a race, they would transfer their favour and enthusiasm and rapidly desert the famous drivers and horses whose names they shout as they recognise them from afar. Such is the popularity and importance of a worthless shirt [in the colour of the faction] – I don't mean with the crowd, which is worth less than the shirt, but with certain serious individuals. (Pliny the Younger, *Epistulae* 9, 6)

The circus factions were very profitable economic

96
**Sarcophagus panel with Cupid chariot-race**
*C.* AD 140
Marble
Musée du Louvre, Paris,
MA 1640

and wealth in their profession. 'That Scorpus am I, the glory of the clamorous Circus, thy applause, O Rome, and thy short-lived darling. Me, snatched away in my ninth three years' span, jealous Lachesis, counting my victories, deemed old in years.' (Martial, *Epigrammata* 10, 53.) This obituary of the famous *auriga* Scorpus was composed by Martial, to whom we owe so much information on the circus and the amphitheatre. Scorpus was one of the few charioteers to be *miliarii*, drivers who had won over a thousand races, and could boast of victory in no less than 2,048 events.

It was perfectly usual for professional charioteers to switch from one faction to another, although most of them committed themselves entirely to one of the *factiones* sooner or later. The inscription placed by the Roman charioteer Polyneices on the tomb of one of his two sons, who both died in racing accidents, probably reflects a typical situation: 'Marcus Aurelius Polyneices, born a slave, lived 29 years, 9 months and 5 days. He won the palm 739 times: 655 times for the Reds, 55 times for the Greens, 12 times for the Blues and 17 times for the Whites.'

We may note that just as in modern football, the loy-

enterprises. They were managed by *domini factionis* (faction masters), usually of the knightly class. Their headquarters (*stabula factionum*), with extensive accommodation and stabling, were on the Campus Martius in Rome, in the area of the present-day Campo dei Fiori, and they kept stud farms and training establishments in the country. In late antiquity there was a growing tendency for the factions to become state-run bodies which also took over the organization of theatrical performances, gladiatorial contests and animal hunts, so that the entire entertainment industry came under state control. The *domini factionis* of the private economy were replaced by state-appointed *factionarii*, quite often ex-charioteers.

Successful charioteers could amass huge fortunes. The prizes for chariot-races in the city of Rome were 15,000 to 60,000 sestertii a race (in the early imperial period a legionary's annual pay was 900 sestertii). Gaius Appuleius Diocles, who took part in 4,257 races in a twenty-year career and won 1,462 of them, made no less than 35,863,120 sestertii and retired at the age of forty-two.

Naturally the profession of *auriga* entailed great risks

In the second quarter of the second century AD the custom of inhumation (burying the dead) became established in Rome; previously, the dead had usually been cremated. Small Cupids have assumed the role of the charioteers here and are racing in two-horse chariots in the Circus Maximus, identifiable by the decoration on the *spina*. The childish charioteers, unlike their human adult counterparts, do not wear tunics with leather lacing and have not slung the reins round their bodies, but hold them in their hands. Cupids performing human activities were a popular pictorial motif in the art of the imperial Roman period.

to life and limb. Many tombstones bear the information that the dead man was killed in a racing accident. One such victim was Scorpus, mentioned above; Martial wrote that he himself earned little in a whole day, 'whereas in a single hour Scorpus, a winner of the race, bears off fifteen bags of gleaming gold' (Martial, *Epigrammata* 10, 74), but that the charioteer's life ended at the turning point of the circus, 'that goal,

**97**

**Lamp with *quadriga***

First century AD

Pottery

Antikensammlung, Staatliche Museen zu Berlin, TC 951

A *quadriga* gallops towards the *meta*, the turning post with its three conical finials. In the background is the *spina*, with several statues on columns, Augustus's obelisk and the apparatus with dolphin figures used to count laps.

whereto thy car sped ever in brief course' (ibid. 10, 50).

However, considering that many of these charioteers had been on the starting line hundreds or even thousands of times before they met with such a fate – and death in the circus was by no means certain – it is clear that by comparison with a gladiatorial career chariot-racing may be considered quite safe. If we compare the chances of survival of an *auriga* with those of a modern racing driver, the charioteer's profession was of course a good deal more dangerous, but the difference can be described as one of degree rather than absolute.

## The horses

The horses to which the charioteers owed their victories enjoyed no less fame. 'I, that Martial who am known to the nations and to Rome's peoples … am not known better than the horse Andraemon.' (*Epigrammata* 10, 9.) Shockingly brutal as the Roman attitude to animals could be, as we saw in the discussion of *venationes* (pp. 70–73), they were also capable of a positively sentimental love of animals for their own sake, particularly horses, and even more particularly racehorses. '*Vincas, non vincas, te amamus, Polidoxe*' ('Win or lose, we love you, Polidoxus') runs the wording on a mosaic from Constantine in north Africa showing the racehorse of that name.

Nor were the horses forgotten when the victory prizes were awarded. Many depictions show palm branches stuck in the horses' harness. The equine recipients probably felt more appreciative of the gilded *modii* (measures for grain) containing a special portion of barley. At the end of a successful career in the arena a horse could expect not the knacker's yard – the Romans did not eat horsemeat – but retirement on a pension: 'Lest the steed that has won many palms should fall, dishonouring his victories, lazily now he crops the meadow grasses.' (Ovid, *Tristia* IV 8, 19.) And finally the horse had honourable burial: 'Sired on the sandy plains of Gaetulia [an area in north Africa] by a Gaetulian stallion, fast as the wind, incomparable in your life, you now, Spendusa, dwell in the realm of Lethe' (inscription for the gravestone of the African mare Spendusa – herself a rare exception, since most racehorses were stallions).

These expensive racehorses were bred and trained on imperial and private stud farms. By far the most successful horses in the circus came from North Africa and Spain, but Cappadocia (an area of eastern Asia Minor), Greece and Sicily were also outstanding sources of animals for racing in the arena. The African and Spanish horses probably resembled today's Libyan and Iberian animals (Andalusians and Lusitanos). Contrary to a widespread myth, those modern and almost identical types were not created by cross-breeding with Arabian horses in the early Middle Ages, but had already existed and were highly regarded in classical antiquity, when Arabs were still entirely unknown. The bedouin rode camels until Islam began to make triumphant headway; only then did they acquire horses from the old breeding regions of Syria, Asia Minor and Egypt, where the Arabs known to us today originated.

The myth of the Arabian desert horse also makes an appearance in *Ben Hur*: the eponymous hero gets his horses from the bedouin Sheikh Ilderim. In fact the horses in the film version are not Arabs, but Lipizzaners from Yugoslavia, and since Lipizzaners have been much cross-bred with Iberian horses, the film did in fact use a breed of historically similar appearance to the originals.

Iberian horses today, however, are rather larger than their ancestors of the Roman period; we know a great deal about the size and physique of Roman horses from finds of skeletons. They were stocky horses of medium size standing 135–55 cm high (the average was about 142 cm), and were thus large animals for their time. By today's standards, most of the horses were somewhere between a large pony and a small full-sized horse. In

## THE CHARIOTS

The standard vehicle in chariot-racing was the *quadriga* adopted from the Greeks, with four horses harnessed to it side by side, as shown on the starting line in *Ben Hur*. Racing with the *biga*, the two-horse chariot, was also common. After the late republican era the *triga* (three-horse chariot), much used under

98
**Charioteer and chariot**
First to third century AD
Bronze, gilded
Landesmuseum Mainz, 0,462

Many of the surviving small figurines of charioteers probably originally stood in model racing chariots drawn by teams of horses, which have been preserved only in a few cases. It is likely that this chariot, now in Mainz, once had two bronze horses pulling it. The wheels are modern additions that do not follow classical models. Such statuettes of *bigae* were used as decorative items or toys. The historian Suetonius tells us that the emperor Nero was often found in his rooms playing with miniature ivory racing chariots, instead of seeing to the government of his empire.

performance they were inferior to their modern counterparts only in their ability to jump, which depends very much on the length of the legs. However, jumping was a minor consideration in classical antiquity, and need not be considered at all in chariot-racing.

Hard, healthy hooves were of great importance, since nailed horseshoes were not used at the time. None the less, frequent racing on the very hard track of the circus arena must have meant considerable wear and tear. In addition, the horses' joints were subject to great stress on the sharp 180-degree bends at the turning posts (*metae*). There was also the risk of injury, which must have been greater for the horses than the charioteers in the frequent crashes. Above all, injuries meant that losses of animals were high, since broken bones in horses were practically impossible to mend, and a horse with a fracture usually had to be put down. None the less, many horses survived hundreds of races and went into honourable retirement.

Etruscan influence in the early Roman period, ran only in a few chariot-races with religious connotations. Occasionally chariots had six horses (*seiugae*), eight horses (*octoiugae*) or ten horses (*decemiugae*), and there are even pictorial depictions of vehicles drawn by twenty horses. Since in all these cases the horses were harnessed to the chariot side by side, the difficulty of driving the team increased enormously with the number of animals, particularly when taking the bends. Racing with such large teams served mainly to demonstrate the bravura skills of individual star charioteers, and did not by any means result in higher speeds.

Contrary to a commonly held opinion, the Romans knew perfectly well how to harness several pairs of draught animals behind each other, but they used this method of harnessing a team only to transport heavy loads over the roads on carts. With chariots for ceremonial display or sport, the aim was to make as strik-

**99**

**Burial canister with racing chariot**

First century AD

Lead

British Museum, London, PRB 1993 1-2 1

This lead canister contained a glass cinerary urn holding a cremation burial. It is decorated with a panel showing the sun-god Sol riding in his chariot, which is depicted as a *quadriga*: the imagery of the circus was widely and commonly used throughout the Roman world.

ing as possible a visual impression, and give the charioteer a chance to show his skill in difficult circumstances.

There is also a persistent prejudice to the effect that riding and driving in antiquity was inefficient because the slave-owning mentality of the Greeks and Romans discouraged innovation, and that the horse was not properly exploited until the Middle Ages, which saw the invention of the horseshoe, the stirrup, the horse collar and other new introductions. On closer examination, such theories turn out to be greatly exaggerated and in some cases pure fiction. The harness used on horses in antiquity is a case in point.

The harness of the Greeks and Romans is said to have consisted of a strap around the neck and a girth around the belly, exerting a strangulatory effect on draught animals and preventing them from pulling loads weighing more than half a metric tonne. Racehorses certainly had lighter loads to pull, but it is still claimed that at high speed the harnessing system had the effect of slowing the teams down.

Practical experiments, in particular those carried out by Jean Spruytte, have shown that these claims are inaccurate. These experiments proved that two horses, harnessed in the girths they would have worn in classical antiquity, could pull loads weighing a metric tonne even over heavy ground, and there were no obvious disadvantages by comparison with modern harness, since the supposed 'neck strap' was really a broad girth around the chest which did not affect the horse's breathing or circulation in any way.

The girth around the belly met the chest girth on the withers and stabilized it. At this point the two girths

were fixed to the yoke (*iugum*) placed over the withers. Only the two central horses of a chariot with a team of more than two were beneath the yoke, and were therefore called *iugales*. All the other horses were harnessed to the chariot to left and right of the *iugales* by traces, and were called *funales*. In a *quadriga* they were the animals on which security and speed depended in taking bends, while the *iugales* bore the main burden of pulling and stabilizing the chariot.

The yoke was a transverse bar about a metre in length, positioned on the withers of the two *iugales* and fixed to the front end of the pole, which had a pronounced curve and slanted upwards. The pole was not much more than about 2.3 metres long, and allowed the horses to be harnessed quite tightly, making them easier to control. This explains why the Romans often tied up the tails of their racehorses with ribbons, for otherwise the long, flowing hair of the tail could easily have caught on the pole, the chariot or the traces.

Except in Jean Spruytte's experiments, practical modern reconstructions have never harnessed the horses to the yoke correctly. In most cases the traces, starting from the sides of the belly girth rather than the withers, have been fastened to a crossbar running in front of the body of the chariot, the swingle-tree, which had not been invented in classical antiquity. A swingle-tree means that it is unnecessary for the pole to curve up to the height of the horses' withers, since instead it can simply run horizontally between the two middle horses and be loosely fixed to their chest girths. The chariot is actually pulled by the shoulder muscles, not the chest.

There are other respects in which the copies of racing chariots in classical antiquity built for *Ben Hur* (and indeed other productions) are so imperfect that they could not possibly function in a historically correct manner. The chariots built in Rome by the Danesi brothers for the race in the film of *Ben Hur*, several of which still adorn the garden of a restaurant in Ostia Antica, look more like heavy armoured vehicles than sports equipment. They are massive structures made of steel tubing and thick, carved wood. The high body of the chariot has been brought down to make it sit lower over the iron axle, and its floor consists of a tangle of steel strips. With a total weight of around 8 metric hundredweight, it is not surprising that during filming the teams could run only four races of a single lap each in a day (as compared to the seven laps of a real Roman chariot-race), and even so some of the horses were spitting blood. As we shall see, Roman racing chariots weighed little more than half a metric hundredweight.

Even apart from such technical cinematic constraints as fitting hydraulic brakes for the scenes of accidents, the chariots built for the film are much too heavy because when the designers studied extant depictions of such vehicles they picked the wrong type as their model: the triumphal chariot (*currus triumphalis*), not the racing chariot (*currus circensis*). Both types did indeed originate in the two-wheeled war chariot of the second and early first millennia BC, but they had lost all military significance in the sixth century BC in both Greece and Italy, and subsequently developed in very different ways.

While the remains of over 250 original vehicles from the transitional phase between the war chariot and the impressive ceremonial chariot have been found in tombs of the Etruscan and Italian nobility of northern and in particular central Italy, no identifiable remains of either triumphal or racing chariots from the republican and imperial periods have been found. We therefore have to depend entirely on visual sources for the period concerned here.

The most monumental and familiar pictorial records, as might be expected, show triumphal chariots. Since

nature of the racing chariot. It certainly had a very long, straight axle, but the wheels were small and light, features that helped to stabilize the vehicle as it took sharp bends. The body of the chariot, which unlike the war chariot or triumphal chariot had to hold only one man, was small and low. It was not of massive construction and had no carved ornamentation, but consisted of a kind of wooden framework. The spaces in this framework were filled in with interwoven straps (for the floor) or with stretched fabric or leather (for the breastwork). The woven floor was not only light in weight but provided a kind of springing.

The miniature bronze *biga* found in the Tiber (fig. 100) is probably the best representation we have of a Roman racing chariot, clearly illustrating the details described above. If we take its proportions and those

100
**Model of a two-horse chariot (*biga*)**
First to third century AD
Bronze
British Museum, London,
GR 1894.10-30.1

The figure of the charioteer and one of the horses are now missing from this detailed model. It was said to have been found in the River Tiber and shows the normal type of Roman racing chariot. Built for speed, it had a light wooden frame covered with fabric or leather. The small wheels and low centre of gravity combined manoeuvrability with stability.

these, too, were two-wheeled vehicles drawn by a team of four horses harnessed side by side, at a fleeting glance there is a danger of mistaking them for racing chariots, and the film-makers promptly made that mistake. The triumphal chariot, however, was a completely non-functional development of the war chariot, which became a vehicle used solely for purposes of prestige, a kind of state coach in which the *triumphator* rode through the streets in all his finery. So did other high officials on occasion, and naturally the emperor himself during the imperial period. Triumphs were processions, and the chariot, controlled by a separate driver, moved solemnly in time with the rest of the procession.

Reliefs and mosaics showing chariot-racing in the circus present a completely different picture of the

of several other good depictions as a guide, then we can assume that the measurements of a typical racing chariot were much as follows:

Total length of axle: 180 cm
Gauge: 155 cm
Diameter of wheels: 65 cm
Height of chariot breastwork: 70 cm
Width of chariot body: 60 cm
Depth of chariot body: 55 cm
Total length of pole: 230 cm

The wheels had six or, more frequently, eight spokes; it is probable, although not certain, that they had thin iron tyres. Apart from that, the builders of chariots would certainly have been sparing in their use of metal components, which we may assume were most likely to be found in the region of the toe of the axle and the

**101**

**Knife-handle in the form of a charioteer**

First to fourth century AD
Bronze
British Museum, London,
PRB 1856.7-1.1249

Found in London, this ornate knife-handle shows a victorious charioteer with characteristic helmet, tunic and protective strapping around his waist. London and Colchester are the most likely venues for chariot-racing in Roman Britain, but as yet no circus has been identified.

top speed on the straight, and the stallions, harnessed side by side, must have incited each other to a very high degree.

## EQUIPMENT AND RACING TECHNIQUE OF THE CHARIOTEERS

The great difference between Greek chariot-racing and the Etruscan and Roman form of the sport is also evident in the equipment and driving style of the charioteers. While Greek drivers of the classical period wore a long chiton and no protective clothing, Etruscan frescoes of the same period already show charioteers in a short chiton and a helmet-like cap. The Romans developed protective clothing of almost modern appearance for their drivers, including a crash helmet made of leather or felt (*pilleus*), a lacing of straps around the torso, and *fasciae*, wrappings of leather or linen on the legs (figs 102 and 103). This clothing was intended to protect the driver in collision with the breastwork of his own chariot or in a fall, particularly if he were dragged by his own horses. To avert that danger, the *auriga* also had a curved knife which he carried stuck in the straps of his torso lacing, so that in an emergency he could cut the reins slung around his body.

The danger of being dragged over the ground of the circus arena was considerably greater for Etruscan and Roman *aurigae* than for their Greek counterparts, who held the reins in their hands, while Etruscan and Roman charioteers wrapped the reins around their waists and tied them fast. They braced their entire bodies against the reins, steering the chariot by shifting their weight and using the left hand only to correct course, while the right hand was entirely free to wield the whip. This driving style was more dynamic and flexible than that of the Greek charioteers, but more dangerous too.

Undoubtedly the racing technique was aggressive and ruthless. A charioteer would cut across the path of an adversary's chariot, trying to force it aside and up against the central barrier, and dangerous collisions were an accepted part of the race. Such situations were exacerbated by the teamwork between charioteers of the separate factions, who would try to help their top team to victory by shielding it, blocking opposing teams and forcing them aside. The situation was of course particularly critical at the turning posts (*metae*), where the chariots had to drive round a bend of 180 degrees. Such light vehicles could go into pronounced skids, which the *auriga* had to calculate skilfully. Since every team tried to take the bend as tightly and as fast as possible, that was where the danger of mass collisions was greatest (cf. fig. 104).

In the film *Ben Hur* the charioteers wear fantastically designed garments, partly Hellenistic and partly exotic oriental, with helmets to match. The eponymous hero looks more like a Roman charioteer than the others with his leather helmet, leather strapping and dagger,

hub. Iron axles were still unknown. A racing chariot certainly weighed less than the Egyptian war chariot, which was intended to carry two men in battle but still weighed only around 35 kg including the pole, as finds of original chariots show. We can therefore estimate that the weight of a Roman racing chariot was 25–30 kg. Since the charioteers will certainly have been rather lightly built men, the entire weight the horses had to pull in the race can be put at a maximum of 100 kg. In a *biga*, then, each animal had to pull 50 kg, in a *quadriga* 25 kg. Since this weight was drawn along absolutely firm, level ground, the burden on the animals was minimal, and in any case very much less than in a horseback race. The horses could reach their

102 (FAR LEFT)
**Charioteer**
Second century AD
Bronze
Römisch-Germanisches
Museum der Stadt Köln,
95,1996

This figure was once part of a
miniature chariot-racing team
(see fig. 82). The charioteer
held his team's reins with his
arms outstretched. His
protective clothing of helmet,
leather strapping and *fasciae* is
reproduced in detail.

103 (LEFT)
**Charioteer**
Imperial Roman period
Bronze
Musée du Louvre, Paris,
BR 714

The dating of this outstanding
bronze statuette is
controversial, since various
details of the charioteer's
equipment, such as his curious
protective headgear and the
way the leather lacing divides
in front, are not found in
comparable pieces. Because
of this, some scholars have
assumed that the statuette really
dates from the Renaissance
period in the fifteenth to
sixteenth centuries. The palm
branch held by the charioteer
shows that he has just won a
race.

although he stupidly takes off his helmet at the beginning of the race, in line with the ridiculous cinematic convention of allowing the protagonist to defy danger bareheaded. All the charioteers are driving in the Greek style with the reins in their hands, and no one has slung them around the body, so it is rather surprising that in his fatal fall Messala never thinks of simply letting go of the reins, instead of clinging on and being dragged for some distance.

The frequency of spectacular accidents in which the chariot teams were a total write-off was of course extremely high – the Roman technical term was *naufragium*, shipwreck. While Fred Niblo's 1926 film version of *Ben Hur* was content with four *naufragia* out of ten teams on the starting line, Wyler's film shows six of nine teams totally written off, not to mention a soldier being run over. Surprisingly, four teams still manage to reach the finish, something the present author noticed only when repeatedly re-running the video of this scene, a possibility that could not have been anticipated in 1959.

However, the actual filming was considerably less brutal in 1959 than 1926, since by the late 1950s it was necessary to bear in mind the protests of animal protection organizations. While about a hundred horses died in the filming of the race arranged by B.

Reeves Eason in 1926 – there are even photographs showing extras posing in the arena beside great piles of dead animals – thirty-three years later, when the arrangement of the race was supervised by Andrew Marton and Yakima Cannutt, the filming passed off without a single serious injury to either man or beast.

Most of the accidents during the race in Wyler's film are of a very realistic character, particularly the first, when a bend is taken too tightly at one of the turning posts. However, the 'Greek' chariot driven by the villain Messala, with rotating blades on the axles intended to cut at the spokes of his adversaries' chariots, is an unfortunate product of the imagination. In view of the carefully devised system of equal chances that lay behind the whole concept of Roman chariot-racing, any man who turned up in such a vehicle would have been disqualified by the referee or lynched by the crowd as certainly as a modern footballer who attacked the other team's goalkeeper with a heavy club outside the penalty area.

## THE CIRCUS

Of all large Roman buildings intended for mass entertainment, the circus was by far the most expensive, and consequently the one least often found outside Rome

104

**Relief with chariot crashing**

First half of the first century AD
Terracotta
Kunsthistorisches Museum
Wien, Antikensammlung,
ASV 49

Terracotta reliefs of this kind
were used to face the eaves of
houses or as wall decoration.
This panel was part of a series,
together with that shown in fig.
105. The example above, now
in Vienna, shows an accident at
the turning post. The driver has
fallen backwards out of his
chariot, and must now try to
cut through the reins to avoid
being dragged by the horses.

itself. The arena of the Circus Maximus had an area of
about 45,000 square metres, making it twelve times
larger than the arena of the Colosseum, the biggest
Roman amphitheatre, while the tiers of the *cavea*
would accommodate at least 150,000 spectators, as
against a maximum of 50,000 in the Colosseum.

The Circus Maximus served as the model for other
sporting venues of its kind. They did not reach their
definitive form until the beginning of the second century AD, under the emperor Trajan, but the crucial step
from provisional racetrack without permanent buildings to a self-contained architectural work was taken in
the late republican period (first century BC). The monumental circus was a Roman innovation. The Greeks,
Etruscans and indeed the Romans of the early period
ran their races on improvised tracks (hippodromes),
preferably laid out in broad valleys that could be over-
looked by spectators sitting on the slopes. Once it had
been drained, the valley between the Palatine and
Aventine hills in which the Circus Maximus lay fulfilled these conditions ideally. From the fourth century
BC onwards the Romans began to equip their most
important racetrack with permanent buildings, first of

wood and then of stone. Until the later part of the first
century AD, moreover, the circus was not just the scene
of chariot-racing but also of athletic contests and
animal hunts, since it was not until the Flavian period
(AD 69–96) that special buildings were erected for
these events.

The form of the circus arena resembled that of the
stadium, with two parallel long sides, one curved
narrow side and one straight narrow side, but the long
sides of the circus were of considerably greater extent.
In the state it achieved under Trajan, the arena of the
Circus Maximus was 550–580 metres long and about
80 metres wide. The smallest public circus known to
us (at Gerasa in Jordan) had an arena measuring 244 x
51 metres.

The straighter narrow side, which did in fact have a
slight concave curve, contained the twelve starting
boxes (*carceres*), flanked by towers. The larger part of
the arena was divided down its length by a double
wall forming a barrier (*spina* or *euripus*). In the Circus
Maximus it was 335 metres long and 8 metres wide. It
was around the *spina* (literally, backbone) that the
teams raced after their starting spurt. The *metae*, or

turning posts, stood at its two ends; they were platforms with a semi-circular ground plan, each of which bore three pillars tapering up to an egg-shaped finial. The *spina* was richly ornamented between the *metae* with statues of gods (although not of such monstrous dimensions as in the film of *Ben Hur*) and with palms and obelisks (cf. figs 106, 107). The empty space between the two walls forming the barrier was sometimes filled with water, hence the name *euripus*, canal. Platforms with frames containing seven egg shapes and seven dolphin shapes also stood on the *spina*; these devices were used as counters, signalling the number of laps that had been driven. A second set of eggs stood at the edge of the arena, where it probably relayed information to the charioteers.

The distance from the *carceres* to the nearest *meta* was 170 metres in the Circus Maximus. The charioteers drove this part of the course only once, at the start, as their teams made for the area on the right of the *spina*, round which they had to drive seven times anti-clockwise for the rest of the race. The curved line along which the starting boxes stood was asymmetrically designed by the Roman architects, so that all the

teams would travel the same distance before reaching the white chalk line marked on the ground between the first of the *metae* and the right-hand outer wall (*podium*) of the arena. In this way none of the contestants was at a disadvantage.

When the chariots reached this line, after a starting spurt along the straight, it can be assumed that most of them were still approximately level, forming a broad front. The architects therefore did not position the *spina* precisely down the lengthwise axis of the arena but gave it a slight bias, so that the distance between the *podium* and the *metae* to the right of the *spina*, a width of 42 metres, was considerably greater than on the other side, a width of 30 metres. In this way the teams were guided into a racecourse narrowing like a funnel, for it was to be expected that the field would string out in the course of the first lap, and less space would then be needed. In the late Roman period the track was widened further at the white line by giving the *podium* an outward bend at this point. The carefully considered construction of racetracks in the imperial period is one of the most impressive examples of the famous functionalism of Roman architecture.

105
**Relief with chariot-racing**
Early first century AD
Terracotta
British Museum, London,
GR 1805.7-3.337

A four-horse team (*quadriga*) approaches the three cones of the turning post (*meta*), which a *hortator* (a rider who encouraged the contestants) has already passed. The turns were the point of maximum danger, where the charioteer and the inside lead-horse played a critical role, and the maker of the plaque has skilfully captured the tension of the moment.

**106**

**Circus beaker with chariot-racing**

First century AD
Glass
British Museum, London,
PRB 1870.2-24.3

This mould-blown glass beaker from Colchester shows four *quadriga* teams racing in the circus. The middle zone depicts the central barrier (*spina*) with obelisks, lap-counters and other monuments, while the inscribed upper zone records that the charioteer Cresces beat his opponents Hierax, Olympaeus and Antilocus.

**107**

**Relief with Cupid chariot-race**

Mid-second century AD
Marble
Museo Archeologico Nazionale di Napoli, 6712

The race is in its deciding phase. The apparatus with the eggs shows that there is only one lap left to go. Four chariots in all are racing for victory, each accompanied by a man on horseback (the *hortator*). The charioteer in front is about to win; his *hortator* is waving to him. The charioteer behind is falling forward over the breastwork of his chariot, and in view of the accident about to happen, the rider behind him clutches at his head in despair. The following teams cannot now influence the outcome of the race, however much the accompanying Cupids urge them on. Assistants are sprinkling the ground of the circus with water; one of them has lost his straw-covered container and fallen under the hooves of the last team.

If we are to calculate the actual distance of a race of seven laps in the Circus Maximus, the position of the finishing line must be determined. John H. Humphrey has convincingly shown that it was probably on the right-hand side of the track, just before the end of the *spina*, where one of the two referees' boxes was placed. The teams therefore drove around the two *metae* seven times, and the race symmetrically ended with a repeat performance of the distance covered in the spurt at the start. A good charioteer who kept close to the *spina* and took the bends around the *metae* as tightly as possible had to drive 5,200 metres at the very least. Modern racetracks (for mounted horses) are usually 2,000–3,000 metres.

The consistency of the surface in the arena was of the utmost importance for a good race. It has been ascertained that the circus at Arles had a foundation of stamped mud, covered with a layer of coarse gravel (diameter of the stones 2–4 cm) to a depth of 10–20 cm. The circus at Sirmium had a 30-cm layer of fine gravel over a foundation of lime mortar with a thin

layer of crushed brick on top. The very top layer may be assumed to have been of sand, probably not laid very thickly (and in Sirmium brick-dust may have been a substitute), but little or nothing of that top layer has been preserved. Of course the subsoil, well levelled, must have had some kind of provision for drainage, or the arena would very soon have turned into a swamp. Traces of drainage devices have indeed been found in various places, for instance in Caesarea and Carthage.

For the race in the 1959 film of *Ben Hur* 25 cm of crushed lava was first laid on a levelled stone surface, and on top of that 20 cm of yellow sand with a total weight of 40,000 tonnes. This proved to be far too deep, and it was all removed except for 4 cm of crushed lava, a layer that proved sufficient to give the horses a soft, stable footing and achieve controllable skids at the bends. None the less, there were problems with ruts, for which the over-heavy chariots will have been chiefly to blame.

To look briefly at the film of *Ben Hur* again: the size and shape of the arena and the design of the *spina* are

108
**Lamp with lap counter**
First century AD
Pottery
Antikensammlung, Staatliche
Museen zu Berlin, TC 7481

The apparatus contains the dolphin figures used to count laps during a race.

basically correct apart from the monumental sculptures, which are badly miscalculated in both style and dimensions. The lap counter device with the dolphins is pretty, although the eggs were ignored. However, the function of the starting boxes and therefore the whole beginning of the race are entirely misrepresented.

## ORGANIZATION AND STAFF

In the imperial period there were normally twenty-four races a day during the *ludi* (games) of the city of Rome. The organizational expense involved was enormous and was mainly borne by the circus factions. If all twenty-four races had the maximum number of entrants, twelve *quadrigae*, there would have been 1,152 horses a day racing. But since as a rule some of the races were run with *bigae*, and it was quite usual for four or eight teams to be on the starting line instead

boys standing around the edge of the arena trying to refresh the horses and drivers of their own teams with water. Several reliefs show them going under the chariot wheels. Other members of staff included referees, officials to count the laps, trumpeters and so on.

The function of the *hortatores* or *iubilatores* is not quite clear: they were individual horsemen wearing protective clothing similar to that of the *aurigae*. They appear in many depictions, and each seems to have been assigned to a particular team. They probably rode ahead to act as guides, showing the charioteers the way in the dust and confusion of the race, indicating good opportunities ahead and warning of dangers. Except round the bends, they were no faster than the teams themselves, but they could move with much more agility, making use of gaps, and since they had to concentrate on managing only a single horse they had a better view than the drivers. We do not know

**109**

**Relief with chariot-racing**

Third century AD

Marble

British Museum, London,
GR 1805.7-3.134

The front of a child's sarcophagus, showing four charioteers racing in *bigae* (two-horse chariots) in the circus at Rome. Each charioteer is accompanied by a mounted escort (*hortator*). The *sparsores*, who watered the horses and tended the track, can be seen lying or kneeling on the ground.

of twelve, the actual number will have been more like 700–800 horses, still a very large number, particularly as additional horses, probably 200–300 of them, had to be available for the use of the staff and the acrobatic riders.

The horses were well prepared and groomed for the race in the stables belonging to the factions, which were 1–2 km away from the Circus Maximus on the Campus Martius. Hundreds of stable lads and grooms were employed, as well as cartwrights and saddlers to look after the chariots and harness, not to mention doctors and veterinary surgeons.

A great many more staff were needed in the circus itself. The starting boxes and in particular the mechanism for unbolting them had to be serviced, the arena had to be tidied up between races, and there must be men ready to clear wrecked chariots and move injured men and horses away from a *naufragium* (collision) as quickly as possible and give first aid – a very dangerous task while a race was still running (the realistically presented operations of the recovery team in *Ben Hur* provide several exciting episodes in the race). Another risky activity seems to have been that of the *sparsores*,

whether they were present in all races or at all phases of a race. In any case, they were purely auxiliaries; the teams alone determined victory or defeat.

Unlike the activity of the *hortatores*, the performances of the *desultores* were a separate part of the programme performed between chariot-races. The *desultores* were acrobatic riders, clothed in loincloths and conical caps and carrying long whips, who raced around the arena at a full gallop, each leading a second horse beside him and leaping from one horse to another in a certain rhythm – probably after each of the seven laps. Acrobatic horsemen jumping on and off their mounts at high speed, often carrying weapons, are known to us from Greek and Etruscan culture, but only the Romans rode with two horses each. The Greeks and Etruscans did use an additional horse in military operations, but it was the Romans who seem to have made a sporting performance out of the practice.

It is a remarkable fact that the simplest and most natural form of horse-racing, with mounted jockeys racing each other on single horses, does not seem to have been practised by the Romans at all in public competition. Among the Greeks such races were as common as chariot-racing, but pictorial depictions show that they fell out of fashion with the Etruscans in the course of the sixth century BC. As Jean-Paul Thuillier has demonstrated, this is one of the clear indications that Roman equestrian sports developed under Etruscan rather than Greek influence.

## THE CONDUCT OF THE RACE

In the city of Rome chariot-racing was the most spectacular part of the *ludi*, the games in honour of specific deities usually lasting several days and regularly held on certain fixed dates. Chariot-races could also be held independently of the festive calendar on special occasions, for instance to celebrate a triumph.

The *pompa circensis*, the great procession preceding the competition, was the feature most clearly illustrat-

their opponents. Allocation of the boxes was by drawing lots, a process conducted publicly in full view of the audience. A ball for each team was placed in a revolving urn. The charioteers then chose starting boxes in the order in which their balls were picked out of the urn, and only the outcome would show whether a decision had been good or bad.

Once the positions of the teams had been determined, they entered the boxes (*carceres*). As the name (meaning 'prisons') indicates, these were closed, cell-like areas. The gates (*ostia*, meaning 'mouths') opening on to the arena were over 6 metres wide in the Circus Maximus, so that even teams of eight horses could get through. In other circuses the *ostia* generally measured only 3–3.5 metres, providing space for teams no larger than the *quadriga*. It has been worked out that each horse needed about 67.5 cm.

The *ostia* had double swing doors, closed under ten-

110
**Relief with *tensa***
Third century AD
Marble
British Museum, London,
GR 1805.7-3.145

A section of the lid-panel of a sarcophagus, restored in the eighteenth century, showing part of the ceremonial circus procession at the start of the games. The *tensa*, a chest for sacred objects which is depicted here as a shrine with images of Jupiter, Castor and Pollux on the sides, is being taken on a four-horse cart from the Capitoline Hill to the Circus Maximus.

ing the religious context in which the racing had originated. Accompanied by musicians and dancers, members of youth organizations, men carrying the statues of gods, and many other groups, the holder of the event stood in a triumphal *quadriga*, the racing teams and the athletes entered the arena, and then preparations for the racing itself could begin.

First the factions had to have their starting boxes assigned to them, a matter of considerable importance for the conduct of the whole race, since depending on their situation teams could shelter their favourites, and block or impede the progress of those favoured by

sion, that would suddenly spring out towards the arena when unbolted. The tension was produced with the aid of twisted bundles of sinews, a system adopted from torsion artillery weapons. They were unbolted centrally with the aid of cords pulled back so that all twelve gates opened at the same moment, and it was as if the 'mouths' were actually spitting the teams out into the arena (figs 111, 112). Thanks to this ingenious method, devised by the Romans in the late republican period (first century BC), there could be no false starts. The famous starting signal given by the holder of the games when he threw down the *mappa*, a piece of cloth, was

**111**

***Ostia* with *quadriga***

Reconstruction

Drawing: Nikolaus Grohmann

**112** (RIGHT AND OPPOSITE)

**Frieze with chariot-racing**

*c.* AD 125–30

Marble

British Museum, London,

GR 1805.7-3.133

Musée du Louvre, Paris,

MA 152, MA 151, MA 1575

All four panels of this frieze
came from the Emperor
Hadrian's villa at Tivoli. They
show Cupids in racing chariots,
but driving fantastic teams of
hounds, antelopes, camels and
wild boar. The British Museum
panel shows the beginning of
the race and the starting boxes
(*carceres*) with their open gates.
In the other panels can be seen
an obelisk and the dolphin lap-
counter, which were part of the
decoration of the *spina*.

for the men working the unbolting mechanism and
above all for the public, but not for the charioteers,
who could not see it in their 'prisons', although they
were able to hear the accompanying trumpet fanfare.

The circus in the film of *Ben Hur* does have
*carceres*, but they are not partitioned off from each
other and serve only as a place for the teams to stand
ready. After a lap of honour like a parade the chariots
start in the middle of the right-hand half of the track. A
realistic view is presented of the confusion resulting
from the nervous state of the horses and charioteers –
including a false start – in fact, those very conditions
that the Romans had succeeded in avoiding with their
starting boxes.

As described above, once the teams had left the
*carceres* they made for the white line between the
*spina* and the right-hand wall of the *podium*. So that
there would be no crashes on this open stretch before
the white line, the teams had to drive straight towards
it and not cut in across each other, but once they had
crossed the line each charioteer could choose his own
route. Naturally they all tried to get as close to the
*spina* as possible, in order to keep the bends short and
tight.

What speeds were reached and how long did a race
in the Circus Maximus last? Racing straight up the long
side of the *spina*, the teams could temporarily reach
speeds of up to about 75 kph, but they had to slow
down considerably before the *metae*, probably to
25–30 kph. Of course a charioteer had to take into
account the very long total distance to be covered – at
least 5.2 km – and must not tire his horses too soon.

To calculate the duration, we can take as a point of
reference a race on horseback staged in 1989 by the
present author and some friends in the well-preserved
late Roman Circus of Maxentius on the Appian Way.
We used Camargue horses of very much the same size
and build as the Roman horses. The Circus of Maxentius is rather smaller than the Circus Maximus; the
length of the spurt from the *carceres* at the start is 159
metres, the *spina* measures 296 metres, so that after
seven laps a horse has gone about 4,570 metres. The
fastest of our horses reached top speeds of up to 70
kph, but the average speed, in a racing time of 10 minutes 20 seconds in all, was only 26.5 kph. Transferred
to the Circus Maximus, these calculations would make
the length of the race 11 minutes 45 seconds. Considering that our horses, carrying the full weight of their
riders on their backs, had a considerably heavier load
than *quadriga*-pulling horses, which would also have
been better trained, and finally that the ground of the
arena had not been specially prepared for us and was
bone-hard, it may certainly be assumed that the average speed of Roman racehorses was more like 35 kph,
which would make the duration of a race 8–9 minutes.
This coincides exactly with the time taken by the race
in the film of *Ben Hur* (8 minutes 20 seconds).

Once the race was over the victory celebration took
place (cf. fig. 113). The successful *auriga* climbed up to
the box of the holder of the games and received his
prizes in the form of a palm branch, a wreath and
money. Instead of the traditional laurel wreath, wreaths
of flowers or circlets of thin metal often seem to have
been used in late antiquity. The victor then drove a lap
of honour past the applauding crowd and left the
arena.

To conclude this chapter, I will quote two more
sources that give a good idea of the drama of chariot-
racing in the circus, and of the dark passions aroused
by this sport. The most detailed and lively account left

by any classical author of a chariot-race is in a poem by Sidonius Apollinaris, writing in the fifth century AD. It describes an amateur race in the court circus won by Consentius, the poet's friend, but the conduct of the race differs only very slightly from that of a professional event. There are only four *quadrigae* at the start, with the colours White and Blue racing together against Red and Green, as was often the case:

Brightly gleam the colours, white and blue, green and red, your several badges. Servants' hands hold mouth and reins and with knotted cords force the twisted manes to hide themselves, and all the while they incite the steeds, eagerly cheering them with encouraging pats and instilling a rapturous frenzy. There behind the barriers chafe those beasts, pressing against the fastenings, while a vapoury blast comes forth between the wooden bars and even before the race the field they have not yet entered is filled with their panting breath. They push, they bustle, they drag, they struggle, they rage, they jump, they fear and are feared; never are their feet still, but restlessly they lash the hardened timber. At last the herald with loud blare of trumpet calls forth the impatient teams and launches the fleet chariots into the field ... The ground gives way under the wheels and the air is smirched with the dust that rises

in their track. The drivers, while they wield the reins, ply the lash; now they stretch forward over the chariots with stooping breasts, and so they sweep along, striking the horses' withers and leaving their backs untouched. With charioteers so prone it would puzzle you to pronounce whether they were more supported by the pole or the wheels. Now as if flying out of sight on wings, you had traversed the more open part, and you were hemmed in by the space that is cramped by craft, amid which the central barrier has extended its long low double-walled structure. When the farther turning-post freed you from all restraint once more, your partner went ahead of the two others, who had passed you; so then, according to the law of the circling course, you had to take the fourth track. The drivers in the middle were intent that if haply the first man, embarrassed by a dash of his steeds too much to the right, should leave a space open on the left by heading for the surrounding seats, he should be passed by a chariot driven in on the near side. As for you, bending double with the very force of the effort you keep a tight rein on your team and with consummate skill wisely reserve them for the seventh lap. The others are busy with hand and voice, and everywhere the sweat of drivers and flying steeds falls in drops on to the field. The hoarse roar from applauding partisans stirs the heart, and the contestants, both horses and men, are warmed by the race and chilled by fear. Thus they go once round, then a second time; thus goes the third lap, thus the fourth; but in the fifth turn the foremost man, unable to bear the pressure of his pursuers, swerved his car aside, for he had found, as he gave command to his fleet team, that their strength was exhausted. Now the return half of the sixth course was completed and the crowd was already clamouring for the award of the prizes; your adversaries, with no fear of any effort from you, were scouring the track in front with never a care, when suddenly you tautened the curbs all together, tautened your chest, planted your feet firmly in front, and chafed the mouths of your swift steeds ... Hereupon one of the others, clinging to the shortest route round the turning post, was hustled by you, and his team, carried away beyond control by their onward rush, could no more be wheeled round in a harmonious course. As you saw him pass before you in disorder, you got ahead of him by remaining where you were, cunningly reining up. The other adversary, exulting in the public plaudits, ran too far to the right, close to the spectators; then as he turned aslant and all too late after

113
**Lamp with circus victory procession**
First century AD
Pottery
British Museum, London,
GR 1856.12-26.479

Said to be from Pozzuoli, this lamp shows a victorious lead-horse from a chariot team surrounded by jubilant supporters, some with palm-branches. The figure in front carries a banner or placard that bore the horse's name and the number of races it had won.

**114**

**Jar with chariot-race**

Second century AD

Pottery

British Museum, London,
PRB 1857.8-6.1

This colour-coated pottery Jar
from Colchester is decorated
with a lively depiction of a
*quadriga* race. The four factions
are shown, each charioteer
clad in helmet, jerkin and
trousers and holding whip and
reins. No circus has yet been
identified in Britain, but the
spirited rendering of the race
shown on this locally made pot
indicates a familiarity with the
sport in the province.

long indifference urged his horses with the whip, you sped
straight past your swerving rival. Then the enemy in
reckless haste overtook you and, fondly thinking that the
first man had already gone ahead, shamelessly made for
your wheel with a sidelong dash. His horses were brought
down, a multitude of intruding legs entered the wheels,
and the twelve spokes were crowded, until a crackle came
from those crammed spaces and the revolving rim
shattered the entangled feet; then he, a fifth victim, flung
from his chariot, which fell upon him, caused a mountain
of manifold havoc, and blood disfigured his prostrate brow.
(To Consentius, Letters 13, 305–4260.)

The other text is from a lead curse tablet probably of
the third century AD found in a tomb in Carthage. Such
tablets, bearing texts in which charioteers or their fans
invoke demons, asking them to bring misfortune on the
horses and drivers of the other factions, were found in
considerable numbers in many parts of the Roman
empire:

I invoke you, spirit of one untimely dead, whoever you are,
by the mighty names SALBATHBAL AUTHGEROTABAL

BASUTHATEO ALEO SAMABETHOR ... Bind the horses
whose names and images on this implement I entrust to
you; of the Red [team]: Silvanus, Servator, Lues, Zephyrus,
Blandus, Imbraius, Dives, Mariscus, Rapidus, Oriens,
Arbustus; of the Blues: Imminens, Dignus, Linon, Paezon,
Chrysaspis, Argutus, Diresor, Frugiferus, Euphrates,
Sanctus, Aethiops, Praeclarus. Bind their running, their
power, their soul, their onrush, their speed. Take away their
victory, entangle their feet, hinder them, hobble them, so
that tomorrow morning in the hippodrome they are not
able to run or walk about, or win, or go out of the starting
gates, or advance either on the racecourse or track, but
may they fall with their drivers, Euprepes, son of
Telesphoros, and Gentius and Felix and Dionysios 'the
biter' and Lamuros. Bind their hands, take away their
victory, their exit, their sight, so that they are unable to see
their rival charioteers, but rather snatch them up from their
chariots and twist them to the ground so that they alone
fall, dragged along all over the hippodrome, especially at
the turning points, with damage to their body, with the
horses whom they drive. Now, quickly.

# 'Give us your applause!' The World of the Theatre

Today, the mention of public entertainment in Rome almost inevitably evokes ideas of its most spectacular manifestations: chariot-racing and gladiatorial contests. The Romans themselves, however, regarded stage plays in the theatre as almost equally important, particularly plays in the form of tragedy and comedy, two genres of highbrow but also popular entertainment that had been taken over from Greece. The theatre of Rome had far more influence on European culture than its violent gladiatorial games and chariot-racing: the present state of drama and the theatre is unimaginable without the example of the Romans. They showed that it was possible to make those great achievements of Greek cultural life their own, and the Latin dramas of Plautus, Terence and Seneca set a more direct example for the early modern period than even the Greeks themselves.

The Romans were in fact the only people of classical antiquity in a position to adapt Greek literature into their own language, thus making it generally accessi-ble. The literary language of the other peoples of the Mediterranean area was Greek itself, as the international cultural language of the time. In the second century AD, for instance, when the Jewish dramatist Ezekiel wrote a play about Moses, the greatest leader of his people, he wrote in Greek as a matter of course. But in the third century BC, when the poet and drama-tist Gnaeus Naevius wrote a tragedy called *Romulus* about the founder of the city of Rome, he allowed his hero to speak the language of Rome itself, Latin – nor did Romulus stand alone, for even the figures of Greek mythology, Achilles and Agamemnon, Clytaemnestra and Iphigeneia, had to speak Latin on the Roman stage so that the whole audience could understand them, follow their stories and become acquainted with Greek mythology themselves. For the Roman theatre was not predominantly for a certain class of society as it is today, when only comparatively few people are regular theatre-goers: it was for everyone. Behind the senators and knights in the grander seats sat the common

115
**Bowl with a mime**
*c.* 350 BC
Pottery
Antikensammlung, Staatliche
Museen zu Berlin , 1969.7

The people of the Greek cities of southern Italy were passionately fond of the theatre. Besides tragedies and comedies, there were popular farces caricaturing themes taken from classical mythology. The vase painters of Campania often decorated their wares with scenes from these productions or with depictions of individual actors, as in the case of this bowl now in Berlin. The inscription gives the mime's stage name, Philopotes, meaning 'he who likes drink'. The picture shows every detail of his costume; he wears a close-fitting leotard leaving only his hands and feet uncovered. A cord is worn as a belt fastening the short doublet above the stuffing of his false stomach.

people, freedmen and even slaves. Women could go to the theatre, too: 'They come to see and to be seen themselves,' says Ovid (*spectatum veniunt, veniunt spectentur ut ipsae*).

## THE BIRTH OF ROMAN DRAMA

A Roman did not have to travel far to see a Greek play. Greece was only next door, for until the third century BC Sicily and most of southern Italy had been Greek. Sicilian and southern Italian cities, like all the cities of Greece, had theatres where a Roman soldier posted to those parts because of the war could see a comedy by Menander or a tragedy by Euripides. It must have seemed a good idea to appropriate these Greek treasures, along with other loot, and bring them to Rome.

A year after the end of the First Punic War (241 BC), and a year after Sicily had become the first Roman province, the Greek Livius Andronicus was the first to offer Rome a Latin drama on the Greek model. He came from the city of Tarentum, famous for its theatre, but spent most of his life in Rome. There are good reasons why 240 BC is regarded as the year when Roman poetry and indeed Roman literature as a whole was born. The development of drama in early Roman culture itself did in fact have certain antecedents, and later historians made much of them for reasons of patriotic pride: Etruscan ritual dances combined with improvised Latin texts were said to have given rise to 'satires filled with music' (*saturae modis impletae*). It is true that a good deal of Etruscan influence can be traced in the language of the Roman theatre, but these pieces lacked the unity of plot (Greek *mythos*, Latin *argumentum*) that is the authentic feature of drama. Livius Andronicus was the first to write a genuine play with a plot on the Greek pattern. As the extant fragments of his works show, he even employed the various rhythms of Greek metre, observing its fundamental distinction between long and short syllables.

This approach was not necessarily to be taken for granted, since the Romans themselves had a native Italian verse form, the rather ungainly saturnian metre, which did not reflect the sophisticated Greek rules of syllabic quantity. When Livius Andronicus translated Homer's *Odyssey* into Latin, he was still using this traditional metre. However, plays were not only to be set in Greece but must sound like authentic Greek drama, echoing the sound to which audiences in Greek theatres were accustomed. The 'barbarous' Latin language thus gradually acquired Greek sophistication. Two centuries later the philhellenic poet Horace saw this as a paradox which he summed up in a phrase that is still a classic saying: 'Conquered Greece itself conquered its uneducated conquerors, and brought the fine arts to Latium' (*Graecia capta ferum victorem cepit et artes / intulit agresti Latio*). Rome learned from the Greeks it had overthrown.

**116**
**Vase in the form of an actor**
*c.* 150 BC
Terracotta
British Museum, London,
GR 1873.10-20.2

A comic actor, perhaps representing Priam at the sack of Troy, is seated on an altar, where he has sought refuge. Asylum was granted to those who placed themselves under the protection of the gods in a temple. However, the character's comic mask and large belly give this theme a ridiculous aspect.

## THE FURTHER HISTORY OF ROMAN DRAMA

Like Livius Andronicus, the two Roman dramatists who followed him did not come from Rome, and Latin was not their mother tongue. We have already mentioned Naevius, who began writing plays in 235 BC and came from Oscan-speaking Campania. He was also the first author writing in Latin to deal with national Roman subjects, from the time of Romulus onwards. One of these so-called (*fabulae*) *praetextae*, meaning 'plays in the *praetexta*, the purple-bordered toga' (the garment of Roman governmental officials), took as its subject a Roman victory over a chieftain of the Gauls in the year 222 BC. Naevius also wrote tragedies on themes from Greek mythology, following the examples of Aeschylus, Sophocles and above all Euripides. It is possible that in addition he was the first to write (*fabulae*) *togatae*, 'comedies in the toga'. These comedies were performed in Italy but interestingly it seems not in Rome itself. Like his predecessor Andronicus, Naevius wrote both tragedies and comedies, whereas all the dramatists of Greece had specialized in only one of those genres.

Quintus Ennius of Calabria (239–169 BC) also wrote both comedy and tragedy, although he was far more important as a writer of tragedies. Speaking three languages, he said he had 'three hearts', *tria corda*: one

Oscan, one Greek and one Latin. Although unfortunately none of the early Roman tragedies has been preserved complete, the abundant fragments of his plays that survive give an impression of the verbal power and magical sound he could present on stage. '*O poetam egregium!*' ('O wonderful poet!'), exclaimed Cicero a century and a half later while reading Ennius, but adding that some of his contemporaries did not think as highly of the dramatist as he did.

It was in the generation of Ennius that specialization on the Greek model became more usual in Rome. Plautus (d. 184 BC), who came from Umbria, the Gaul Gaius Statius Caecilius (d. 168 BC) and Terence (Publius Terentius Afer, of African origin, d. 159 BC) wrote only comedies based on Greek originals, while other dramatists a generation later specialized in *togatae* (Titinius, Afranius and Atta; many titles of their plays but only some 600 lines in all have been preserved). On the other hand Pacuvius of Brundisium (d. around 130 BC) wrote only tragedies, as did the even more famous Lucius Accius of Umbria, known for his polished phrases. One of his sayings, spoken by a tyrant, was well known from its application to the later Caesars, '*Oderint dum metuant*' ('Let them hate me so long as they fear me' – not as neat in a modern European language as those mere three words in Accius's original Latin).

There is still no totally satisfactory explanation of the way in which the productive development of Roman drama lapsed for at least half a century after the death of Accius in 86 BC (and of the *togata* writer Atta in 77 BC). It cannot have been for lack of interest on the public's part, for the dramas of the older classics such as Ennius and Plautus were very successfully revived in new and expensive productions far grander than anything available to the original dramatists in their own time, but the creative writers of Rome were no longer writing plays. Perhaps they were now anxious to seek the approval of literary critics, and felt the popularity of drama was beneath them. (Much the same may be said of opera today; the genre is kept alive predominantly through new productions of recognized masterpieces.) Be that as it may, at the end of the first century BC the emperor Augustus tried to revive the drama through patronage, and Horace, with Virgil the greatest poet of the age, supported him – not by writing plays himself, but by giving young poets good advice in his *Art of Poetry* (*De arte poetica*). Horace suggested that thorough study of the Greek models would enable them to create a drama suitable for the educated public of Augustan Rome. These endeavours were not immediately successful; only two tragedies of the period have stood the test of time, including the famous poet Ovid's *Medea*.

Yet Horace's efforts did bear fruit, although only later. No less than the philosopher and statesman Seneca (d. 65 BC), tutor and friend of the art-loving emperor Nero, wrote a whole series of tragedies. They almost perfectly matched the criteria set out by Horace and thus, at least in terms of language and metre, the standards of the great Greek classic poets.

## THE HOLDING OF PERFORMANCES

Anyone living in a large, modern European city would have no difficulty in going to the theatre daily. Every evening, he would find either a subsidized national theatre or a commercial theatre open to him. It was very different in ancient Rome, where plays were performed only on the occasion of public state games (*ludi*) or festivals, and were part of a religious context. There were special festivals such as the *ludi votivi* (games held in fulfilment of a vow), for example on the occasion of triumphs and the consecration of temples, and above all there were *ludi funebres*, funeral games for famous people (in the religion of antiquity it was not felt that a muted atmosphere had to prevail on such occasions). The expenses of these funeral games were met by the dead person's relations, who thereby added to the family's reputation. Regular state games were organized and financed by the aediles, officers of state who still had to enter upon the higher and more exacting stages of their professional careers (as praetors and consuls); and with an eye to future elections they were well advised to prove themselves generous as holders of the games, in which the public was offered all kinds of amusements. A dramatist did not, therefore, have to beat other writers and win the approval of a jury panel, as in the drama competitions of ancient Athens, but he did have to compete with less highbrow and even more popular forms of entertainment such as the gladiatorial contests described above, or sporting competitions and similar events.

An instance is a performance of the fine comedy *The Mother-in-Law* (*Hecyra*) by Terence, which had to be broken off not, as is sometimes claimed today, because the public felt bored and walked out: what really happened was that hordes of fans stormed the theatre on hearing that tightrope-walkers and boxers were to appear there later, and fought so ruthlessly for seats that no one could pay attention to the play. On another occasion the announcement of forthcoming gladiatorial contests similarly interrupted a performance.

## DRAMATISTS, DIRECTORS, ACTORS

There was no protection of intellectual property in classical antiquity, and authors' royalties were very rare indeed. A dramatist was the only kind of Roman writer who could make any money out of his work on the open market. He sold his drama to a company of actors (*grex*), or rather to the head of the company (*dominus gregis*), who was both manager and director. He in turn was paid for staging it by the holder of the games at which it was performed. An author's popularity was thus reflected in his income. Horace later claimed that Plautus had been solely concerned to earn as much money as he could by making audiences laugh as much as possible, regardless of artistic considerations.

While most Roman authors had to be well off before they could indulge in the pleasures of writing, dramatists were usually poverty-stricken foreigners who

**117**
**Actor in the part of a silenus**
First century AD
Bronze
Ny Carlsberg Glyptotek,
Copenhagen, 2828

Sileni, half-man, half-goat creatures, were among the retinue of the god of wine, Bacchus (Greek: Dionysos). The actor is playing the part of one of these creatures. His costume is made of animal fur, while his mask has a twisted beard reminiscent of a goat. Fifth-century performances of classic Greek tragedy consisted of three serious plays and a concluding comic satyr play, in which such creatures took on the role of the chorus.

depended on their earnings, and were consequently not of very high social standing. Naevius was sent to prison for offending the noble family of the Metelli by making suggestive remarks about them in a comedy. He died in exile in Africa. Plautus is said to have worked as a labourer in a mill after failing to make his way in the wholesale trade. Only men who, like Ennius and Terence, found noble patrons were in a rather better and more independent situation.

The lowest reputation of all, however, was that of the actor (*actor* or *histrio*), because he had to earn money with his body (*corpore quaestum facere*), which the Romans regarded as a disgrace. In addition, singing and dancing in general were considered rather unrefined activities. While distinguished citizens of classical Athens had themselves been both writers and actors, the actors who appeared in Rome were professionals – as in fact they were in the Hellenistic Greece of this period – and were often slaves or freedmen. The mere fact that their manager was described as *dominus gregis*, literally 'owner of the flock', is significant. It is not true, as some scholars have claimed, that when a

free man became an actor he lost his Roman citizenship, but he did become *infamis* (meaning 'without honour') and incurred various legal disadvantages. Only one actor of the republican period succeeded in rising above this lowly status and acquiring a great reputation: Roscius, Cicero's friend, whom the dictator Sulla even made a knight. In return, however, he had to relinquish any wages. (He then taught slaves to act and put them to work for him.)

## THE THEATRE AND THE STAGE

Despite – or because of – Roman enthusiasm for the theatre, for almost two hundred years the authorities, in other respects very keen to provide popular entertainment, would not allow any permanent theatre to be built. Perhaps this was partly a matter of national pride, for the theatre was still regarded as very Greek, and Rome did not want to give any impression of being a Greek city; similarly, Roman diplomats abroad would pretend ignorance of the Greek language and use interpreters. Pompey built the *theatrum Pompeii*, named for him, only after the hellenization of Rome in the late republican period.

In the earlier republican period plays were performed on makeshift stages erected either in the circus, which already had seats available, or very often outside a temple, where there were flights of steps that could be used like tiers of seats. The later stone-built theatres had a proper auditorium (*cavea*) divided into rising wedge-shaped sections (*cunei*). The stage itself (*proscaenium* or *pulpitum*) was very broad but quite shallow, so that the action seemed almost two-dimensional. This made it easier for actors in comedy to address remarks directly to the audience. In addition, the width allowed several *dramatis personae* who were on stage at the same time to appear not to notice each other, without straining the audience's credulity too far. Since the singing and dancing chorus played little part in Roman tragedy, and even less in comedy, there was no 'dance floor' or *orchestra*, the round area in front of the stage characteristic of the Greek theatre. When an *orchestra* was built at a later date it was not round but semi-circular or horseshoe-shaped, and contained grand seats for senators. The most important theatrical innovation to be introduced on the Roman stage was the curtain (*aulaeum*), which unlike a modern theatrical curtain sank into a pit in front of the stage at the beginning of the play and rose again at the end.

The term *scaena*, from which our modern words 'scene' and 'scenic' derive, means strictly speaking not the stage itself but its backdrop, the wall that also divided it from the backstage area. Audiences could tell at once from the sets and scenery whether the play was a tragedy or a comedy. In tragedy the characters regularly acted against the façade of a royal palace, in comedy in front of a set showing two or three citizens'

118
**Roman theatre, Aspendos**
Second century AD

This building, in present-day Turkey, is the best-preserved Roman theatre we have. The backdrop of the stage (*scaenae frons*) still stands to its full height, and only the pillars that originally stood in front of it are missing. A pillared hall (*porticus*) crowns the semi-circular auditorium (*cavea*).

houses. Distinction between the two genres did not depend on whether a play had a 'tragic' ending; that meaning of the word is modern. The crucial point was the social class from which the characters came: ordinary citizens featured only in comedies, and as a result comedy was defined as a 'mirror of life'. Princes and persons of high rank appeared only in tragedies, and their lives, sufferings and deaths had different, 'tragic' dimensions. Rome, which was in essence under aristocratic rule, retained these conventions of Greek drama, and indeed they remained in force until modern times: it was not until the late eighteenth and early nineteenth centuries that such authors as the German dramatists Lessing and Schiller began writing 'bourgeois tragedies', plays in which ordinary people staked their claim to lives and sufferings as important as those of the nobility.

## PERFORMANCE ON STAGE

As in Greece, no women actors appeared in serious Roman drama; the female parts were taken by men. None the less, in the early period of the Roman theatre actors do not seem to have worn the masks usual in Greece. According to an account by Cicero, the introduction of masks was contemporaneous with the stage career of his friend Roscius, mentioned above, at the end of the second and the beginning of the first century BC. Older spectators, Cicero tells us, were sorry that they could no longer appreciate the changing expressions on the great actor's face. It seems likely, then, that the change came not because Roscius had a

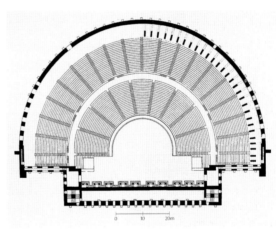

119
**Roman theatre, Aspendos: ground plan**
Second century AD

squint, as writers in antiquity claimed, but was connected with his rise in the social scale. As a Roman knight, he may have thought it more appropriate to keep his face hidden on stage, whereas he had shown it without a second thought when he was still a lowly actor. If he did in fact bring in the general custom of wearing masks in this way, it may indicate a general rise in the status of actors.

The costumes typical of certain roles were particularly important in letting audiences know what kinds of characters they were. These costumes and their attributes also gave the different types of dramas their names. The *praetexta* and *togata*, the national Roman forms of tragedy and comedy, have been mentioned above (p. 104). Besides tragedy on subjects from Greek mythology, there was the (*fabula*) *palliata*, comedy in the *pallium*, the everyday garment of Greece, which

120

**Mask**

First century BC

Terracotta

Württembergisches
Landesmuseum Stuttgart,
Antikensammlung, 2.894

Remnants of the original
painting in red on a white
ground remain in the crevices
of the face. The mask belongs
to one of the stock characters
of the New Comedy. Even in
the second century AD the
author Pollus mentioned over
forty different stock figures,
including grandfathers,
youthful heroes, slaves and
courtesans.

121 (RIGHT)

**Actor**

Third century BC

Terracotta

Museum für Kunst und
Gewerbe, Hamburg,
1917.1054

The plays of Greek New
Comedy had an enduring
influence on Graeco-
Hellenistic and Roman theatre
alike. Consequently the
traditional masks and costumes
worn by certain types of
characters remained in use over
a long period. The figure of this
actor, now in a Hamburg
museum, wears the costume
of an Attic citizen, as the knotty
staff in his right hand shows.
A similar elderly character is
shown in action on a marble
relief from Naples (cf. fig. 128).

## ROMAN COMEDY AND ITS GREEK MODEL

Roman comedy is known to us from a body of twenty
plays by Plautus and six by Terence. These works are
the oldest, great literary monuments of Rome. Their
model was the New Comedy then fashionable on the
Greek stage. The outstanding writer of such comedies
was Menander (342–291 BC), and other names were

the Romans themselves often wore in their leisure
hours (the toga is attractive but extremely impractical).

The performance probably often began with a brief
overture played by the *tibicen*, a player on the *tibia*.
This instrument, with its reed or double reed, resembled a modern clarinet or oboe, but the sound volume
must have been more like that of a saxophone, since
the *tibia* was solely responsible for all the incidental
music, and in particular had to accompany the arias
(*cantica*) and the verses spoken to music like recita-
tives. It was probably also required to play brief interludes between acts when the stage was empty. The
divisions between acts were not themselves as clearly
distinct in early Roman drama as in the Greek model,
since the chorus that sang between the acts of Greek
plays was usually absent in Rome. Not until the time of
Seneca and his tragedies was the play again divided
into five acts with four choral songs between them, in
accordance with the precepts of Horace.

We still know the names of the composers who
wrote for the comedy writers Plautus and Terence (the
music was 'composed out', i.e. elaborated from a basic
tonic structure). They are slave names, as one would
expect. We have no kind of musical notation, for the
plays are preserved as texts, not stage manuscripts. The
musicians of antiquity, unlike the writers and composers of today, do not seem to have hoped that their
works would be immortal. Yet the music was obviously specially suited to every play, and we can still
deduce its rhythm from the texts of the songs. Cicero
mentions musical experts who recognized the music
for Pacuvius's *Antiope* as soon as the first note was
played on the *tibia*.

Diphilos, Philemon and Apollodoros. Their comedies
took ordinary Greek family life as a subject and
reflected bourgeois existence. A famous saying ran: 'O
Menander! O life! Which of you copied the other?'
These plays were not really at home in the city of
Rome, which was still by Greek standards somewhat
unsophisticated, but they did present a world that the
Romans could imagine, and one that fascinated them
just because it differed from theirs in many ways.
Menander, who with Homer was probably the ancient

Greek writer most read in modern Europe, was known for centuries only through Roman adaptations of his works. Not until the twentieth century did finds of papyri in the Egyptian desert restore to us a series of his plays almost complete, or with large parts preserved, enabling us to form a better idea of him.

His comedies were very elegant in form. In portraying his characters he started out from certain stock figures (the stern father, the mild father; the impudent slave, the faithful slave; and so on), but he avoided cliché. His plays were set in a world ruled by the capricious goddess of fortune, Tyche (Fortuna), but it was a world in which human beings often suffered adversity through their own fault, instead of showing consideration and feeling sympathy for others. Before Cicero coined the word 'humanity' (*humanitas*) two hundred years later, no other author wrote with such warmth and sympathy of mankind: 'How amiable is man when he is only human!' runs a well-known phrase of his.

However, there was plenty to laugh at in Menander, too: human weaknesses, and in particular that most dramatically productive weakness of all, love (*eros*). 'Not a piece by the entertaining Menander is without love ...', says Ovid, who certainly knew what he was talking about (*fabula iucundi nulla est sine amore Menandri*). Ovid adds 'and yet he is commonly read by boys and girls'. That was not surprising, for Menander kept eroticism within the bounds of decency, and in line with traditional ideas of morality, even though he depicted high-class prostitution in the characters of the hetaerae, or courtesans, although not, surprisingly, the traditional Greek love of men for boys.

In Menander, as in his Greek colleagues and the Roman writers who adapted their work, the action regularly turns on the story of a pair of lovers. The man is middle class and of course usually young (*adulescens*). The woman is a middle-class girl herself (*virgo*), very occasionally a young married woman (*uxor*) – in both cases decency forbade her actual appearance on stage – or a hetaera (*meretrix*, literally 'woman who earns money') from the outlying areas of Greece. This character is in the hands of a pimp who exploits her (*leno*), or she is being kept by a man, or (less usually) she has a household of her own. The action of the plot runs to a pattern in which the lovers are separated by various different people or events – hostile fathers, unscrupulous pimps, pirates, misunderstandings, pregnancies outside marriage and so forth – but in the end they are reunited. Single middle-class lovers marry, young married couples make up their quarrels, or the courtesan enters into a long-term relationship with her lover.

An important part in the reunion of the lovers is played by intrigues chiefly concerned with acquiring money or getting rid of unwanted rivals, and often devised and carried out by ingenious slaves. The feature known as 'recognition' (*anagnorisis*) also promotes the happy ending: as a rule a supposed courtesan is revealed to be after all a respectable girl who by some miracle has remained untouched and is therefore eligible as a wife. These plots may be improbable and full of coincidences, with the goddess of fortune playing a large part, but the behaviour of the characters is very human. The obligatory love story does not by any means occupy the entire foreground of these comedies; there are also timeless conflicts between fathers

**122  Head of Menander**
Lived 342–293 BC
Marble, AD 30–50
Museum für Kunst und Gewerbe, Hamburg, 1964.327/St. 207

Menander, the most famous writer of the New Comedy, came from Athens. In the Athenian festivals, which were also competitions, his plays repeatedly won prizes. This portrait was done in the Roman period from a statue erected to the dramatist after his death at the scene of his successes, the theatre of Dionysos in Athens.

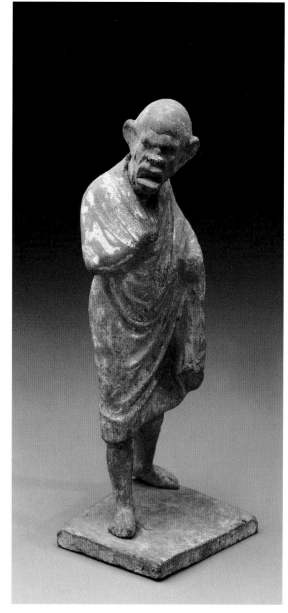

**123**
**Orator**
Second half of the third
century BC
Terracotta
Museum für Kunst und
Gewerbe, Hamburg, 1898.52

This grotesque figure has
assumed the attitude of an
orator. The exaggerated features
are in comic contrast to what
may be a serious speech. This
was probably an actor in the
New Comedy, if we assume
that the figure is wearing a
mask. However, it is possible
to interpret it as pure caricature
with no direct link to the stage.
Such distorted images were
popular in the Hellenized Egypt
of the third century BC.

considers himself irresistible and is indeed positively megalomaniac on the subject. One is inclined to suspect that Plautus went further than his Greek model in introducing this characteristic into the figure of his central military character and the title of the play itself. At the time of the great Punic War, which had plunged Rome into the deepest crisis of its history, he may have intended to give his piece a piquant touch of topicality. When the soldier boasts of his own prowess he uses the vocabulary of Roman heroes known to us in particular from inscriptions dealing with the Scipio family – a Scipio did in fact defeat Carthage soon after the première of the play.

Admittedly Plautus refrained from introducing any further topical relevance into the play. The object of his mockery is not the Roman consul doing his patriotic duty by waging war. Instead, and as usual retaining the background of his Greek original, his butt is a professional soldier, an Ephesian mercenary captain with the grandiloquent name, invented by Plautus, of Pyrgopolynices ('conqueror of tower and city'). He is recruiting soldiers for King Seleucus, but rests on his supposed laurels in order to get all the enjoyment he can from the city of Ephesus, which as he puts it is famed 'for leisure and for women'. It was perfectly permissible to laugh at this man and his way of life, only too Greek by Roman standards – *pergraecor*, to revel in the Greek fashion, was the term used when someone spent the night indulging in wine, women and song – and a good many of Plautus's comic effects in general derive from mockery of Greek oddities.

## THE *MILES GLORIOSUS*, PART 1:
AN EARLY CASE OF BRAIN-WASHING

However, one must look above all at the love story, which is the driving force behind the plot, as it almost always is in such comedies, at least on the surface. The lovers are the young Athenian Pleusicles ('hero at sea') and the girl he loves, Philocomasium ('party-loving girl'). As with all the lovers in Plautus, and in contrast to Menander's young lovers, Pleusicles cuts a poor figure – Plautus and his Roman audience obviously thought the fuss the Greeks made about love, not to mention the money they would expend in pursuit of it, was particularly funny. The girl is a beautiful courtesan looking for a permanent relationship or relationships. She first belonged to Pleusicles, but has been abducted during his temporary absence by Pyrgopolinices and taken by sea to Ephesus. The abduction was against her own will, although with the connivance of her mother acting as a bawd.

The aim of the plot is therefore to restore the girl to her former lover, and he has already come to Ephesus to find her when the play opens. The goddess Fortuna or Tyche has given the lover two great advantages: first, his former slave Palaestrio ('man with the wrestler's tricks'), who is still devoted to him and is a

and sons, masters and slaves, husbands and wives, pimps and their customers, soldiers and civilians, or old and young courtesans.

## THE EARLIEST ROMAN COMIC HERO

To understand how the Romans handled these originally Greek plots, let us look at the earliest work of Latin comedy – indeed, of Latin literature in general – that can be dated: *Miles gloriosus*, 'The Braggart', 'The Swaggerer' or literally 'The Boastful Soldier', written for the stage by Titus Maccius Plautus (possibly the writer's full name) in the year 205 BC, and perhaps based on a model by Menander.

The boasting of the eponymous military hero, which is very amusingly presented, especially in the brilliant opening scene, plays no part in the far from pacifist action of the play. Rather, the plot is based on the soldier's particular boastfulness in matters of love, for he

The first intrigue, then, consists in preventing the guard Sceledrus from revealing all. Palaestrio does everything he can to intimidate his fellow-slave, subjecting him to a kind of brain-washing operation – probably the first known to us in literature – to persuade him that he never saw what he really did see at all. Palaestrio's structure of lies rests chiefly on the invention of a twin sister for Philocomasium, said to have just arrived in the company of her own lover to visit her sister. That, most importantly of all, explains the incriminating kiss. Unfortunately Sceledrus, whose mind works slowly, still believes the evidence of his own eyes, and an elaborate scene has to be staged to convince him that he is mistaken. Philocomasium comes out of one door as herself and out of the other as her twin sister – a trick made possible by the hole in the internal wall. The incredulous harem guard physically attacks her, but at last, accused of impudent slander and of insulting the foreign lady, and threatened with severe punishments, he becomes mentally confused, decides he cannot trust his own eyes and begs forgiveness. Although it is generously granted, he flees the house in alarm and is thus out of action for the second part of the play.

124 (LEFT)
**Mask**
First century BC
Terracotta
Württembergisches
Landesmuseum Stuttgart,
Antikensammlung, 2.894

This New Comedy mask represents a brothel-keeper.

125 (BELOW)
**Mask**
First century BC
Marble
Lent by the Syndics of the
Fitzwilliam Museum,
Cambridge, GR 10.1865

This comic mask, from a relief, was that of the slave, a very important stock character in the New Comedy. Asymmetrical eyebrows enabled the mask to assume different expressions, depending on the spectator's angle of vision.

central character in the play, happens through an outrageous coincidence to be in the soldier's service. Second, the soldier's next-door neighbour, a *bon viveur* called Periplectomenus ('man who embraces all'), is an old friend of the family of Pleusicles. Pleusicles can therefore stay with Periplectomenus, next door to his beloved, and the soldier, under threat both at home and from next door, is at a hopeless disadvantage. But for all his ridiculous airs he is a rich and influential man, and represents a real threat to the lovers until the play is almost over.

The girl has to be liberated, or re-abducted, without too much obvious illegality, which would be dangerous, since as a hetaera she is contractually bound to the soldier. Her rescue is achieved by two intrigues that in essence occupy the whole play. As almost always in Plautus, they are both engineered by a cunning character, the slave Palaestrio, acting as a double agent or the servant of two masters. In the first intrigue the lover and his supporters are on the defensive. Out of friendship, although illegally, Pleusicles's host Periplectomenus has made a hole through the wall into the house next door, so that the lovers can get through it and visit each other. However, it looks as if this cunning trick and the whole planned rescue may fail, for the slave Sceledrus ('squatter on his haunches'), whom the soldier has set to watch the girl as a harem guard, happens to have looked down from the rooftop and seen his master's mistress kissing a strange young man in the house next door – what a scandal that will cause if the soldier finds out! And how unfortunate it will be for him, the negligent guard, if the soldier learns of it not from him but from other people.

111

Reading Plautus over two thousand years later, one is amused not only by the cunning with which the artful string-puller Palaestrio finally outwits his simple-minded fellow slave but also by the skill with which the writer lets his audience into the secret of the intrigue and the whole *quiproquo*. Obviously the Romans were not yet very well accustomed to such dramatic subtleties of deception, and the crucial point on which the intrigue turns, the hole in the wall, could not be shown on stage, since the scene had to be set in the open air outside the house. Plautus was therefore clearly afraid that the audience might fall for the deception themselves, along with Sceledrus. He keeps dropping hints that of course there is really only a single girl, who appears now in one place and now in

courtesan called Acroteleutium ('best of all') pretends to be the wife of Periplectomenus, the soldier's neighbour. The soldier is persuaded, particularly by her ostentatious gift of a ring, that she is desperately in love with him. Amorously inflamed (for where the first part of the drama dealt with emotions of fear, the second deals with desire), the soldier is now anxious to be rid of his former mistress Philocomasium. He is even ready to send her back to Athens with the slave Palaestrio and a financial settlement, since he is a snob and prefers a respectable married woman to a hired courtesan. So far so good.

But what happens when the deception comes to light, as it inevitably must in the end? Plautus has provided for that contingency, too. Philocomasium leaves

126 (RIGHT)

**Head of an actor**

Early second century BC
Terracotta
Museum für Kunst und
Gewerbe Hamburg, 1981.409

This head with its mask originally belonged to a statuette of a slave in the New Comedy, a stock character identical with the one in fig. 125; in spite of the small scale, all the essential features can be seen.

127 (FAR RIGHT)

**Mask**

Second to first century BC
Terracotta
Württembergisches
Landesmuseum Stuttgart,
Antikensammlung, 2.835

This mask does not conform entirely to any of the known stock characters. The huge (damaged) ears and bulbous forehead suggest grotesque caricatures from the Hellenistic period (cf. fig. 123).

another in different costumes, and to reinforce those hints he has even turned what was obviously an improvisation in the Greek original – the invention of the twin sister – into an elaborate plan worked out on stage by Palaestrio in a long scene of pantomime. The audience is told about the plan in advance, so that they can keep up with it.

## THE *MILES GLORIOSUS*, PART 2:
### ENTRAPMENT OF THE LADY-KILLER

The same process is at work in the second part of the play, where the supporters of Pleusicles, who only now makes his appearance, go on the offensive to rescue Philocomasium. Again, the new developments of the intrigue are carefully explained in advance, and parts of it are rehearsed on stage so that even an inattentive audience could hardly fail to grasp it. An Ephesian

with her lover Pleusicles, who disguises himself as a seaman and spirits her away to board a ship in a scene of almost Hitchcockian suspense, for up to the moment of departure they risk premature discovery of the deception, in time for the soldier to retaliate. Once they have gone, the boastful lady-killer is lured into the house next door to visit his new mistress, who claims to have separated from her husband, and falls into the disastrous trap set for him. The alleged cuckolded husband rushes in and has the soldier dragged on stage; he makes it clear that the man who has dishonoured him will be deprived of his most vital weapon by castration. Drooping already, and struggling pitifully, the soldier is threatened by Periplectomenus's cook with a terrible knife, but eventually buys his freedom. He is exposed to general ridicule, and on learning from his slaves when they get back from the harbour how his former mistress has tricked him, he can no longer contemplate revenge. In a sudden fit of unmotivated repentance, he pronounces the moral epilogue of the play:

My finding is, 'A true bill.'

If other adulterers were so greeted, adulterers
would be fewer here

and their appetite for such affairs less. Home we go.

Give us your applause!

This early play by Plautus, which has its *longueurs* and is far from being his best, is none the less characteristic of his later work in many respects. His treatment or rather non-treatment of erotic elements in the second part is very typical. While Menander presented love affairs in a distinctly sentimental light, everything in Plautus strikes a comic, even grotesque note. The audience is not invited to take any particular interest in the fate of the lovers, or feel for them in their hopes and fears and the joy of their reunion. In fact, Plautus never wrote a play where a reunited pair of lovers with whom the audience can identify is on stage at the end.

The one big love scene in the *Miles gloriosus*, the soldier's encounter with the apparently enamoured wife of his neighbour, in reality the hetaera Acroteleutium, is based on pure deception. The soldier, in his overweening vanity and in order to heighten his erotic market value, acts coyly at first, although he is hot with lust for the courtesan. She herself mocks him by pretending not to see him at first, and announcing that she will break down the door of his house in her amorous frenzy. Then she claims that, since love has given her a wonderful sense of smell, she can tell by smell alone that he is not at home but on stage, and when she finally sees him, she pretends to be dazzled. Her lady's maid has to woo him for her. No wonder the soldier, flattered by these theatricals, promises that he 'will not loathe her as I do the others', as he puts it, but will 'alleviate' her lovesickness.

Here and in his other plays Plautus carefully deprived his love scenes of any depth of feeling that might invite sympathy. Even in his most serious passages, he makes his effect through exaggeration and the occasional metaphorical use of language, or sometimes by means of ironic asides as third persons comment on the dialogue. Above all, he wants to make his audiences laugh, and consequently, unlike Menander who always observed the proprieties, he sometimes includes smutty jokes (the subject of homosexuality, usually excluded from Roman drama, may also feature). Whole scenes, for instance in the particularly risqué *Casina*, strike a note of indecency. (It can be shown that the scene in which the boastful soldier narrowly avoids castration was not present in that form in the Greek original of the *Miles gloriosus*.) It is particularly interesting in this context that Plautus dwelt on plot elements involving courtesans in his comedies more than his Greek models did. The second part of the *Miles gloriosus* depends largely on the sometimes

suggestive scenes with the hetaera, and in the *Pseudo-lus* there is a scene that is usually called 'parade of courtesans'. But there was nothing comparable to the Greek hetaerae in the Rome of Plautus, only some relatively primitive brothels. The Roman audience for these plays sought not so much the mirror of their own lives, in the classic definition of comedy quoted above, but an image of Greek life which they relished for its exoticism and which they could also mock.

Much the same is true of the presentation of slaves, particularly when they are involved in intrigues. Palaestrio, who hoodwinks the ridiculous and unsympathetic soldier, behaves with relative decorum. Many other comedies, for instance Plautus's *Mostellaria* (*The Haunted House*), present dignified fathers of families being despised and fooled by their slaves, who regularly outdo them in cunning and get away scot-free at the end of the play. Of course this does not reflect real conditions in Rome, where strict domestic discipline was the rule; it is a distorted image of the situation in Greece. The masters of Athenian slaves were known to have allowed them considerable liberties, and the plays of the New Comedy reflected that attitude. But it seems to have been only in Plautus that the boisterously high-spirited slave comes to dominate the stage with his bold intrigues, showing himself superior to his master in many ways. This is a topsy-turvy world that does not correspond to the realities of either Greece or Rome, but obviously arose from a need to find release – at least in the enjoyment of a comic play – from the stressful life of a serious Roman citizen. The foreign background of the subjects made that release possible, and so they were retained. It is significant that in the less frequent *fabulae togatae*, comedies performed in the costume of the Romans, slaves were never depicted as cleverer than their masters.

## MUSIC AND DANCE IN PLAUTUS

The most noticeable difference between Plautus and his Greek predecessors, however, is in the setting of his plays to music. Menander's comedies were almost entirely spoken, with occasional incidental music on the *aulos* (corresponding to the Roman *tibia*), while the chorus performed only brief interludes between the acts. As far as we know, Menander wrote no texts for the chorus at all, but left the chorus itself to choose songs from its own repertory. Plautus, on the other hand, added so much music in his comedies that they almost became operettas or musicals. Only about a third of his plays have no music. The rest included either recitation to musical accompaniment at emotional high points in the text or actual singing (as we can deduce from the verse metre). The *Miles gloriosus* is not typical, for there is singing in only one scene, when Palaestrio is negotiating with both his master the soldier and with the pretty maid of the supposedly enamoured wife of the soldier's neighbour, speaking

alternately and separately to both of them. Both the strong metrical rhythm of the verse, and the stage directions for movement that can be gleaned from the text, suggest that these interchanges were arranged as a formal dance scene – an idea that could present a challenge to modern composers and choreographers. Otherwise, the piece confines itself to recitative with background music, whereas the later comedies of Plautus are full of songs, duets and ensembles, with attractive rhythmic variations that always fit expressively to the text. When Plautus died, according to the epigraph on his tombstone, the mourners included *numeri innumeri*, 'unnumbered numbers' (i.e. countless measures of verse), all pitifully lamenting the loss of their great music master.

There are various theories for the origin of this kind of musical adaptation: it may derive from the songs of Greek 'Old Comedy', from an increase in the musical

element in later Hellenistic drama or from native traditions of musical stage plays. But it is clear that this preference for songs over spoken monologue must have met a need felt by the Roman public. Although singers and actors alike were of low social standing in Rome, their art at least was enjoyed no less than in Greece.

## FROM PLAUTUS TO TERENCE

We move from Plautus to his most outstanding successor, Terence, who died only a quarter of a century after him in 159 BC, still very young, for he was only twenty-five or thirty-five at his death. Yet it is like moving to another world, or as a scholar has cogently put it, from the fairground into the church. Outwardly, the same kinds of plots and characters appear in Terence's works, which comprise six comedies performed between 166 and 160 BC: they contain young men in love, beautiful courtesans, stern fathers and so forth. But the treatment is very different indeed. The bright, boisterous, loud and farcical aspects of Plautus are almost entirely gone. The effect of Terence's comedies on stage is soft and muted. Music has now lost its dominant position (although it is still more important than in Menander). The plots, which in Plautus often had a tendency to stray into the episodic, pursuing comedy for its own sake and disregarding the structure of the play as a whole, are now strict and often perfect in their formal construction. The conduct of the characters is decorous. Young men show tender sensitivity, courtesans are often positively noble-minded, and fathers are less absurd and above all never in love (a situation presented by Plautus as especially ridiculous). Sometimes even a pimp, to Plautus the lowest of the low, if he is too mercilessly fooled by the young people in the play, becomes a sympathetic figure or at least arouses pity.

This is indeed another world, and the real outside world had changed, too. In particular, the victory of the Romans over Perseus of Macedonia in 169 BC brought a new wave of Greek education and civilization to Rome. The man who had conquered Perseus, Aemilius Paullus, was himself a lover of Greek culture. He surrounded himself with Greek philosophers, rhetoricians and philologists, even Greek sculptors and painters as tutors for his children (one of whom was the younger Scipio, later to be a friend of Terence). The advent of these higher forms of Greek intellectual culture went hand in hand with the Hellenization of other areas of life through Greek gastronomy, medicine and the culture of the symposia (banqueting), together with the acceptance of hetaerae and pederasty.

In this new world Hellenism lost the attraction of exoticism that it still unmistakably held in Plautus. With that development, however, came an opportunity for writers to concern themselves more closely and seriously than in Plautus with the psychological and humane aspects of Greek comedy, particularly the comedy of Menander (whom Terence, more than Plautus, revered above other writers), presenting on stage the eternal problems encountered by ordinary people, in Rome as elsewhere, in their marriages, their family lives and with their neighbours. By suppressing all excessively Greek or Attic local colour, Terence, who could quite well be played in modern dress today, tried to import even more of the true spirit of Menander into Rome. Later, like Menander himself, Terence was much studied in schools, and in the early modern period students learned Latin, particularly spoken Latin, from his plays. However, he was no slavish imitator of his model Menander. It was Terence who introduced a subsidiary pair of lovers into comedy, a feature that became almost a cliché in his work (it is a convention familiar to modern theatre-goers chiefly from operetta), and in general he did much to enrich

the plot with lively elements. Even in his lifetime, critics blamed him for 'contaminating' (contaminare) the Greek originals in his adaptations. He skilfully defended himself against this accusation in the prologues to his plays, pointing out that he was doing no more than Plautus and Naevius had done before him. It is more difficult to dismiss another criticism levelled against him by Caesar, who had a good literary education and said that, for all the linguistic subtlety Terence was generally admitted to possess, he lacked the *vis comica*, the 'power of comedy', and was only 'half' a Menander (*dimidiatus*). Caesar can only have meant by this that Terence was rather more serious than his Greek model, and there was considerably less to laugh at in his plays. However, no one disputed his mastery of characterization.

## AN UNUSUAL COMEDY – THE *HECYRA*

The greatest difference between Terence and Plautus is in the relationship they try to foster between the action on stage and the audience. Plautus ensured that his style of presentation, for instance when his characters directly address the spectators, set a distance between them and the course of the action. Conversely, Terence was anxious to make the spectators identify with his characters and feel moved by them.

He introduces suspense into his subjects, too, in a manner that not only affects the plot – for it is obvious well in advance roughly how the play will end – but sometimes, and in an unusual way for the literature of classical antiquity, also changes the audience's perception of what has gone before. His most adventurous play in terms of form is the *Hecyra* (*Mother-in-Law*), which was successful only on its third performance (in 160 BC). In this play neither the audience nor the characters know that the young husband Pamphilus raped his wife Philumena before their marriage, unrecognized by her, while he was drunk. The play begins, while Pamphilus is away, with the surprising revelation that his young wife has left the house of her mother-in-law (the eponymous heroine) to go back to her own mother. On his return her husband Pamphilus learns the partial truth at the same time as the audience: Philumena is giving birth to a child who, she thinks, cannot be her husband's, since for the first two months of their marriage, when he was still in love with a beautiful courtesan, he never touched her – a fact that, in turn, is known only to the young couple and the wife's mother. In the first part of the play, then, Philumena tries to keep her husband Pamphilus in the dark about the birth of her illegitimate child; in the second half Pamphilus tries to hide the existence of the baby from the rest of the world – in Philumena's own interests, he tells himself. Injured in his masculine pride, he feels he cannot possibly stay with the wife whom he now, despite everything, loves dearly, but he wants to spare her the shame of having brought an illegitimate

128 **Relief with a scene from a comedy**
First century BC
Marble
Museo Archeologico Nazionale di Napoli, 6687

This famous relief shows a typical New Comedy situation: a young man is on his way home from a tavern. Since he is drunk, he is leaning on his slave, gesticulating with his right hand, and singing a song to the accompaniment of the girl flute-player. Disaster looms in the shape of his father, who has come out of his ornately decorated house with a stick to receive his son with a beating. A second man is trying to restrain him. Today it cannot be said whether this scene was from some particular play or of a general nature, for most of the texts of the New Comedy are lost. Menander alone wrote over a hundred works, of which only one has been preserved in anything like a complete state.

child into the world. Pure chance brings enlightenment. Pamphilus had given the courtesan with whom he was in love the ring that he took from Philumena when he raped her. Recognition of the ring makes all clear: it was the husband himself who raped his future wife, and now all is well.

In this play Terence wrote a work unique in the literature of antiquity, one in which the spectators know only as much at any time as the protagonist Pamphilus, so that they will inevitably to some extent feel and suffer with him. The attraction of the drama depends on this feature and on the extraordinary subtlety of Ter-

**129**
**Mask**
Third to second century BC
Terracotta
Lent by the Syndics of the
Fitzwilliam Museum,
Cambridge, GR 67.1984

This New Comedy terracotta
mask could be worn during
theatrical performances.
The holes in the ears would
have taken a strap or ribbon
to tie it in place.

ence's characterization, for the amount of action on stage is minimal. While in the Greek original of the play (by Apollodoros) the recognition of the ring by the mother of the violated girl was the dramatic culmination of the action – as we know from an account dating from classical antiquity – Terence merely reports the incident; he was interested only in the psychological reactions to it of those involved. Particularly surprising is his elimination, in his treatment of the story, of the moral message present, in all probability, in the Greek play: Pamphilus has acted very badly in waxing self-righteously indignant over his wife's involuntary indiscretion, forgetting his own pre-marital adventure. Menander's play *Epitrepontes* (*Arbitrators*), which is similar in this respect, ended with expressions

of remorse from the young husband; in Terence the audience becomes aware of the outrageous nature of his behaviour only belatedly and in retrospect, if at all. Since moralizing was a national passion among the Romans, we may perhaps suppose that here Terence (who is said to have died on a study tour of his beloved Greece) was trying to be even more Greek than the Greeks.

He did not continue further artistically down the *Hecyra* route; his subsequent comedies, of which the *Adelphoe*, dealing with the problem of education, is rightly the most famous, approached the more familiar type again. The *Eunuchus*, probably the most frequently performed of his plays, has elements of slapstick, as the title itself suggests.

## ATELLAN FARCES AND MIMES

The *togata*, performed in Roman costume, belongs to the period after the death of Terence in 159 BC. He was the last of the great writers of *palliatae*. He was also closest of them all to the Greek originals, and is perhaps the most undervalued of classical Roman writers today. The master of the *togata* – known to us now only from some four hundred single lines – was most probably Afranius. It is said that like Terence, whom he admired, he was particularly close to Menander, and transplanted plots modelled on his plays to Italian soil. However, he took the liberty of using the love of men for boys as a major element in his plots, and in this he too was to some extent more Greek than the Greeks.

After Afranius other forms of comic drama began to appear in the literary sphere. One of them was the Atellan farce (*fabula Atellana*), so called from its origin in the town of Atella near Capua. Such farces were coarse and rustic in content. They were originally introduced into Rome in the Oscan language, probably in the early third century BC – that is, some time before Greek dramatic forms. Typically, they contained four stock characters, each with a comic double consonant in his name: *Maccus*, the fool; *Bucco*, the babbler; *Pappus*, the grandfather; *Dossennus*, the glutton or doctor. This dramatic form developed next as Latin amateur theatricals performed by Roman youths (much as rustic farces are often played today by amateur groups). To appear in Atellan farces was not considered any disgrace: all the actors wore masks. At first the plays were improvised; then, around the end of the second and beginning of the first century BC, they developed into literary works in verse. The main writers of such plays were Lucius Pomponius of Bologna and Novius, who between them have left us over three hundred extant lines of verse. The language remained plebeian and often indecent. It is interesting that the Atellan farces were used as humorous epilogues to tragedy, a kind of counterpart to the Greek satyr plays that concluded a trilogy of tragedies in Athens, and also tended to be obscene. There were obviously no real Latin satyr plays (although Horace laid down rules for such plays, probably in the hope that some dramatist would eventually fill the gap – a hope that remained unfulfilled).

Another form of comedy is to be distinguished from the Atellan farce: this was the *mimus*, originally from Hellenized Sicily, and probably first performed in Greek when it came to Rome in the third century BC. Its subjects involved the realistic and faithful portrayal of the everyday life of the lower classes, particularly in towns. Adultery loomed large, whereas it was not a subject of comedy proper. Its claims to organized dra-

matic structure were modest. Cicero describes the end of a *mimus* thus: 'If no one can think of a way to end the play, someone makes his escape, there is a clatter of castanets and the curtain comes up.' The actors never wore masks, and female roles were taken by attractive women – an unusual development on the stage of classical antiquity. At the spring festival of the Floralia, regularly held from 173 BC onwards, it was even customary for the actresses in these mimes to take off their clothes by public demand at the end of the play.

Around the middle of the first century BC the *mimus*, by now written in verse, had become a literary form and superseded the Atellan farce as the comic epilogue to a tragedy. Two writers of mimes were particu-

larly famous: a Syrian called Publilius Syrus, who acted in his own plays, and the Roman knight Decimus Laberius. When Syrus once challenged all the dramatists of Rome to a competition in improvisation (probably at the games held in the year 46 BC), the dictator Caesar, as if in derision of conventional Roman morality, urged Laberius to take the stage. We still have the prologue to his piece, in which he laments having left his house as a knight in order to return as a mime without honour (that is, having lost the rank of knight). In the play itself he is said to have avenged himself in the lines: 'Citizens, forward! We give up our liberty!' and, ominously in view of the coming Ides of March, 'He needs must fear many whom many fear!' whereupon all eyes were turned on Caesar. However, the dictator was gracious enough to pretend he had not heard, and immediately and publicly restored Laberius to his former rank by giving him the golden ring of a knight as well as a gift of money. We know that in mimes comments that would normally have been daring (*mimorum dicta*) had something of the satirical function of modern political cabaret, and continued to do so in the imperial period, when the mime flourished. It is also known that the reaction of the public to such remarks was carefully noted.

## THE PANTOMIME

The *pantomimus*, however, seems to have been more popular than any other kind of stage entertainment in the imperial period. Pantomime was an expressive dance said to have been introduced to Rome in the year 22 BC, but this probably means only that it was first given then in what later became its standard classic form, one that is linked to the names of the two great pantomime actors Pylades and Bathyllus. Apart from the fact that performance was in dumb show, the pantomime actor had little in common with what we understand by a mime or pantomime artist today – an actor like Marcel Marceau who performs little scenes from everyday life, usually of a comic nature. Instead, the pantomime actor was a man – later sometimes a woman – dancing solo to a poetic text and taking different roles. The text was sung by a chorus to the accompaniment of a small ensemble of stringed, wind and percussion instruments. The texts, mainly in Greek – and the famous pantomime actors themselves regularly came from the east of the empire – were sometimes comic, but only at first; later, the subjects were almost always serious and tragic. They dealt not only with stories from Greek mythology but with historical themes, and sometimes even incidents from the early history of Rome (for instance the tales of Dido and Turnus from Virgil's famous *Aeneid*). They might be taken from an existing work of poetry or tailor-made as a new libretto designed for a certain dancer. Since some of the most popular pantomime actors were paid enormous sums, writers had a chance of additional

130
**Silenus mask**
Second century AD
Marble
Museum für Kunst und
Gewerbe Hamburg, 1999.106

This mask, from Campania or possibly from the city of Rome, was purely decorative. It could never have been worn because of its great weight and the absence of any eyeholes. The pointed ears show that this is a silenus figure, half man, half goat. As companions of the god of wine Bacchus (Greek: Dionysos), sileni were considered to bring luck. Consequently such masks were popular for the decoration of houses.

**131 Relief of an actor**

Marble, last quarter of the first century BC

Staatliche Kunstsammlungen Dresden, Skulpturensammlung,
ZV 1914

This famous relief depicts an actor, identifiable from his long
chiton with sleeves and the built-up soles of his shoes (*cothurnae*).
The ivy wreath with its band, the animal skin over his chest, and
the thyrsus wand show that he played the part of Bacchus.
Beside him are a boy playing the flute and a Maenad, a woman
from the retinue of the god of wine. The rocky chasm, the statue
of a god almost completely missing from the column on the right,
and the curtain indicate that this is a sacred precinct. The mime,
whose face shows portrait-like features, may have won an actors'
competition as he carries a wreath of flowers round his body.
Alternatively, he may have been the head of a guild of actors who
was also a priest of the wine god Bacchus.

earnings as librettists. A famous instance was the fee
received by the poet Statius, a master of the epic form
who did not usually write for payment, for a version of
*Agave* which he sold to the famous pantomime actor
Paris; the sight of the mother of Pentheus dancing in
Dionysian ecstasy with the head of her son torn from
his body must have made an effect comparable with
Richard Strauss's *Salome*.

These pantomime artists, assisted only by changes of
masks and costumes, had to dance the parts of several
different interacting characters – in the story of the
Judgement of Paris, for instance, the three rival god-
desses and the appropriate reactions of Paris to each.
They filled not only recital halls but the huge theatres
of the Roman empire with such performances, holding
audiences enthralled. Their art, as in the dance of the
ancient world in general, must have depended less on
the movement of the legs (usually invisible) than on
the expressive ability of their arms and hands, and was

probably superior to anything we can imagine in dance today. It called for an artistic perfection of the body that could be achieved only by strict dieting and an ascetic training programme. The enthusiasm aroused among the women spectators in particular, and not just the young women in the audience, seems to have been equal to anything the fans of 1960s pop music showed for the stars they worshipped. 'When the supple Bathyllus dances the part of the gesticulating Leda,' mocked the satirist Juvenal, thinking of course of Leda's intimate relations with the swan, 'Tuccia cannot contain herself; your Apulian maiden heaves a sudden and longing cry of ecstasy, as though she were in a man's arms.' If there were no games for a long time, he added, the fans would caress the masks and underwear of the dancer they adored. It is strange, for this and other reasons, that no modern dancer has yet tried breathing new life into the fine artistic genre of Roman pantomime, which integrated as it did music, dance and poetry.

## SENECA'S TRAGEDIES – FORGOTTEN DRAMAS

It seems likely that classical tragedy, a flourishing form of art in the old republic, fell out of public favour in the imperial period and was cast into the shade by these quasi-tragedies in dance, for it can be no coincidence that our sources, which speak with such enthusiasm of the *mimus* and *pantomimus*, have less to say about tragedy. However, ten complete tragedies bearing the name of the great philosopher Seneca are extant, and in the opinion of scholars today eight of them are undoubtedly genuine. Seneca, therefore, together with Plautus and Terence, is one of only three Roman dramatists about whom we really know much today. But while as a rule people have heard of the works of those two writers of comedy, the tragedies of Seneca hardly feature at all in our general knowledge. This is surprising, since they exerted a strong influence – often stronger than that of Greek drama – on the greatest dramatists of the early modern period such as Shakespeare and Racine (and it can sometimes still be detected in later writers like Anouilh). The main reason for this ignorance may be sought in the nineteenth century and the literary pronouncements of the witty German writer August Wilhelm von Schlegel, famous as the translator of Shakespeare; many of his verdicts were wide of the mark, but they were brilliantly expressed and are therefore still accepted today.

On Seneca Schlegel commented that he wrote not for the stage but for the school of rhetoric, an opinion still echoed by at least some modern critics. In fact Seneca's literary style, like that of most writers of the imperial period, did bear some similarity to that of Roman teachers of rhetoric. He not only has a tendency to powerful hyperbole, particularly in presenting anything frightful and terrible, but also likes short and often paradoxical punchlines with startling antitheses, for instance *scelus aliqua tutum, nulla securum tulit* ('Criminals are often secure, but never free of care'). In addition, he uses circumlocutions for horrors that make them seem even more horrifying. When Thyestes, on learning that he has eaten his own sons, breaks into wails of despair and is about to beat his breast in the conventional fashion, he refrains out of consideration for the dead whom he has consumed, with the words *parcamus umbris* ('let us spare the shades'). Such a macabre punchline is not, of course, to everyone's taste, but it cannot be said to lack dramatic effect.

It is often thought today that a number of incidents in Seneca's tragedies show they were not written for the stage or intended to be performed on it at all. However, although such senes as the display of a man's entrails in *Oedipus*, the reassembly of the body parts of the dismembered Hippolytus like a kind of jigsaw puzzle in *Phaedra*, or the moment when the eponymous heroine of *Medea* stabs her two children before the eyes of the audience and then flings them at her husband Jason's feet may go beyond anything in Greek tragedy, modern productions have shown that they can be perfectly well performed on stage, and they usually work well in their dramatic context. In *Medea*, for instance, Seneca demonstrates that he can make it appear plausible for a woman, maddened by the delusions resulting from her earlier crimes, to turn a knife on her own flesh and blood. (In Euripides Medea is merely a cold and calculating avenger, and her action is therefore so difficult to understand as to provide another reason why it should take place offstage.) The fact that the youth Hippolytus is made unrecognizable by his dismemberment gives visible expression to one of the main themes of *Phaedra*, the transience of beauty. To a public familiar with gladiatorial contests, moreover, such horrors certainly seemed less objectionable than they do to us. Much of what initially appears strange, therefore, can not only be defended but may even prove powerfully effective in performance.

## STAGE PLAYS OR DRAMAS FOR RECITATION?

And if Seneca did not write for the theatre, what was he writing for? Since there are no records in classical antiquity of a dramatic genre intended to be read rather than performed (as with the initial plans for Schiller's *Die Räuber* and various other plays in the modern period) but we do know of public recitations of tragedies, it is usually thought that Seneca had such performances in mind and was writing dramas for recitation. However, the theory overlooks the fact that the usual *recitationes* recorded in the imperial period, including the recitation of epics, elegies, poetry and even legal speeches, were never regarded as the real presentation or performance of those works, and they are also to be distinguished from other kinds of reading

aloud. These *recitationes* were in the nature of work-shops. The author presented a literary piece on which he was working to try it out for effect and elicit praise or criticism. That hypothesis is supported by the fact that the authors themselves and not other speakers regularly did the 'recitation', and, most important of all, only unfinished and unpublished works featured on these occasions. If they had been dramas intended for recitation, finished texts would have been performed by professional speakers.

The more closely one studies the tragedies the more obvious it becomes that Seneca always had the contingencies of stage performance in mind. In his *Hercules furens*, for instance, he makes sure that, when the frenzied Hercules shoots or strikes down his children, the victims fleeing before him are not actually killed until they are offstage. Certain important incidents on stage can be gathered from the text alone only when one reads later parts of it, which means that the plays were not meant for readers but for spectators, who would be able to grasp everything at once.

Probably more important than any of this, however, is the fact that Seneca went even beyond the Greek writers of tragedies in ensuring that the action and indeed the principal ideas of his plays could take visible shape on stage. One critic rightly said of the *Hercules* mentioned above – a play in which the hero first rescues his family from a tyrant, then kills his own children in a fit of madness and after that tries to commit suicide, but is prevented by his own father – that thanks to Seneca's stage presentation even a deaf spectator could have understood the broad outline of the plot.

Although Seneca's plays as a whole follow the classicizing rules (for the number of acts, the chorus, accounts brought by messengers, characterization and above all metre) laid down by Horace, who derived them from Greek drama, he may well have integrated features from other dramatic genres into his tragedies. In the *Troas* (often wrongly called *Troades* today) the Trojan women captured in war bare their breasts in a moment of emotion as they sing their lament for the fallen city; there would have been some risk of unintentional comedy if the chorus were played by men in the usual way, even if they wore artificial bosoms. It is possible that for these parts Seneca engaged some of the actresses who usually performed on stage in the *mimus* genre and were accustomed to taking off even more of their clothes (see above, p. 117 ).

Some use of the *pantomimus* genre seems even clearer, especially at the beginning of the *Medea*, when after the opening prologue the chorus sings the eponymous heroine a wedding song, or epithalamium, for her unfaithful husband and his new wife Creusa. If the chorus, as is usually assumed, came on stage for this purpose, the wedding procession would inevitably lead to a meeting between Medea and her former husband which is dramatically impossible, since they do

not in fact come face to face until later. However, she comments on the song only, 'We are undone! Upon my ears has sounded the marriage-hymn!'. Since nothing suggests that she leaves the stage during the song and then comes back, and anyway such a departure would be completely unmotivated, we may assume that the chorus sang offstage and remained invisible, while Medea, on the stage, expressed her horror at the wedding and the sometimes very obvious sexual suggestions made in the song in a pantomime dance or play of gestures. If the actor playing the part had some training in pantomime, that would have presented no problem; if not, perhaps a double was used for the heroine in this scene.

## SENECA'S *TROAS* – A DRAMA OF DEATH

Let us look at one of Seneca's plays rather more closely. His *Troas*, that is *The Tragedy of Troy*, which has had occasional productions in the modern era, proclaims itself to be a drama of death and disaster even in its stage set. The backdrop is the magnificent entrance to the tomb of Hector, once the champion of Troy. Beyond it the ruins of the city are still smoking behind its breached walls (an effect presenting no technical problems in the time of Nero, when a whole house was once burned down on stage in a *togata*). The play, which to some extent is a combination of the *Hekabe* and *Troades* of Euripides, describes the sad fate of two children killed in the aftermath of the destruction of the city. Polyxena, daughter of king Priam and his wife Hecuba, is slaughtered as the future bride of the dead Achilles in a terrible act of ritual murder; Astyanax, the son of Hector and Andromache, is thrown from the top of a tower as a preventive measure, since he might live to avenge his native city. Unlike the two children, the adults, particularly their mothers Hecuba and Andromache and the chorus of Trojan women, remain alive, making the point that in this case those who die are more fortunate than the survivors.

The drama begins with a prologue, consisting of Hecuba's lament, that may be regarded as the first act and is followed by a ritual, wildly despairing dirge performed by the chorus of half-naked women and accompanied by a dance, as described above. The first reference to one of the dead – in this case Priam – as happy occurs in this song. After the powerful presence of women in this act, the second introduces the Polyxena strand of the plot among the Greek warriors. Talthybius, herald of the Greeks, announces that the dead Achilles demands the human sacrifice of Polyxena, who had once been promised to him as his wife. The classic form of a messenger's account, which was the conventional way of dealing with such subjects, leaves it intentionally uncertain whether the apparition of the dead Achilles should be considered real or only imaginary. The Greek commander Agamemnon and

132
**Two actors in a tragedy**
First century AD
Fresco
Museo Archeologico Nazionale di Napoli, 9039

The costumes and masks of both actors belong to the genre of tragedy. The colour of the Pompeian fresco gives a good impression of the splendour of the costumes to be seen on stage. The scene cannot be definitely identified as coming from a particular play or a myth. The figure on the right, a woman played by a man (as for all female parts in tragedy), is holding a baby in her arms and speaking to the figure opposite, who has a ewer in his right hand of a kind that was used for sacrificial purposes. Both actors wear *cothurnae* (built-up shoes) to make themselves look taller.

the hero Pyrrhus, son of Achilles and very conscious of his own prestige, then discuss whether or not to carry out the dead man's injunction. Agamemnon, putting forward ideas found in Seneca's own essay *De clementia* (*On Clemency*, regarded as a princely virtue), has the better arguments on his side, and for reasons of humanity wishes to spare Polyxena. But Pyrrhus, with scarcely veiled threats of mutiny and violence, wins the dispute. On being asked to deliver his verdict the priest Calchas not only demands the sacrifice of Polyxena, as was to be expected, but the death of Astyanax as well. In sombre mood, the chorus of Greek soldiers sings of the fate of the soul after death. While the Trojan women had believed in another life beyond the grave, the sceptical Greeks and philosophers come to the conclusion that the soul perishes at death and a human being becomes nothing, as he was before his birth. The question of which alternative is right remains undecided, in line with the uncertainty in Seneca's own mind.

After one act devoted to women and another devoted to men, the third act could be said to bring both sexes and Greeks and Trojans alike together on stage. Andromache, with a presentiment of the tragedy to come, hides her little son Astyanax in his father's tomb, in order to preserve Hector's heir so that he may avenge Troy. But Ulysses, using a virtuoso technique of questioning and intimidation in what could be described as the first criminal investigation in literature, and one of the most telling scenes in the drama of classical antiquity in general, succeeds in discovering the child's hiding place, and after a shattering farewell from his mother, who feels less sorrow for her son himself than for the crushing of her hopes of revenge,

Astyanax is led off to execution. The chorus of Trojan women enters again, this time with a song that comes almost as a relief after so much emotional strain, evoking images of the different parts of Greece to which they may now be dispersed as captives taken in war.

The fourth act returns to the interrupted Polyxena strand of the plot. The fair Helen, disastrous cause of the war that has just ended, is sent by the Greeks to put up a show of persuading the young Polyxena to marry Pyrrhus, although she is really to be killed to placate his father Achilles. Only when Polyxena realizes this does she willingly allow herself to be adorned as a bride and led away by her supposed betrothed, who seizes her brutally as her mother Hecuba falls into despair. The visible contrast between the two women clearly symbolizes the basic idea of the play. After a final song by the Trojan women, promising themselves comfort in the knowledge that they share their sorrows – the more dreadful the course of events, the gentler their songs become – a messenger brings the two strands of the plot together by giving an account of the heroic death of both children. Astyanax has cast himself off the tower before Ulysses could throw him down. Polyxena died with the fearless demeanour of a Roman gladiator. Hecuba utters the despairing conclusion: why must it be she, an old woman and tired of life, who does not die? The call to go on board ship is heard, and as the Trojan women part from each other the curtain comes up: Troy, the subject and title of the play, has finally been destroyed.

Even this brief summary of the tragedy shows that it is has more than a superficial connection with Seneca's own thinking (he was probably among the most important philosophers writing in Latin before St Augustine of Hippo over three centuries later). The theme at the heart of the play – death and the psychological preparation for death (*meditatio mortis*) – is also prominent in his prose writings, which are marked by the philosophy of the Stoics. He staged his own death – his suicide was forced on him by the emperor Nero and was really a kind of execution – as a drama following the Greek example of Socrates. The tragedy thus contains an easily understood message of stoic wisdom, yet it is more than merely stoic. If children (whom the Stoics singled out as being incapable of reason, *ratio*) could free themselves of the fear of death like Polyxena and Astyanax, not through philosophical considerations but out of national and family pride, then how much more must an adult human being endowed with reason be able to do so, considering how often death is preferable to life? The fact that Seneca made two mute parts the heroes of his drama is a brilliant touch on the part of a true dramatic author.

Another point deserving mention in this context is the fact that in the tragedy *Octavia*, which has come down to us under Seneca's name and is the only extant example of a *praetexta*, the philosopher himself appears as tutor and mentor of the emperor Nero, and

to some extent the guardian of Nero's conscience. However, the authenticity of this play has been almost entirely dismissed today, and not without good reason.

The high poetic worth of Seneca's tragedies, which are magnificently constructed and psychologically subtle in their detail, makes us painfully aware of what we may have lost in the old tragedy of the republican period, a genre that enjoyed a higher reputation in classical antiquity than did Roman comedy.

To sum up, there cannot have been many periods in the cultural history of mankind when a form of mass popular entertainment could achieve such a high artistic level as it did in this ancient Rome that was hungry for education, in love with the Muses, and both alienated and fascinated by the Greeks. Seneca's tragedies, even if they were for stage performance and perhaps deliberately intended for the common people, certainly lost any popular appeal in a period when mimes and pantomimes dominated the entertainment industry. But if, in a later tradition, they could hold their own with the earlier tragedies, it was probably because as products of a more cultured period they were in the last resort simply better than the works of the past – another reason why it may be useful to regard them not just as historical curiosities but as works of art of enduring value, ripe for rediscovery on the modern stage.

## 'What These Women Love is the Sword':
## The Performers and their Audiences

### GLADIATORS – THE DARLINGS OF THE CROWD

Who were the men who fought to the death during performances in the amphitheatre? A great many of them were convicted murderers, arsonists or desecrators of temples. The sentence for these crimes was condemnation *ad gladium* (to the sword) or *ad bestias* (to the wild beasts). The unusual marble relief now in Oxford (fig. 136) shows the end of a trial: two men in trousers, tunics and helmets are leading away four other men clad only in loincloths, with ropes round their necks. The animals fighting in the lower field of the relief indicate that they are probably criminals who have been condemned *ad bestias*, a penalty that almost always meant certain death. Only if a man put up a particularly courageous and dramatic show in the arena or managed to defeat the animals' superior strength, could he hope for pardon, and such decisions were certainly very exceptional. One case is mentioned with obvious awe by the historian Tacitus in his *Annales* (12, 56, 5): during the legendary mock naval battle staged by the emperor Claudius in the year AD 52 on Lake Fucino, east of Rome, 'the battle, though one of criminals, was contested with the spirit and courage of freemen; and, after much blood had flowed, the combatants were exempted from destruction.'

When a man was condemned *ad ludum* (to the gladiatorial school), on the other hand, he had a better chance of escaping death by giving a brilliant performance, since he was trained for gladiatorial combat before his first fight. In one of his letters (7, 3–5) the Roman philosopher Seneca describes the regular execution of criminals in the amphitheatre for the entertainment of the audience. Their death agonies were interludes filling the mid-day break between contests, and the sensation-hungry audience made loud comments as accompaniment to these dramatically staged executions. From the accounts of the biographer and imperial official Suetonius it seems that persons who had committed less serious crimes could also meet such an end on the whim of the emperor. Claudius punished bad cases of deception by making the offenders fight wild beasts, and Vitellius sold his favourite Asiaticus to a gladiatorial school when annoyed by his behaviour.

Christians died in the arena, too. Their religion prohibited them from taking part in the imperial cult and worshipping their deified rulers, and their refusal to recognize one of the state's major festivals made them guilty of high treason, one of the worst crimes punishable by death in the amphitheatre. At first only a few Christian communities were affected, but systematic persecution began under Nero and Domitian. In the second century AD a decree of the emperor Trajan ruled that individuals could be condemned on the grounds of denunciation alone if they failed to abjure their faith, and from the beginning of the third century AD persecution increased throughout the empire, ending only with the recognition of Christianity by Constantine in the early fourth century AD.

According to several contemporary eyewitnesses, performers in the arena included women. If Suetonius (*Domitian* 4, 1) is to be believed, Domitian made women fight by torchlight at night. In one gladiatorial event held by Nero, the historian Cassius Dio (*Rhomaike historia* 62 [63] 3, 1) tells us, only Ethiopians appeared, including women and children. During Nero's reign not only slaves but 'women of rank' took part in the performances, according to Tacitus in his *Annales* (15, 32). The guests at *Trimalchio's Banquet*

135
**Relief with gladiator**
Second century AD
Stone
British Museum, London,
GR 1847 4-20 18

The Greek inscription on this relief from Halicarnassus gives the gladiator's name: Hilaros.

136
**Relief with prisoners**
Third century AD
Marble
Ashmolean Museum, Oxford,
Michaelis 137

Men condemned *ad bestias*
are led away with ropes.
(See text pp. 73–4.)

by Petronius discuss a woman who was to fight from a chariot (45, 7). The marble relief now in London (fig. 137), from Halicarnassus in Asia Minor, was carved on the occasion of the *missio* of two women fighters, 'Amazon' and 'Achillia', who had earned their freedom by giving a series of outstanding performances. In the year AD 200 Septimius Severus banned appearances by women. This decree probably applied to women athletes as well as female gladiators, who were loudly mocked, as Juvenal makes clear (*Saturae* 6, 246–60).

A great many gladiators were recruited from the ranks of those who had been captured in war and enslaved. The successful wars waged by Rome in the middle of the republican period greatly increased their numbers. Around 50 BC it is estimated that there were 100,000 to 200,000 slaves living in Rome alone, out of a population of about a million. These slaves might come into the hands of owners of gladiatorial schools through auction or purchase.

Gladiatorial contests in the arena to celebrate notable victories were popular. The historian Flavius Josephus, in his account of the Jewish war (7, 3, 1), tells us that after the destruction of Jerusalem in AD 70 the Romans set thousands of Jews to fight each other. Such demonstrations of power were based on an old tradition, and persisted into late antiquity. The first performances of this kind were obviously in the fourth and third centuries BC when the Romans, after a war of changing fortunes, defeated the Samnites, an Italian

**137** (TOP RIGHT) **Relief with female gladiators**
Stone, first or second century AD
British Museum, London, GR 1847.4-24.19

This relief, from Halicarnassus, shows two female gladiators in combat. They have the same equipment as male gladiators but are depicted without helmets. The Greek inscription tells us that their names (probably stage names) were Amazon and Achillia and that they had been granted an honourable release from the arena.

**138** (CENTRE RIGHT) **Inscribed plaque**
Bone, AD 88
British Museum, London, GR 1889.5-20.1

If a gladiator fought well and was successful over a long period in many events he might be granted an honourable discharge. This inscribed plaque from Lanuvium has been interpreted as a ticket of release for a gladiator called Moderatus, granted by his owner Lucceius, on 5 October AD 88.

**139** (RIGHT) **Dwarf gladiator**
Bronze, first to second century AD
British Museum, London, GR 1922.7-12.4

Dwarfs were popular in fashionable Roman households and they were retained by several Roman emperors. This small figurine appears to depict a dwarf armed with the equipment of a *hoplomachus*.

tribe living in Campania. Over 500 years later, in AD 310, Constantine sent prisoners of war from the Germanic Bructeri tribe into the arena to fight wild beasts. Organizers of expensive mass spectacles involving thousands of performers were particularly likely to use prisoners of war when staging such events as mock naval battles, which enjoyed extraordinary popularity. The first event of this nature was held by Caesar in the year 46 BC. The historian Appian of Alexandria describes his creation of an artificial lake where two fleets fought, manned by 6,000 soldiers in all, whose numbers included a large number of prisoners of war.

Gladiatorial contests were so enormously popular that certain individual fighters achieved fame and fortune, and such prospects might even tempt volunteers to try their luck in the arena. At the beginning of their training these so-called *auctorati* swore an oath that was incompatible with the dignity of a Roman citizen: from then on they must be subject to 'burning, imprisonment, or death by the sword', as Seneca put it in his letters (37, 1 f). After a successful fight they received not only a palm branch as the trophy of victory but money and other gifts from the holder of the games. Many a gladiator was able to live for a long time on the proceeds of his former fame, as we know from Suetonius (*Tiberius* 7, 1).

Before he became emperor Tiberius held gladiatorial contests in honour of his grandfather Drusus, and on this occasion persuaded fighters who had already gone into honourable retirement to appear for a fee of 100,000 sestertii. Volunteers were by no means always destitute men hoping to make their fortune in the arena; even members of the upper classes felt the fascination of this dangerous form of single combat. At a *munus* given by Caesar (Suetonius, *Caesar* 39, 1) a former senator and a man from a family of praetorian rank fought in the arena. Even emperors enjoyed making personal appearances. Caligula not only took several *thraeces* into his bodyguard but entered the arena as a *thraex* himself, conduct which displeased his contemporaries. The passion of Commodus for gladiatorial contests was proverbial, and many rumours sought to explain it by saying that his real father was not the emperor Marcus Aurelius, who made no secret of his distaste for the cruelty of spectacles in the amphitheatre, but a gladiator whom his mother Faustina had loved. 'The form of contest that he [Commodus] practised and the armour that he used were those of the *secutores* ... he held the shield in his right hand and the wooden sword in his left, and indeed took great pride in the fact that he was left-handed,' wrote Cassius Dio (73, 192) in an account of the emperor's fighting style. Such imperial performances, however, were the exception. Both men, Caligula and Commodus, presided over reigns of terror to which an end was finally put by their assassinations. At the age of thirty-one Commodus was killed on 31 December AD 192 in the Villa Vectiliana, a gladiatorial

**140**

**Clasp-knife**

Second to third century AD
Bone and iron
Römisch-Germanisches
Museum der Stadt Köln, 44,105

This folding knife has an iron blade and a bone handle ornamented with carving. The grooves in the carving were lined with a mixture of wax and pitch to make them clearly visible. The handle is in the shape of a *secutor*, identifiable chiefly by his large, rectangular shield and smooth-crested helmet.

**141**

**Lamp in the form
of a *murmillo* helmet**

Second century AD
Pottery
Römisch-Germanisches
Museum der Stadt Köln,
N 2147

This lamp depicts the metal surface of a *murmillo* helmet with small indentations.

school near the Colosseum, where he was training for his own appearance next day.

The gladiators belonged to schools that were at first owned by private people, but became imperial institutions after the first century AD. In Rome alone there were four gladiatorial schools under the ruler's patronage, one of them specializing in training men for animal hunts. The members of these schools travelled around as well as fighting locally. Performers in the Pompeian amphitheatre, for instance, were not only gladiators from the school in the city but came from all over Campania. Precise statistical records were kept for each man, and after death their tombstones summarized their careers. The stela of a dead *retiarius* in the museum in Split gives the story of his life: he came from Aquileia, where there was a famous school with which he toured northern Italy. He then crossed the Adriatic to Dalmatia and died of his injuries in Salonae. The modest monument to Danaos (fig. 143), now in Vienna, shows the bold gladiator, victor in nine contests, in an idyllic domestic setting, taking his evening meal with his family. Father and son recline, while the mother sits in an armchair in front of them.

This curious contrast of the gladiatorial career, symbolized by the man's weapons and his nine wreaths of victory, with his private life strikes an oddly discordant note. Unfortunately we do not know whether Danaos won permission through his victories to marry and have a family, or whether he voluntarily chose the career of a *thraex*.

## SPARTACUS – THE GLADIATORS' REVOLT

The revolt led by Spartacus in the Campanian town of Capua has a chapter to itself in the history of gladiatorial contests. The events of the years 73 to 71 BC bring the fate of prisoners of war who were sent into the arena as gladiators dramatically before our eyes. The deeds of Spartacus were already legendary in classical antiquity, and his name is still generally known today. In his biography of the consul Licinius Crassus the Greek historian Plutarch gives a detailed account of the revolt. Spartacus, who came from Thrace in the Balkans, was forced to join a gladiatorial school. To avoid the imminent certainty of death he and seventy other gladiators escaped, and with a Celt called Krixos

142
**Roman amphitheatre, Nîmes**
AD 70–100

The amphitheatre in Nîmes is smaller than the large complexes in Rome, Capua and Verona, but in a considerably better state of preservation. The building was probably erected in the Flavian period. The Romans built some 200 arenas around the Mediterranean, an obvious indication that gladiatorial contests were popular throughout the Roman empire.

he assembled a large group of prisoners. When they had defeated a praetorian army at Vesuvius the revolt spread to the whole area, until its adherents numbered some 40,000 men. Krixos fell in battle in Apulia, and Spartacus marched to northern Italy, probably hoping to lead his men back to their homes. After winning several victories, however, the rebels went no further but marched south again, and at first their successes continued. However, Spartacus was killed in the deciding battle against Licinius Crassus. Six thousand of his defeated men were crucified along the Via Appia between Capua and Rome.

The public example made of the rebels may have been connected with the danger presented by well-trained gladiators if they banded together in a powerful fighting troop. For instance, the politician Sallustius Crispus (*De coniuratione Catilinae* 30, 7) feared that Catiline would succeed in carrying out the *coup d'état* he was planning in 63 BC with the aid of gladiatorial reinforcements. Nor were such fears entirely unfounded. In his controversial candidature for the post of consul in 52 BC the senator Titus Annius Milo surrounded himself with a retinue of some 300 slaves, including tried and tested gladiators. Fear of such organized groups was so great that in AD 63 a law was passed requiring all potential candidates for political office to refrain from holding games for a period of two years before applying.

The revolt led by Spartacus marks the culmination of mass slavery in the late republic. Despite that event, however, we must remember that the fate of slaves was not necessarily an unhappy one. They might work on large landed estates or belong to prosperous urban households, where they could pursue many different activities and where their daily lives were not so very different from those of the free common people. Only the decrease in the number of wars during the imperial period reduced the slave supply. The emperor Hadrian in particular limited autocratic power by introducing more humane laws, one of which banned the practice of selling slaves to gladiatorial schools without giving a reason.

## THE AUDIENCE – CRITICISM AND ACCLAIM

The comments of several contemporary writers suggest that intellectuals and many members of the upper classes disapproved of the cult of gladiators and its influence on the people. The philosopher Epictetus (*Encheiridion* 33, 2), who came to Rome from Asia Minor in the first century AD and was one of the last major Stoics, appealed to the rational faculties of the audience, deploring the fact that even respectable citizens enjoyed discussing incidents in the arena and participating in common gossip. Several generations earlier, the highly esteemed poet Horace (Quintus Horatius Flaccus) had expressed similar sentiments in one of his letters (1, 18, 19). The low status of gladiators is clear from a law mentioned by the historian Tacitus in his *Histories* (2, 62, 2), where he tells us that the emperor Vitellius forbade all Roman knights to bring their rank into disrepute by taking part in gladiatorial games.

Not so the influential statesman and orator Marcus Tullius Cicero, who expressed a different opinion of gladiators in the early first century BC. Part of his *Tusculan Disputations* discusses the subject of physical pain and how to deal with it, and he comes to the conclusion that a Roman who wishes to possess *virtus*, one of the most important of qualities, will scorn both pain and death. The examples of this authentic manly virtue that he names include gladiators as well as old soldiers of the Roman army (2, 38–41). Cicero regards these swordsmen only as individuals, figures of power and strength, and does not concern himself with other aspects of the games as a whole: as he expressly points

out, he distinguishes between the courage of an individual man and the general cruelty of the games. He might well have come to a different conclusion if he could have foreseen the more outrageous features and increasing perversity of performances in later years.

Despite sporadic negative criticism, however, it seems that a visit to the amphitheatre was extremely popular not only with the common people who made up the bulk of the audience but among all social classes. The oldest stone amphitheatre known to us today is in Pompeii (fig. 145), one of the larger cities of Campania, a region where gladiatorial games attracted particularly large numbers. When performances became increasingly crowded, Augustus laid down general rules for the allotment of seats, described as follows by the biographer Suetonius (*Augustus* 44, 1–3): the front rows were reserved for senators; soldiers and civilians sat separately; married men of the lower classes had special seating areas, as did boys and their tutors; while women sat separately from men in the top rows at the back.

The holders of the games found them a good way of winning public favour, since gladiatorial contests and animal fights in the arena had an overwhelming fascination for the Romans, who were anxious never to miss a performance. The comic dramatist Terence suffered the insult of having a production of one of his

144
**Lamp in the form of a *thraex* helmet**
c. AD 200
Pottery, glazed
British Museum, London,
GR 1885.4-18.4

The helmet is of the type worn by *thraex* gladiators, with a broad brim, griffin crest and high, arched visor grating.

**146** (BELOW) **Graffito of a gladiator**

Stucco, first century AD

Museo Archeologico Nazionale di Napoli, 4697

This small sketch shows a *murmillo* attacking his opponent with shield raised.

**145** (ABOVE)

**Amphitheatre, Pompeii**

80 BC

This amphitheatre, the oldest stone-built example known, was erected in Pompeii by the magistrates Gaius Quintius Valgus and Marcus Porcius shortly after 80 BC. It served for the entertainment of the veterans who settled in the city the same year, having been given land in the region as a farewell gift on their discharge from army service.

plays threatened by loud and excited spectators, because someone had spread a rumour that gladiatorial games were about to be staged. Emotions ran even higher in the amphitheatre, where spectators urged the gladiators on. 'Kill him! Lash him! Brand him!' are some of the comments reported by Seneca in his letters (7, 5). The loser earned a final, 'He has it!' The winner, on the other hand, could be sure of an enthusiastic ovation, the palm branch of victory, a sum of money to an amount determined by the giver of the games, and other rewards in kind. It was part of the crowd's pleasure to take a hand in deciding the loser's fate: only if a defeated gladiator had fought with exceptional courage could he hope for the goodwill of the merciless audience. By enabling spectators to participate in this way, the holder of the games gave everyone the uplifting sense of being a judge with the powers of life or death. The performers were not only of interest in the arena but also a subject of conversation outside it, as is shown in *Trimalchio's Banquet* by Petronius (45,

4–7), where there is extensive discussion of a future performance as well as disparaging comments on the last show. Graffiti of gladiators found on painted walls are evidence that their fortunes were part of the daily lives of the spectators. One drawing depicting the end of a fight between a *retiarius* and a *secutor* comes from a house in the southern French town of Vaison-La-Romaine.

The women in the audience seem to have found gladiators particularly attractive. In his *Art of Love* (1, 163–176) Ovid recommends the amphitheatre, with the theatre and the circus, as a likely place for young men to meet pretty girls. The rumours mentioned above about an affair between the empress Faustina and a gladiator show that even ladies of very high rank admired them. The satirist Juvenal (*Saturae* 6, 110 ff.) tells us of the amorous feelings of a lady called Eppia for one of these heroes of the arena; his many wounds did not trouble her, for after all he was a gladiator. The satirist comments, resignedly: 'What these women love

is the sword.' A particularly piquant scene was discovered by the excavators of the gladiatorial school in Pompeii, who found a richly adorned society lady among the fighting men. The eruption of Vesuvius had brought her love affair to a terrible end. A sculptural group from Pompeii (fig. 147) alludes rather more broadly to the charms of the swordsmen: the gladiator is leaning on a figure of the god of fertility, Priapus, identifiable by his huge phallus. This group stood in front of a tavern near the amphitheatre, and probably served as a sign informing thirsty fans of the nature of the establishment.

A whole independent branch of the art industry exploited the popularity of gladiators. Souvenir shops sold everyday utensils with scenes of contests in the amphitheatre. Fighting scenes ornamented knife handles, lamps, pottery and much more. The fans bought these items and took home a souvenir of their heroes. The little pocket mirror (fig. 148) comes from a tomb of the third century AD, and its back bears a relief showing a *venator* fighting a powerful wild boar. The man wears the armour of a *murmillo* with sword, shield, *manica*, helmet and greaves. The helmet of a *secutor* was the model for the dropper-flask from Cologne (fig. 149). Such luxury items were made by the glass-blowing workshops of Cologne, which had an outstanding reputation.

Even after death, gladiators were remembered. A funerary stela now in the Louvre in Paris (fig. 150)

**147**
**Gladiator and Priapus**
First century AD
Tufa
Pompeii, Deposito
Archeologico, 11739

The gladiator is identifiable as a *hoplomachus* by his round shield. He is standing in an attacking position though also leaning on a figure of the fertility god Priapus, who can be recognized by his large phallus and the way he has girded up his garment. The god was thought to bring luck and the gladiator would have hoped for his protection. But the statues also suggest the appeal of the gladiator, for the stars of the arena were considered extremely attractive. Countless graffiti in Pompeii praise them as lovers and the objects of young girls' enthusiasm.

148 **Pocket mirror with a *venator***
Bronze, third century AD
Römisch-Germanisches Museum der Stadt Köln, 25,1057

This little mirror (diameter 6 cm), whose back shows a *venator* fighting a wild boar, had a polished side in which the owner's face could be reflected. Mirror glass was only rarely used by the Romans.

**149**
**Dropper-flask in the form of a *secutor* helmet**
Third century AD
Glass
British Museum, London,
GR 1881.6-24.2

This small glass container for perfume, found in Cologne, was made in the shape of a *secutor* helmet with its distinctive small eye-holes and smooth low ridge.

133

The careers of certain outstanding charioteers are recorded in inscriptions: when Marcus Aurelius Polyneices died at the age of thirty, he had 739 victories to his name in all, 655 for the Reds, the others for the factions of the Greens, Blues and Whites (CIL VI 10049). Even more successful was Publius Aelius Gutta Calpurnianus. He was one of the *miliarii*, charioteers who had won over a thousand times; in fact he had come first in the race 1,127 times, on over 1,000 of these occasions driving for the Green faction. His highest single prize was between 30,000 and 50,000 sestertii (CIL VI 10047). By comparison, a highly educated *grammaticus* working as a tutor could earn at best a top salary of 100,000 sestertii a year (Suetonius, *De grammaticis et rhetoribus* 17, 2). The names of the factions reflected the colours of the clothing worn by the charioteers. Drivers obviously did not work for only a single racing association, but might move to a new employer if offered a higher fee. Money was more important than loyalty to a certain faction.

## 'IT IS THE RACING-COLOURS THEY REALLY SUPPORT AND CARE ABOUT'

The spectators were drawn from all sections of the population. Even in aristocratic circles games in the circus were so popular that Marcus Aurelius, that philosopher among emperors, expressly comments in his *Meditations* (1, 5) that he has been neither a Green nor a Blue. Not so with Caligula, of whose passion for chariot-racing Suetonius tells us (*Caligula* 55, 2f.): 'Caligula supported the Green faction with such ardour that he would often dine and spend the night in their stables and, on one occasion, gave the driver

**150 (ABOVE)**

**Relief with a gladiator**

Second century AD

Marble

Musée du Louvre, Paris,

MA 4492

The *thraex* Antaios is so well entrenched behind his shield and greaves that no unprotected parts of his body are exposed to his adversary's attack.

shows a man called Antaios as a *thraex* in a defensive attitude. His wife set up this relatively expensive monument in memory of her dead husband, whose obviously successful career had enabled him to achieve a certain prosperity.

## CHARIOTEERS – THE STARS OF THE CIRCUS

Chariot-races had a long tradition behind them and consequently enjoyed a higher reputation among the upper classes of Rome than gladiatorial contests. The attraction of the sport – high earnings and a calculable amount of risk – tempted not only slaves but volunteers, especially freedmen, to sign on as charioteers. Victorious drivers won fabulous amounts of prize money and enjoyed high social standing; they were even allowed to drive through the city of Rome at certain times committing crimes and go unpunished. This traditional privilege was abolished only by Nero, as Suetonius tells us in his biography of the emperor (*Nero* 16, 2). Like gladiators, charioteers received valuable gifts in kind as well as prize money, together with the inevitable palm branch and wreath of victory.

**151 (RIGHT)**

**Head of a charioteer**

Second to third century AD

Bronze

Museum für Kunst und

Gewerbe Hamburg, 1999.164

Eutychus presents worth 20,000 gold pieces.' It has been suggested that the fine ivory statuette (fig. 152) may represent the emperor Caracalla as a charioteer.

Games in the circus were almost as popular as gladiatorial contests in the amphitheatre. Before the beginning of the race the crowd would inspect the drivers and horses, and then decide where to place their bets. Although the Circus Maximus could take about 150,000 people, many spectators queued overnight to get a seat. Juvenal (*Saturae* 9, 142 f.) advises taking two strong slaves along for protection in the crowd. According to the Christian apologist Tertullian (*De spectaculis* 16), emotions ran very high during the racing, and a deafening noise filled the circus as the spectators shouted angrily, cried out and rejoiced at the misfortunes of the teams they did not support. If necessary, the *hortatores* accompanying the teams would whip up the enthusiasm of adherents of the factions even further. Unlike the drivers, spectators did not change sides. Once you had decided which colour to support, you identified entirely with it, feeling for all its successes and failures. It was the faction that mattered rather than the victory of individual charioteers. The Younger Pliny describes this fanaticism in his letters (9, 6, 2 f.), where he comments: 'It is the racing-colours they really support and care about.' Chariot-racing and support of a particular faction was an excellent way to escape from the frustrations of daily life. A man who could give vent to his aggressive feelings in the circus would become less agitated about political events. Not for nothing did Juvenal (*Saturae* 10, 81) comment on the Roman *plebs* that it 'now meddles no more and longs eagerly for just two things – bread and circuses.'

152 (BELOW LEFT)
**Bust of a charioteer**
Early third century AD
Ivory
British Museum, London,
GR 1851.8-13.175

The leather lacing over the tunic identifies the figure as a charioteer. The precious material of which it is made – ivory – and the high quality of craftsmanship distinguish this piece, which is said to be from the amphitheatre at Arles, from such souvenir items as terracotta figurines and lamps. It has been suggested, probably erroneously, that it is a portrait of the emperor Caracalla as a charioteer.

153 (LEFT)
**Lamp with a charioteer**
Pottery
Antikensammlung, Staatliche
Museen zu Berlin,
TC 8217/107

The pictorial part of the lamp portrays the head and shoulders of a charioteer, identifiable by the leather lacing over his tunic. His life-like face, reproduced in detail, shows clear features of genuine portraiture, rare in decorated Roman lamps. This lamp seems to have been a souvenir for sale to fans, like other lamps and contorniates (cf. figs 15 and 20) that also show famous drivers.

154 (LEFT)
**Gladiator**
First century AD
Terracotta
Römisch-Germanisches
Museum der Stadt Köln,
27,4111

Many terracotta statuettes of gladiators have been found in tombs. It is hard to determine their original function, but they were probably either decorative items or toys. Some of them had removable helmets. The *secutor* can be identified by his large shield and smooth-crested helmet. The statuette would have looked different in antiquity, since its original painting has not been preserved.

Like gladiatorial contests, chariot-racing gave rise to an industry selling souvenirs of every kind to the fans of the various factions. You could buy everyday utensils and souvenirs of your day at the races in the shops around the circus arenas. Such items included lamps (fig. 153), pottery and statuettes (fig. 154) showing the successful stars.

## ATHLETES – GREEKS IN THE SERVICE OF ROME

The heavy athletics disciplines deeply rooted in Greek culture were at first difficult to establish in Rome. In the second and first centuries BC there were occasional events of this kind; among them, the shows presented by Lucius Cornelius Sulla in the year 80 BC aroused most interest. For the celebrations of his triumph over Mithridates VI, which made him ruler of all the east, he had so many athletes brought from Greece that the Olympic Games could not be held that year for lack of competitors. Augustus introduced the first regular contests, and the people of Naples founded the *sebasta* in his honour in the year AD 14, an event with athletic contests as well as musical performances. The emperor Augustus held no games in Rome itself, although he was particularly fond of boxing matches and always gave the contestants rich prizes, as Suetonius notes in his biography (*Augustus* 45, 2). But it was not until the time of Caligula and Claudius that the Romans had another chance to watch boxing matches and other attractions held, in the same way as animal hunts, for the entertainment of the crowd. In AD 60 Nero introduced the *neronia* called after him, games including musical performances and athletics, although they, too, came to an end after his violent death in AD 68. It was Domitian who finally established athletics in Rome, when he founded the *capitolinia*, a sporting event featuring various disciplines. This took place every four years and was soon among the great sporting contests of the ancient world.

Most of the athletes came from Greece, particularly in the early years, as the account given by the historian Appian of the triumph of Sulla (*Bella civilia* 1, 99) suggests. Greek athletes will have continued to make up a large part of the competitors later. But by the time of Augustus there were Roman professional sportsmen, as Suetonius points out (*Augustus* 45, 2). Augustus especially enjoyed boxing matches between Greek and Roman opponents. To entertain the men in the audience, women, too, took part in certain disciplines, for instance foot-races and wrestling matches. The bronze statuette now in Hamburg (fig. 155) shows a woman athlete with her hand raised, probably to hold a *strigilis*, a curved instrument for scraping sand and dust from the athletes' oiled bodies after exercising.

The opinion of Roman authors on sporting competitions was unanimous. They were totally opposed to them: they feared that Greek decadence would lead to the decline of Roman virtues. Cicero (*Tusculanae dis-*

putationes 4, 70) and Tacitus (*Annales* 14, 20, 4) condemn the nudity of the athletes. Tacitus feared that the young men of Rome, led astray by foreign influences, would 'strip to the skin as well, put on the gloves, and practise that mode of conflict instead of the profession of arms'. Plutarch (*Quaestiones Romanae* 40) blames the Greek gymnasia for the political decadence of the Hellenes. Seneca gives it as his opinion in his letters

(15, 3) that physical exertion dulls the mind. The Greek doctor Galen (*Opera* 1, 28 f.) argues against heavy athletics on medical grounds, and compares the lives of the sportsmen who practised them with those of pigs. They were indeed very well fattened up, and many extant statuettes show that they could become obese.

In spite of sharp criticism by such intellectuals, athletic contests had a certain popularity, although the number of their fans could not be compared with the crowds who flocked to the amphitheatre or the circus. Boxing, wrestling, the pancration and foot-races, however, were an important branch of the Roman entertainment industry. The stadium built by Domitian in Rome would take about 15,000 spectators, evidence of the attractions of athletics. Even Seneca, in one of his letters (80, 2), says that these games attracted a large number

**155**

**Woman athlete**

First century AD

Bronze

Museum für Kunst und
Gewerbe Hamburg, 1917.362

This statuette proves that women sometimes took part in sporting events. Unfortunately we cannot tell what kind of athlete she was. She holds either a curved sword or a *strigilis* in her raised hand, and has a bandage around her knee.

of people. 'The people demand contests in the Greek style', adds Tacitus in his *Annales* (14, 21, 4).

Women were not allowed to join the audience; since the athletes appeared naked, there were fears for morality and decorum, and female spectators were banned as early as the time of Augustus. Some exceptions were made under Nero, who allowed the presence of the six priestesses of the goddess Vesta, the Vestal Virgins vowed to a life of strict chastity, on the grounds that the priestess of Demeter was allowed to attend the Olympic Games in Greece (Suetonius, *Augustus* 44, 3 and *Nero* 12, 4). In spite of this prohibition, women obviously did have contacts with the athletes, gave them presents and hoped for closer relationships, as Juvenal (*Saturae* 6, 355 f.) and Tertullian (*De spectaculis* 22) agree.

## ACTORS – LOVED AND DESPISED

Three kinds of plays dominated the Roman theatre in the imperial period: the mime, the Atellan farce and the pantomime. There is evidence for the existence in Rome of the mimes, comedies in simple and often smutty language, from the second century BC; they were extremely popular. The actors in mimes did not wear masks, while the characters in the equally coarse Atellan farces were four stock characters identified by their bizarre masks. Hardly any tragedies were still performed after the first century AD; they had been superseded by pantomimes in which stories on mythological subjects were performed by a single actor playing all the parts.

Public disapproval of such shows, particularly the Atellan farces and mimes, was vehement. Roman writers, like the first Christian authors, were outraged by these coarse plays with their presentations of indecent subjects. Tacitus (*Dialogus de oratoribus* 29, 3) mentioned them in the same breath as gladiatorial contests and chariot-racing, considering them to be vices that kept the people from striving for higher things. Tertullian (*De spectaculis* 17, 1–4) fulminated against the lack of any sense of shame in the senators who would do nothing to put an end to such obscene performances. The verdict on the versatile pantomime actors

156

**Cantharus**

Mid-first century AD

Silver

Museo Archeologico Nazionale di Napoli, 25381

Not only humble everyday utensils but expensive luxury goods were decorated with motifs from the world of entertainment. Wine and love are the themes of this magnificent drinking cup from Pompeii, which also includes theatre masks in its design.

was not so harsh: they received a comprehensive training in dance as well as poetry and mythology in order to perfect their art. The audience expected something more highbrow of their appearances, and if those expectations were not fulfilled the actors would meet with biting mockery.

Actresses were particularly harshly criticized. They were regarded as prostitutes who 'expose themselves to the gaze of the public with their shameless movements until lustful eyes have seen their fill', as the Christian rhetorician Lactantius wrote in horror around AD 300 (*Divinae institutiones* 1, 20, 10, tr.). Marriage to such a woman was dishonourable and illegal (*Digesta* 23, 2, 42).

These condemnations are in clear contrast to the popularity of the dramas themselves. Their suggestive scenes were very much to the audience's taste. Only once, when the respected statesman Cato attended a performance, did the public feel any inhibitions over urging the actresses to strip, according to Valerius Ammianus in his collection of notable sayings and deeds (2, 10, 8). Obviously, official disapproval says nothing about the popularity of the theatre. The actors were only giving the general public what it liked, making drama an important part of the Roman entertainment industry.

The opponents of these shallow plays were sure they had a bad influence on audiences: according to the Christian authors Amobius (*Adversus nationes* 7, 33) and Cyprianus (*Ad donatum* 8), they led people into immorality, and it was their fault that spectators went straight from the brothel to the theatre and were tempted to commit adultery. However, Seneca was of the opinion (*De brevitate vitae* 12, 8) that the vices of everyday life were worse than anything shown in the theatre of his time. This comment seems to get to the root of the matter: such licentious plays were reflecting contemporary society.

What was the status of the actors, and where did they come from? Most of them were slaves and freedmen from the eastern parts of the empire, and in particular from Greece. Their low social standing was reflected in a law allowing magistrates to chastise them anywhere and at any time, although Augustus (Suetonius, *Augustus* 45, 3) amended this law by confining the exercise of such rights to the theatre. To earn their living, actors did not stay with a single theatrical company but went from place to place, as the Greek writer Philostratus tells us (*Vita Apollonii* 5, 9).

Most actors made just enough to live on; only famous stars earned top salaries. For a slave who was a pantomime actor his new owner paid 700,000 sestertii. Pylades, a freedman of Augustus and the most famous actor of his time, accumulated a huge fortune, which allowed him to produce plays himself. In the course of time salaries rose to such heights that Marcus Aurelius felt obliged to set a legal maximum.

Men and women of all walks of life, from slaves to senators, went to the theatre, as cogently described by Ovid (*Tristia* 2, 495 ff.): 'Foul-jesting mimes ... always contain the sin of forbidden love, in which constantly a well-dressed adulterer appears and the artful wife fools her stupid husband. These are viewed by the marriageable maiden, the wife, the husband, and the child; even the senate in large part is present.'

The spectators loved and idolized the heroes of the stage. Women in particular felt ardent admiration for the actors, as Juvenal mockingly describes (*Saturae* 6, 63 ff.): 'Your Apulian maiden heaves a sudden and longing cry of ecstasy ... the rustic Thymele is all attention, it is then that she learns her lesson.' Galen (*Opera* 14, 631 ff.) mentions a woman patient who was suffering from unrequited love for the pantomime actor Pylades. Even women in high society could not resist the charms of the actors. The affair between a famous actor called Paris and Domitia, wife of the emperor Domitian, came to a fatal end when the emperor had him murdered in the open street.

The pantomime actor Mnester was credited with some particularly risqué affairs. First he had a liaison with the emperor Caligula, who did not hide his feelings but caressed Mnester publicly, as Suetonius tells us with some relish (*Caligula* 55, 1). After the emperor's death the actor began a relationship with Messalina, the wife of Claudius, which eventually caused his death, for Claudius had him and many of the empress's other lovers executed.

These relationships between actors and people in high society make it very clear that criticism of the theatre by intellectuals did nothing to affect its popularity. Actors might officially be subject to mockery and derision, but the public loved them.

## ENTERTAINMENT – THE PLEASURES OF THE PEOPLE

If we look at contemporary Greek and Roman comments about entertainment in ancient Rome as a whole, we see a picture divided into two parts: the intellectuals appear in the narrow upper part of the picture, lamenting the bad influence of games on the common people and pointing out that gladiatorial contests, chariot-racing and farces are deleterious to independent thought and encourage mankind's primitive instincts. Instead of intellectual argument, complain the intellectuals, people turn to banalities. Heavy athletic disciplines are bad for morality and promote the decline of Roman virtues. Pagan and Christian authors are united in their condemnation of theatrical performances, which they say endanger decency and decorum, tempting spectators into immorality.

The broad lower part of the picture, however, is occupied by the majority of the population, who are not at all dismayed by such criticism. Not only the common people but the highest circles of society enjoy a good show and help the games to become enormously popular. At the centre of interest are performances in the amphitheatre, but the circus and the theatre, too, enjoy extraordinary popularity. Even the boxing and wrestling matches imported from Greece have their adherents. Although the performers themselves are generally slaves or freedmen, victorious gladiators and charioteers and outstanding actors can rise to become highly paid stars of the show business of the ancient world, as well known as today's footballers or racing drivers.

The rulers of Rome exploited the influence of these pleasures on the people. Augustus was particularly skilful in controlling his subjects and using them for his own ends by constructing an imperial entertainment industry. The high sums he spent on the games, proudly enumerated in his *Res gestae*, were good investments. The public could work off its aggressive instincts, make decisions on life or death in the arena, and enjoy the licentiousness of the theatre; in concentrating on the circus factions and their successes, they steered clear of politics. Seen from today's viewpoint, these were cold, cruel calculations, but they worked, and the emperors used them until the Byzantine period. The Roman rhetorician Marcus Cornelius Fronto, tutor of the emperor Marcus Aurelius, aptly described the relationship between the satisfied people and their popular emperor (*Correspondence* 2, p. 216):

> These very things … seem to be based on the loftiest principles of political wisdom, that the emperor did not neglect even actors and the other performers of the stage, the circus, or the amphitheatre, knowing as he did that the Roman people are held fast by two things above all, the corn-dole and the shows.

**157**
**Gladiator**
First to second century AD
Terracotta
Lent by the Syndics of the Fitzwilliam Museum, Cambridge, GR 120.1984

This figure is remarkable among gladiatorial terracotta statuettes because of its careful execution. The helmet is interesting, since it is not one of the regular types: its smooth crest suggests the helmet of a *secutor* but the perforated visor is like that of the helmet of a *murmillo*.

139

# Money and Circuses: Competitive Sport as Part of the Entertainment Industry

'Perhaps football will now come to an end entirely', wrote Franz Kafka in 1923, forty years before the Federal German Football League was founded. No one knows what impelled him to make that statement, and anyway, brilliant writer as Kafka was, in this case he was wrong. Reality has caught up with him, and football now reigns supreme in the media and on the sports ground. No game has ever been more prominent in the public mind or more of a commercial venture than today's professional football.

And what is true of football is true of other sports as well: the idea of innocence is a thing of the past in competitive sport, and it is the athlete's body that suffers for it. To the collective guilty conscience that likes to see sport presented by the media as mass entertainment, the wealth flowing into the pockets of athletes is a modern way of buying absolution. Whether in the big football matches of the Champions' League, where all that matters is the millions to be earned, or in athletics, tennis, boxing or high-powered Formula One motor-racing, competitive sports have lost all connection with play and relaxation to become part of a monstrously inflated entertainment industry. Its heroes are Ronaldo, Carl Lewis, Boris Becker, Mika Häkinnen. Most of these gladiators of our late capitalist period are men, but that is another story. Competitive sport is big business: money and circuses – for the 'bread' of ancient Rome comes in the form of hard currency today.

The athletes do well out of it: competitive sport pays. It paid in the Rome and Athens of classical antiquity, and it pays today in London, Berlin, New York and Paris. Sportsmen of the past, such as Milo of Croton, a Greek wrestler who won in many Olympic Games, and Gaius Appuleius Diocles, the victorious Rome charioteer, like sportsmen of modern times – for instance the boxer Mohamed Ali – have always won prizes and had incomes many times greater than the earnings of a legionary in the Roman army or a worker in a modern factory. The difference between the athletes of the ancient and modern world is marginal: famous sportsmen can now derive considerable additional earnings from advertising, but if there had been an advertising industry in the ancient world, it would surely have exploited the popularity of athletes, particularly as successful sportsmen in public life have always had very high profiles.

Sporting heroes resort to many methods to keep it that way, not all of them legal. 'Mother's little helpers', as the Rolling Stones song put it, are on the bedside table of many an athlete obsessed with success. When the trainer alone can do no more – and the ancient Greek term for a trainer, *paidotribes*, translates aptly as 'taskmaster of boys' – then the time for biochemistry has come. But doping, for instance in cycling, swimming and particularly in the classic Olympic disciplines of light athletics, is not a modern phenomenon. 'Anything goes' was the maxim centuries ago in antiquity. Athletes would try any means of improving their chances in competition, although of course substances to promote strength and stamina were not yet available in pill form, nor were there any lists of legal and illegal substances; they built up their physique through their daily diet.

The force-feeding of sportsmen was very fashionable in antiquity, and it was severely criticized, just like today's methods. In Plato's *Gorgias* Socrates condemns the trainers of his time who, in his view,

> know nothing about gymnastics; servants you tell me of, and caterers to appetites, fellows who have no proper and respectable knowledge of them, and who peradventure will first stuff and fatten men's bodies to the tune of their praises, and then cause them to lose even the flesh they had to start with.

A classical text has seldom been more apt today, although it overlooks the cynical conclusion to be drawn, for after all, an athlete using drugs is only being honest. He is putting into practice the radical principle inherent in competitive sport in Rome, Athens and elsewhere: the aim of achieving success at any price.

Even the Olympic Games first held in 776 BC in honour of Zeus, undoubtedly with noble ideals in mind, were dominated from the start by the dictates of physical performance. Only their abolition in AD 394 ushered in an era of sport that, as the writer Hubert Ortkemper points out, was probably largely free of the use of stimulants to increase an athlete's powers and lasted for some 1,500 years until Baron Pierre de Coubertin founded the first Olympics of the modern era in 1896.

At this point the ancient and modern worlds joined hands again across the centuries; victory alone was their aim. Although medals are awarded for second and third places today, they are little more than a kind of democratic concession by the victors to the losers.

And a loser is still very much a loser, with his public prestige sinking towards nil, if indeed it registers on the scale at all. In the past, however, the brutality of sporting competitions – and here we do have an important difference between the competitive sport of the ancient and modern worlds – was so great that we could hardly revert to it today, at the beginning of the twenty-first century, now that our perceptions are different. The sociologist Norbert Elias writes, for instance, that Leontiskos of Messana, a champion in the pancration (all-in wrestling), defeated his opponent not by throwing him but by swiftly breaking his fingers. Another case was that of Arrhachion of Phigalia, twice Olympic champion in the pancration, who was throttled by his adversary in 564 BC while he was trying to win the laurel wreath for the third time. Before he died, however, he managed to break his opponent's toes, and the man had to give up in pain, with the result that Arrhachion, although dead, was declared the winner. Among the Greeks and Romans a game had become a battle, and often a bloody one. The 'process of civilization', as Elias describes it, has at least had a good effect on our attitude here: the death of a loser, once publicly accepted and even encouraged for the sake of his personal honour and that of his family, is an idea that now evokes horror.

Yet sport is really much the same as it was in the past: ultimately, only winning counts, and the rest is of no value, mere window-dressing in a carefully staged sporting spectacle designed to keep up appearances. Our admiration for a loser from an unusual background who innocently participates in sport without benefit of drugs, driving his body to the brink of collapse in the marathon or decathlon, is the exception proving the general rule of which that athlete himself is an indispensable part. He represents the pure doctrine of sport for sport's sake – a fig leaf at which we smile tolerantly. Still, the official, highly paid heroes are on show week in, week out, on television or in the stadium just around the corner. That is where we know adventure lies – for real dramas still take place on the turf of the sports ground. It is true that the wars fought there are only mock wars, but for that very reason they have become necessary to us, and while they are actually in progress big business keeps its distance – at least in the hearts and eyes of the spectators.

158

**Exhausted marathon runner at Atlanta in 1996**

This woman marathon runner is close to collapse on the finishing line. Attendants are supporting her and wrapping a blanket round her to prevent her body from cooling down too quickly. The scene is not entirely different to that depicted almost 2,000 years earlier on the great gladiator relief from Pompeii (see fig. 64).

BRITANNIA

Londinium (London)

GERMANIA INFERIOR

Colonia Agrippina (Cologne)

GALLIA
BELGICA

Mogontiacum (Mainz)

Augusta Treverorum (Trier)

GALLIA
LUGDUNENSIS

Lutetia (Paris)

GERMANIA
SUPERIOR

Augusta Raurica (Augst)

RAETIA

NORICUM

PANN
SUP

GALLIA
AQUITANIA

Lugdunum (Lyon)

ALPES  COTTIAE

Arausio (Orange)

GALLIA
NARBONENSIS

Nemausus (Nîmes)
Arelate (Arles)

ALPES  MARITIMAE

Massalia (Marseille)

ETRURIA

DALMAT

LUSITANIA

HISPANIA
TARRACONENSIS

Tarraco (Tarragona)

Emerita (Merida)

Roma

BAETICA

Capua       CAMPANIA
Neapolis
Pompeii

SARDINIA

Tarentum

MAURETANIA

Carthage

SICILIA

NUMIDIA

Syracuse

AFRICA
PROCONSULARIS

THE ROMAN EMPIRE IN THE MIDDLE OF THE SECOND CENTURY AD

Leptis Magna

..................       borders of provinces
NORICUM       names of provinces

0                                    500 km

### THE CITY OF ROME IN THE IMPERIAL PERIOD

0   500 m

Circus of Caligula

Campus
Martius

Stadium
of Domitian

Saepta
Iulia

Odeion of
Domitian

QUIRINAL

VIMINAL

CAPITOL

Theatre
of Pompey

Theatre
of Balbus

ESQUILINE

Tiber

Circus Flaminius

Forum Romanum

Theatre of
Marcellus

Colosseum

PALATINE

CAELIUS

Naumachia
of Augustus

Forum Boarium

Amphitheatrum
Castrense

AVENTINE

Circus Maximus

---

DACIA
POROLISSENSIS

DACIA
SUPERIOR

DACIA
INFERIOR

MOESIA
INFERIOR

MOESIA
SUPERIOR

*BLACK
SEA*

THRACIA

Byzantium (Constantinople)

PONTUS ET
BITHYNIA

MACEDONIA

Ancyra

Thessaloniki

GALATIA

CAPPADOCIA

EPIRUS

Pergamon

Actium (Nikopolis)

ASIA

ACHAIA

Ephesos

CILICIA

Athens

Aphrodisias

Antiochia (Antakya)

Aspendos

LYCIA ET
PAMPHILIA

SYRIA

CYPRUS

*MEDITERRANEAN*

CRETA

Berytus (Beirut)
Damascus

Hierosolyma (Jerusalem)

SYRIA
PALAESTINA

CRETA ET CYRENAE

Alexandria

Petra

ARABIA

AEGYPTUS

# Chronology

753 BC
Legendary founding of Rome by Romulus

509 BC
The first games, the *ludi romani*, held for
the dedication of the great temple of Jupiter
on the Capitol

506/5 BC
Banishment of the last king of Rome,
Tarquinius Superbus; founding of the republic

364 BC
First theatrical performance in Rome

328–290 BC
Samnite war

264 BC
First gladiatorial contests in Rome

264–241 BC
First Punic War

218–201 BC
Second Punic War

186 BC
First games to include animal fights
First appearance of professional Greek athletes
at Roman sporting events

168 BC
Battle of Pydna; victory over the Macedonians

149–146 BC
Third Punic War; destruction of Carthage

133 BC
Death of Attalos III of Pergamon;
founding of the province of Asia

73–71 BC
Revolt of Spartacus

49 BC
Caesar governs alone as dictator

44 BC
Assassination of Caesar

31 BC
Naval battle of Actium; Octavian (Augustus)
defeats Mark Antony and Cleopatra

**Julio-Claudian emperors**
27 BC–AD 14 Augustus
AD 14–37 Tiberius
AD 37–41 Caligula
AD 41–54 Claudius
AD 54–68 Nero

**Flavian emperors**
AD 69–79 Vespasian
AD 79–81 Titus
AD 81–96 Domitian

**Adoptive emperors**
AD 96–8 Nerva
AD 98–117 Trajan
AD 117–38 Hadrian

**Antonine emperors**
AD 138–61 Antoninus Pius
AD 161–80 Marcus Aurelius
AD 180–92 Commodus

**Severan emperors**
AD 193–211 Septimius Severus
AD 211–17 Caracalla
AD 218–22 Elagabalus
AD 222–35 Alexander Severus

AD 235–84
Military emperors

AD 286–305
Tetrarchy (Diocletian, Maximian, Galerius,
Constantius Chlorus)

AD 307–37
Constantine

AD 312
Victory of Constantine over Maxentius
at the Milvian Bridge

AD 313
Edict of Milan; recognition of Christianity

AD 476
Deposition by Odoacer of the last emperor,
Romulus Augustus; end of the western Roman
empire; the eastern empire (Byzantium)
continues in existence until 1453

# Glossary

amphitheatre: building of elliptical shape in which gladiatorial contests were held.

*Atellana fabula*: Atellan farce, popular farce featuring stock characters. In the imperial period they were increasingly superseded by the *pantomimus*. Atellan farces were called after the town of Atella in Campania where they had originated.

*caestus*: boxing glove made of interwoven leather straps over a leather base often reinforced with leather or metal knuckledusters.

*carceres*: starting boxes for the teams competing in chariot-racing in the circus. Also rooms behind the *podium* in the Colosseum.

circus: building and track for chariot-races.

Colosseum: the main amphitheatre in Rome and the largest in the Roman world. Inaugurated by the emperor Titus in AD 80, it could hold up to 45,000 spectators.

comedy: dramatic genre dealing with life in the middle classes of society from which the characters were drawn.

*editor*: holder of games, in charge of the gladiatorial contests. He decided on the pairings of competing gladiators and on the life or death of the losers.

*eques* (pl. *equites*): gladiatorial category. One of these 'horsemen' competed only against other *equites* and was armed with a round shield, helmet, thrusting spear and *gladius*.

*fabula*: general term for all dramatic genres written in Latin.

*galerus*: shoulder-guard worn by the *retiarius*. It was buckled to the *manica*, and with its rim, which bent outwards, offered protection for the gladiator's head.

*gallus*: early gladiatorial category, named after the Celtic Gauls defeated by the Romans.

*gladius*: medium-length sword with a straight blade. The term 'gladiator' was derived from it.

*hoplomachus*: gladiatorial category. The *hoplomachus* wore tall greaves over quilted trousers, a brimmed helmet and a *manica*, and carried a small round shield. He was armed with a straight sword and a lance, and usually fought the *murmillo*.

*lanista*: private entrepreneur who owned a group of gladiators, had them trained in a gladiatorial school (*ludus*) and hired them out or sold them to an *editor*.

*ludus*: game, as in *ludi romani*. Also private or imperial gladiatorial schools in which the gladiators were trained.

*manica*: arm-guard made of leather or lined linen, and in late antiquity armoured with metal.

*mimus*: popular, realistic dramatic representation in verse of scenes from everyday life.

*missio*: the discharge of a defeated gladiator from the arena with his life, granted by the *editor*.

*munus* (pl. *munera*): gladiatorial contests originally held at funerals.

*murmillo*: gladiatorial category. Besides the *manica* on his right arm, and wrappings and a greave on his left leg, he was equipped with a helmet and his characteristic shield (*scutum*). Armed only with the *gladius*, he usually fought the *thraex* or *hoplomachus*.

*naumachia*: mock naval battle elaborately staged as an entertainment.

New Comedy: the late period (end of the fourth century BC) of Attic comedy, consisting of works with a middle-class setting that had a great influence on Roman comedy. Its outstanding author was Menander.

*noxii*: criminals condemned to death who were executed in the arena.

*palliata*: dramatic genre, the adaptation of a Greek comedy called after the everyday garment of Greece, the *pallium*.

*pantomimus*: mimed dance in which a solo dancer assumed various roles with the help of masks and costumes. The accompanying text was sung by the chorus, supported by an instrumental ensemble.

*pompa*: march of the gladiators in solemn procession at the beginning of a *munus*.

*praetexta*: type of Roman comedy called after the toga worn by governmental officials (*praetexta*). The protagonists of these plays were holders of political or military office, and the subjects came from Roman history.

*princeps*: 'first', a term used as a title for the Roman emperors from the time of Augustus onwards.

*provocator*: gladiatorial category. The *provocator* fought other gladiators of his own kind, and his armour, besides the *manica* and helmet, included a breastplate and a half-length greave on the left leg. He carried a rectangular shield and a sword with a straight blade.

*retiarius*: gladiatorial category. This gladiator wore no helmet or any other defensive armour except on his left arm (the *manica* and *galerus*), and was armed with a trident, net and long dagger. He fought the *secutor*.

*samnis*: gladiatorial category for which there is evidence only in the republican period. He was probably the predecessor of the *murmillo* and *secutor*. The name refers to the Italian Samnite tribe overcome by the Romans in the third century BC.

*scutum*: curved rectangular shield with a height of about 100 cm.

*secutor*: gladiatorial category (also called *contraretiarius*), a variant of the *murmillo* and as such specially designed to fight a *retiarius*. The difference between the *murmillo* and the *secutor* was the latter's helmet, completely enclosing the face except for small eyeholes in order to avoid offering any point of attack for the trident of the *retiarius*.

*thraex*: gladiatorial category. The 'Thracian' wore a brimmed helmet and high greaves over quilted trousers; he carried a small rectangular shield and wore the *manica*. Armed with a curved sword, he fought chiefly against the *murmillo*.

*togata*: type of Roman comedy called after the toga of the Roman citizen, since these plays were about Romans in private life who wore civilian clothing.

tragedy: drama with subjects usually taken from mythology, with high-born characters.

*venationes*: animal-fights in which exotic beasts were pitted against each other or against humans.

# Bibliography

**Authors of classical antiquity**

Augustus, *Achievements of Augustus/Res gestae divi Augusti*, ed. P.M. Brunt & J.M. Moore, Oxford 1967

Cassius Dio, *Roman History/Rhomaike historia*, trans. E. Cary, Loeb Classics, London & New York 1914–27.

Cicero, *Tusculan Disputations/Tusculanae Disputationes*, trans. J.E. King, Loeb Classics, London & New York 1927.

Horace, *Epistles/Epistulae*, trans. H. Rushton Fairclough, Loeb Classics, London & New York 1926.

Juvenal, *Satires/Saturae*, trans. G.G. Ramsay, Loeb Classics, London & New York 1918.

Martial, *Epigrammata/Epigrams*, trans. W.C.A. Kerr, Loeb Classics, London & New York 1919–20.

Ovid, *Art of Love/Ars amatoria*, trans. J.H. Mozley, rev. G.P. Gould, Loeb Classics, London & Cambridge, Mass. 1929, 2nd edn 1979.

Ovid, *Tristia*, trans. A. Wheeler, Loeb Classics, London & New York 1924.

Petronius Arbiter, *Trimalchio's Banquet/Cena Trimalchionis*, trans. Michael Heseltine, rev. E.H. Warrington, Loeb Classics, London & Cambridge, Mass. 1913, rev. edn 1969.

Plautus, *The Braggart Warrior/Miles gloriosus*, trans. Paul Nixon, Loeb Classics, London & New York 1924.

Pliny the Younger, *Epistles/Epistulae*, trans. Betty Radice, Loeb Classics, London & Cambridge, Mass. 1969.

Plutarch, *Parallel Lives/Bioi paralleloi*, trans. Bernadotte Perrin, Loeb Classics, London & New York 1914–20.

Sallust, *Bellum Catilinae/The War with Catiline*, trans. J.C. Rolfe, Loeb Classics, London & New York 1921.

Seneca, *Epistles/Epistulae morales*, trans. R.M. Gummere, Loeb Classics, London & New York 1917–25.

Seneca, *Medea*, trans. Frank Justus Miller, Loeb Classics, London & New York 1927.

Suetonius, *The Twelve Caesars/De vitae Caesarum*, trans. Robert Graves, Harmondsworth 1957.

Tacitus, *Annals/Annales*, trans. John Jackson, Loeb Classics, London & Cambridge, Mass. 1937.

Tacitus, *Histories/Historiae*, trans. Clifford H. Moore, Loeb Classics, London & Cambridge, Mass. 1939.

Terence, *Hecyra/The Mother-in-Law*, Loeb Classics, London & New York 1912.

Tertullian, *De spectaculis*, trans. T.R. Glover, Loeb Classics, London & Cambridge, Mass. 1931.

**Roman society and the games**

Bernard Andreae, *Römische Kunst*, Freiburg, Basle and Vienna 1973.

Hermann Bengtson, *Grundriss der römischen Geschichte mit Quellenkunde*, 3rd edn, vol. 1, Munich 1982.

A. Cameron, *Bread and Circuses: The Roman Emperor and his People*, Oxford 1974.

Karl Christ, *Geschichte der römischen Kaiserzeit: Von Augustus bis zu Konstantin*, 2nd edn, Munich 1992.

Andrea Giardina (ed.), *Der Mensch der römischen Antike*, Frankfurt am Main 1991.

Jean Golvin and Christian Landes, *Amphithéâtres et gladiateurs*,

*Caisse nationale des monuments historiques et des sites*, 1990.

Augusta Hönle and Anton Henze, *Römische Amphitheater und Stadien. Gladiatorenkämpfe und Circusspiele*, Lucerne and Herrsching 1981.

K. Hopkins, *Death and Renewal*, Cambridge 1983.

Frank Kolb, *Die Geschichte der Stadt in der Antike*, Munich 1995.

W. Nippel, *Public Order in Ancient Rome*, Cambridge 1995.

A. Olivova, *Sports and Games in the Ancient World*, London 1984.

David S. Potter and Davis J. Mattingly (eds), *Life, Death and Entertainment in the Roman Empire*, Ann Arbor 1998.

Jean-Paul Thuillier (ed.), *Spectacles sportifs et scéniques dans le monde étrusco-italique*, Rome 1993.

J.P. Toner, *Leisure and Ancient Rome*, Cambridge 1995.

Paul Veyne, *Bread and Circuses*, trans. B. Pearce, Harmondsworth 1990.

Paul Veyne (ed.), *Geschichte des privaten Lebens*, vol. 1, 'Vom römischen Imperium zum byzantinischen Reich', Frankfurt am Main 1989.

T. Wiedemann, *Emperors and Gladiators*, London & New York 1992.

Karl-Wilhelm Weeber, *Panem et circenses. Massnunterhaltung als Politik im antiken Rom*, Mainz 1994.

**Gladiatorial contests**

J.K. Anderson, *Hunting in the Ancient World*, 1985.

A. Angelov, S. Conrad, W. Luppe, 'Σεκούτωρ Πολυνείκης: Ein Grabmal fur einen erfolgreichen Gladiator aus Marcianopolis', in *Nikephoros* 9, 1996, 135–44.

Richard C. Beacham, *Spectacle Entertainments of Early Imperial Rome*, New Haven and London 1999.

Filippo Coarelli, 'Il relievo con scene gladiatore (Monumento di Lusius Storas)', in *Studi Miscellanei* 10, 1966, pp. 85–99.

K.M. Coleman, 'Fatal Charades: Roman Executions Staged as Mythological Enactments', in *The Journal of Roman Studies*, 80, 1990, pp. 44–73.

K.M. Coleman, 'Launching into History: Aquatic Displays in the Early Empire', in *The Journal of Roman Studies*, 83, 1993, pp. 48–74.

G. Cozzo, *The Colosseum, the Flavian Amphitheatre*, Rome 1971.

Claude Domergue, Christian Landes and Jean-Marie Pailler (eds), *Spectacula I, Gladiateurs et Amphithéâtres. Actes du colloque tenu à Toulouse et à Lattes*, Lattes 1990.

Domenico Faccenna, 'Rilievi gladiatori', in *Bullettino della Commissione Archeologica Comunale di Roma* 73 (1949–50), appendix, pp. 3–14.

Jean-Claude Golvin, *L' amphithéâtre romain. Essai sur la théorisation de sa forme et de ses fonctions*, Paris 1988.

Marcus Junkelmann, *Das Spiel mit dem Tod – Roms Gladiatoren im Experiment* (in preparation).

Donald G. Kyle, *Spectacles of Death in Ancient Rome*, London and New York 1998.

Christian Landes and Daniel Cazes, *Les gladiateurs*, exh. cat. Lattes and Toulouse, Lattes 1987.

Maria Grazia Mosci Sassi, *Il linguaccio gladiatorio*, Bologna 1992.

John Mouratidis, *On the Origin of the Gladiatorial Games*, in *Nikephoros* 9, 1996, 111–34.

Hermann Pflug, 'Helm und Beinschiene eines Gladiators', in Angelo Bottini et al., *Antike Helme. Sammlung Lipperheide und andere Bestände des Antikenmuseums Berlin*, Römisch-Germanisches Zentralmuseum, Monographien 14, 1988, pp. 365–74.

P. Plass, *The Game of Death in Ancient Rome*, Madison 1995.

Louis Robert, *Les gladiateurs dans l'Orient grec*, Paris 1940.

Patrizia Sabbatini Turnolesi, *Gladiatorum Paria. Annunci di spettacoli gladiatorii a Pompei*, Rome 1980.

Alex Scobie, 'Spectator Security and Comfort at Gladiatorial Games', in *Nikephoros* 1, 1988, pp. 191–243.

Georges Ville, 'Essai de datation de la mosaïque des gladiateurs de Zliten', in Centre National de la recherche scientifique, Colloques internationaux, Sciences Humaines, *La mosaïque gréco-romaine*, 1965, pp. 147–55.

Georges Ville, *La gladiature en occident dès origines à la mort de Domitien*, Rome 1981.

Jürgen Wahl, 'Gladiatorenhelm-Beschläge vom Limes', in *Germania* 55, 1977, pp. 108–32.

Katherine Welch, 'The Roman Arena in Late-Republican Italy: A New Interpretation', in *Journal of Roman Archeology* 7, 1994, pp. 59–80.

**Chariot-racing**

Alan Cameron, *Porphyrius the Charioteer*, Oxford 1973.

Alan Cameron, *Circus Factions. Blues and Greens at Rome and Byzantium*, Oxford 1976.

Michel Eloy, 'Le cirque romain et la course de chars au cinéma et dans la bande dessinée', in Christian Landes (ed.), *Le cirque et les courses de chars Rome – Byzance*, exh. cat. Lattes, Lattes 1990, pp. 189–203.

Adriana Emiliozzi (ed.), *Carri da guerra e principi etruschi*, exh. cat. Viterbo, Rome 1998.

Antonio Blanco Freijeiro, 'Mosaicos romanos con escenas de ciro y anfiteatro en el museo arqueologico nacional', in *Archivo Español de Arqueología* 78, 1950, pp. 127–42.

John G. Gager (ed.), *Curse Tablets and Binding Spells from the Ancient World*, Oxford 1992.

John H. Humphrey, *Roman Circuses. Arenas for Chariot Racing*, Berkeley and Los Angeles 1986.

Ann Hyland, *Equus. The Horse in the Roman World*, London 1990.

Marcus Junkelmann, *Die Reiter Roms I. Reise, Jagd, Triumph und Circusrennen*, Mainz 1990.

Marcus Junkelmann, *Die Reiter Roms III. Zubehör, Reitweise, Bewaffnung*, Mainz 1992.

Christian Landes (ed.), *Le cirques et les courses de chars Rome – Byzance*, exh. cat. Lattes, Lattes 1990.

Claude Sintès, 'La piste du cirque d'Arles', in *Nikeophoros* 3, 1990, pp. 189–94.

Jon Solomon, *The Ancient World in the Cinema*, South Brunswick and New York 1978.

Jean Spruytte, 'L'attelage sportif. Le quadrige de course', in *Plaisirs équestres* 102, 1978, pp. 418–24.

Jean Spruytte, *Etudes expérimentales sur l'attelage. Contribution à l'histoire du cheval*, Paris 1997.

Jean-Paul Thuillier, 'Le programme hippique des jeux romains: une curieuse absence', in *Revue des études Latines* 65, 1987, pp. 53–73.

**Heavy athletics**

Dario Battaglia, 'Pugilatus. L'interattività nell' uso degli arti superiori', in *MACHIA* 3, pp. 92–101, and several other articles on experimental research into fighting techniques of classical antiquity in *MACHIA* 1–4, 1998, 1999.

Norman Gardiner, *Athletics of the Ancient World*, 2nd edn, Oxford 1965.

H.A. Harris, *Sport in Greece and Rome*, London 1972.

Christian Landes, *Le stade romain et ses spectacles*, exh. cat. Lattes, Lattes 1994.

Hugh M. Lee, 'The Later Greek Boxing Glove and the "Roman" *Caestus*: A Centennial Reevaluation of Jüthner's "Über antike Turngeräthe"', in *Nikephoros* 10, 1997, 161–78.

Michael B. Poliakoff, *Combat Sports in the Ancient World: Competition, Violence and Culture*, New Haven 1987.

Werner Rudolph, *Olympischer Kampfsport in der Antike. Faustkampf, Ringkampf und Pankration in den griechischen Nationalfestspielen*, Berlin 1965.

Thomas F. Scanlon, 'Greek Boxing Gloves: Terminology and Evolution', in *Stadion* 8/9, 1982/3, 31–45.

Judith Swaddling, *The Ancient Olympic Games*, London 1999.

Jean-Paul Thuillier, 'Le programme athlétique des ludi circenses dans la Rome républicaine', in *Revue des Etudes Latines* 60, 1982, pp. 105–22.

**Theatre**

William Beare, *The Roman Stage: A Short History of Latin Drama in the Time of the Republic*, 3rd edn, London 1964.

Margarete Bieber, *The History of the Greek and Roman Theater*, Princeton 1961.

Jürgen Blänsdorf, *Theater und Gesellschaft im Imperium Romanum*, Tübingen 1990.

Horst-Dieter Blume, *Einführung in das antike Theaterwesen*, 2nd edn, Darmstadt 1984.

Karl Büchner, *Das Theater der Terenz*, Heidelberg 1974.

George E. Duckworth, *The Nature of Roman Comedy: A Study in Popular Entertainment*, Princeton 1952.

Konrad Gaiser, 'Zur Eigenart der römischen Komödie: Plautus und Terenz gegenüber ihren griechischen Vorbildern', in *Aufstieg und Niedergang der römischen Welt* 2, 1972, pp. 1027–1133.

Barbara Höttemann, 'Phylakenposse und Atellane', in Gregor Vogt-Spira (ed.), *Beiträge zur mündlichen Kultur der Römer*, Tübingen 1993, pp. 89–112.

Josef L. Klein, *Geschichte des griechischen und römischen Drama's* II, Leipzig 1874.

Eckard Lefèvre (ed.), *Das römische Drama*, Darmstadt 1978.

Friedrich Leo, *Plautinische Forschungen: Zur Kritik und Geschichte der Komödie*, 2nd edn, Berlin 1912.

Friedrich Leo, *Geschichte der römischen Literatur*, Berlin 1913.

Walther Ludwig (ed.), *Antike Komödien: Plautus/Terenz*, Munich 1966.

R. Scodel (ed.), *Theatre and Society in the Classical World*, Ann Arbor 1993.

W.J. Slater (ed.), *Roman Theater and Society*, Ann Arbor 1996.

Norman T. Pratt, *Seneca's Drama*, Chapel Hill and London 1983.

Eric Segal, *Roman Laughter: The Comedy of Plautus*, New York 1971.

**Sport and leisure today**

Norbert Elias and Eric Dunning, *Sport im Zivilisationsprozess*, Münster 1986.

Hubert Ortkemper, 'Ein Leben wie die Schweine – Gedopte Vorbilder. Schon in der Antike zeigte der Leistungssport sein wahres Gesicht. Schön ist es nicht', in *Die Zeit* no. 26, 24 June 1999.

# Picture Credits

# Index